Exile and Destruction

Sculpture by Friz Cremer called "Die Trauernde" (The Mourning Woman), created in 1947 for the memorial group honoring the Viennese who were sent to concentration camps. The statue stands in the National Galerie Berlin. Photo by Wayne Geist.

EXILE AND DESTRUCTION

*The Fate of Austrian Jews,
1938–1945*

Gertrude Schneider

Westport, Connecticut
London

Library of Congress Cataloging-in-Publication Data

Schneider, Gertrude.
    Exile and destruction : the fate of Austrian Jews, 1938–1945 /
Gertrude Schneider.
        p.   cm.
    Includes bibliographical references and index.
    ISBN 0–275–95139–1
    1. Jews—Austria—Persecutions.   2. Holocaust, Jewish (1939–1945)—
Austria.   3. Austria—Ethnic relations.   I. Title.
DS135.A9S36   1995
940.53′ 18′ 09436—dc20   94–38563

British Library Cataloguing in Publication Data is available.

Library of Congress Catalog Card Number: 94–38563
ISBN: 0–275–95139–1

First published in 1995

Praeger Publishers, 88 Post Road West, Westport, CT 06881
An imprint of Greenwood Publishing Group, Inc.

Printed in the United States of America

∞™

The paper used in this book complies with the
Permanent Paper Standard issued by the National
Information Standards Organization (Z39.48–1984).

10 9 8 7 6 5 4 3 2 1

Contents

Acknowledgments

Sincere thanks to the Research Foundation of the City University of New York. Its support in the form of a two-year research grant enabled me to examine the large volume of documents concerning the destruction of Austria's Jews and perhaps equally important, to walk in the footsteps of the victims. I visited every place to which they had been sent for extermination, and I describe their fate in detail, just as if I had been there with them. Future generations of Austrians should be able to imagine what their Jewish compatriots felt and should experience their martyrdom in other ways than just through statistics.

Standing at the edge of the mass graves in the forests around Riga, or Maly Trostinec in Minsk, entering the silent gas chambers and crematoria left for posterity in Auschwitz and Stutthof, sifting the ashes mixed with earth at Majdanek, at Belzec, at Sobibor, at Treblinka, at Chelmno, or other such dismal sites, walking through the muddy streets of Opole and Kielce, experiencing the utter stillness of a Sunday afternoon in what used to be the teeming ghetto of Lodz, or offering a silent prayer at the Ring Graves in Buchenwald, where my father, together with many other victims, lies buried, brought the brutal and senseless murder of all the Jewish victims in general, and the Austrian Jews in particular, into focus.

I vowed not to let the world forget that one-third of Austrian Jews fell victim to Hitler and the Austrian henchmen among his followers, who took such bloody vengeance on the Austrian Jews in an attempt to make up for their own inadequacies as human beings.

I would like to thank Dr. Wolfgang Neugebauer and his staff at the Dokumentationsarchiv des Oesterreichischen Widerstandes in Vienna, and I wish to single out their Chief Librarian, Magister Herbert Exenberger. His sympathetic interest in the destruction of the Jewish community, his empathy with the victims, his willingness to spend much time with me and follow up on my requests were done with grace and charm. Not for him the general amnesia prevalent in Austria on the fate of its Jewish citizens! He knows what his fellow Austrians did and he tries to honor the memory of the victims.

My thanks also go to surviving members of my family and friends with whom I spoke about the war. I listened to their stories, and I researched diligently before reporting their experiences in this book.

My appreciation goes to the staff of the World War II archives in Riga, Latvia, for their courtesy and cooperation.

To Hadassah Modlinger, head of the archives at Yad Vashem in Jerusalem, a very special thank-you for making available all the Viennese police documents and especially the transport lists compiled by the very thorough Gestapo. These lists are the harrowing proof of murder, giving names, sometimes dates of birth, and last addresses in Austria of those hapless, unsuspecting Jews about to be "resettled" in the East. Hadassah Modlinger understood and aided my efforts, especially after it became all too clear that the Arolsen archives of the International Tracing Service were not inclined to cooperate with any kind of historical research, even though they had done so during the summer of 1971 when I did the research on the Riga ghetto. I must therefore suppose that the present administrators do not look kindly on those who want to do research on the unspeakable crimes committed during the Nazi era.

I appreciate the help and encouragement I received from Heinz Rosenberg, the author of *Jahre des Schreckens*. Rosenberg is one of the few survivors of the Minsk ghetto. He felt, and I agree, that far too little is known about the Minsk "murder factory."

Thanks also to Frau Heidi Weiss, the overworked archivist of the *Kultusgemeinde* in Vienna, for extending me the benefit of her expertise and the courtesy to let me search at my own speed without bureaucratic restrictions.

Another special thanks goes to Elliott Welles, the director of the Anti-Defamation League's task force on Nazi war criminals, who gave me access to the names of over 5,000 SS officers hailing from Austria. They are contained in eight volumes collected by the authorities in Ludwigsburg and list a total of 42,000 SS officers from all over the German lands, as well as the Ukraine, Latvia, Lithuania, Holland, Italy, Spain, and surprisingly, some

American and British as well. Elliott Welles's foresight in bringing these volumes to the United States is to be applauded.

I could never have pursued my quest in the East to where the Austrian Jews had been sent for annihilation had it not been for my husband, Eric Schneider, who drove me to every hamlet, every camp, every road on which they trod. Acting as my interpreter, he was invaluable when I interviewed older Poles who could best describe what took place almost next door to them, or when I visited the archives in Czechoslovakia and Poland where documents pertaining to the deportees are kept.

To the director of the archives kept at the former concentration camp Stutthof, Magister Janina Grabowska-Chalka, and her assistant, Dr. Marek Orski, many thanks for the excellent treatment I received whenever I made requests. Thanks also for being supplied with valuable photocopies of important material.

I thank all of those who encouraged me, not only my colleagues at the Graduate School of the City University of New York, but also Jews who were once upon a time Viennese and are now citizens of other countries. Thanks also to Albert Sternfeld, a repatriate from Israel and Egon Rothblum, a repatriate from the United States, whose input on life in present-day Austria as seen by Jews who had been forced to go into a bitter exile, contributed to my own edification.

I would further like to thank the Praeger staff: Dr. James Sabin, executive vice president—editorial; Ms. Marcia Goldstein, editorial assistant; Ms. Jay Williams, production supervisor; Ms. Jude Grant, production editor; and last but not least, Ms. Mary Hammer, copy editor. All of them contributed their professional expertise, exhibiting great sensitivity when dealing with the subject of yet another aspect of the Holocaust; their empathy was touching.

Finally, to Dr. George Schwab, friend, colleague, and fellow survivor, my heartfelt thanks and appreciation for his advice and his suggestions on the final manuscript. Despite the many demands on his time as a scholar, professor, and president of the National Committee on American Foreign Policy, he was always there when I needed him.

I dedicate this book to my children David, Barbara, and Peter, so that they may know how the enlightenment in Austria fooled us, the Jews, into being complacent when we should have been agitated, into feeling secure when we should have been wary, and into loving our country which did not love us at all. May they never have to make a choice—but forewarned is forearmed.

Wedding of Anna Peczenik to Willi Zauderer, December 1909, Vienna. Photo by S. Weitzmann, photographer to Her Royal Highness Archduchess Maria Josepha. Photo reproduced and restored by Wayne Geist, New York.

Those individuals whose names are mentioned within the text of this book include:

Front row: (first from left) Bernhard LeWinter, born 1908, died 1982 in New York City; (fifth from left) Laura Merlin, born 1898, died 1942 in the ghetto of Opole, Poland; (sixth from left) Jacob (Bubi) Merlin, born 1904, died 1943 at the concentration camp Mauthausen, Austria; (eleventh from left) Jacques LeWinter, born 1904, died 1942 at the concentration and extermination camp Auschwitz, Poland.

Second row: (first from left) Antoinette (Toni) LeWinter, born 1905, died 1942 at the concentration and extermination camp Auschwitz, Poland; (second from left) Bertha LeWinter, née Mandel, born 1882, died in 1967 in New York City, (fourth from left) Paula Rintel, née Merlin-LeWinter, born 1865, died 1942 at the extermination camp Maly Trostinec, Minsk; (fifth from left) Charlotte LeWinter (author's mother), born 1898, died 1982 in New York City; (sixth from left) Ernestine Peczenik, née Merlin-LeWinter, born 1874, died 1943 at the Lodz Ghetto or in Kulmhof; (seventh from left) Anna Peczenik, born 1892, died 1943 at the Lodz Ghetto or in Kulmhof; (eleventh from left) Chaya Merlin, née Wolfzahn, born 1864, died 1942 at the extermination camp Maly Trostinec, Minsk.

Third Row: (first from left) Abraham Merlin-LeWinter, born 1870, died 1938 in Vienna; (fifth from left) Willi Zauderer, born 1885, died 1939 in Nisko, Poland; (seventh from left) Fanny LeWinter, née Grossman, born 1880, died 1947 in New York City; (eighth from left) Hermann LeWinter, born 1880, died 1938 in Vienna.

Fourth Row: (second from left) Joachim LeWinter, born 1884, died 1942 at the Janowska extermination camp near Lvov, Poland.

Fifth Row: (second from left) Nachman Merlin-Hirschhorn, born 1896, died 1942 at the extermination camp Sobibor, Poland; (third from left) Isadore Spielberg, born 1897, died 1951 in New York City; (fourth from left) Pinkas Hirschhorn (author's father) born 1898, died 1945 at the concentration camp Buchenwald, Germany; (fifth from left   Leon LeWinter, born 1894, died 1985 in Miami, Florida; (sixth from left) Clara Rintel, born 1887, died 1942 at the Theresienstadt Ghetto, Czechoslovakia.

Exile and Destruction

Introduction

Thousands of years ago, the great valley of the Danube River was an important pathway for the tribes who came to Europe from the East, as well as for traders from the North on their way to Rome and Alexandria.

The Romans soon realized the significance of the region's geographic location and set up strong forts at Carnuntum and Vindobona, today's Carinthia and Vienna. Around A.D. 400, Germanic tribes swept over the land and stayed there and so, with the influx of many different people, the area became a true meeting place for East and West.

While there may have been Jewish traders among the Romans, the first historical recording of a Jewish presence in Austria was dated 906. Called the Toll Ordinance of Raffelstaetten, it was a tax imposed upon Jewish merchants passing from Bavaria into the Balkans.

In the eleventh century a small town called Judenburg (Jewish fort) was established in Austria by a group of Jews, and in 1204 the first Jewish synagogue in Vienna, the country's capital, was opened.

For the next two hundred years, the country was ruled by the Babenberg Dukes, and although the few Jews living in Austria were tolerated and could go about their business, they had to pay very high taxes for this privilege. In a charter dated 1244, Duke Frederick I extended legal protection to the Jews under his rule. He went as far as employing not only a Jewish mint master, but also several financial agents with connections outside his dukedom.

Meanwhile, in the other German-speaking lands, owing mainly to the crusades, there were furious riots aimed against Jews, and some of those

who managed to flee were welcomed in Austria. As time went on, additional
Jewish communities were established in Krems, Wiener Neustadt, Tulln,
Klosterneuburg, Innsbruck, and other cities, all of whom combined into a
sort of loose federation with the older communities of Judenburg and
Vienna.

Although the first Habsburg emperor, Rudolf I (r. 1273–1291), confirmed
the Babenberger's charter of 1244, granting Jews his protection for their
lives and property, the growing anti-Jewish sentiment stirred up by the
Catholic church made life in Austria rather unpleasant for its Jewish
minority. In the fourteenth century, the scourge of Europe known as the
black plague was blamed on the Jews. Consequently, in 1348, many Jews
were burned at the stake and slaughtered throughout Austria. Owing to the
fact that they were less affected by the plague than their Christian neighbors
due to strict adherence to their laws of cleanliness, they remained under
suspicion. They could have saved themselves had they accepted conversion,
but very few did so.

After a series of lesser pogroms over the next seventy years, the Jews of
Vienna were subjected to a mass expulsion in 1420 and the immediate
reason given for this event, based on spurious allegations and never confirmed, was that they had aided the Hussite heretics against the Catholic
church.

The synagogue in Vienna was razed shortly after the expulsion and the
stones were preserved to be used for the newly erected building of the
Vienna University, which had been chartered in 1365. They can still be seen,
and half a millennium later, these stones might be considered an omen, as
the university's well-deserved fame rests in no small part on the Jewish
scholars, scientists, and physicians who are a part of it. Today their statues
and busts are in the Hall of Fame.[1] There, among other statues, stands
Sigmund Freud, the founder of psychoanalysis, whose name is synonymous
with Vienna; Adolf Lieben, Professor of Chemistry; Leopold Oser, Professor of Anatomy; Ludwig Mauthner, Professor of Ophthalmology; Emil
Zuckerhandel, Professor of Chemistry; Guido Goldschmiedt, Professor of
Chemistry; Ernest von Fleischl-Marxow, Professor of Physiology; Leopold
Eoves de Dittel, Professor of Surgery; Heinrich von Bamberger, Professor
of Internal Medicine; and Moritz Kaposi, Professor of Dermatology. The
contribution made by Jewish physicians to Vienna's School of Medicine
was described in detail by Alfred Vogl in the *Bulletin of the New York
Academy of Medicine* on the occasion of the six hundredth anniversary of
that famous institution. Vogl credited Emperor Joseph's II Act of Tolerance

for having brought the best and the brightest to Vienna's medial faculty for the next 150 years.

After the expulsion in 1420, 210 Jews were kept in Vienna for the purpose of being forcefully baptized in a public spectacle. When it became clear that they would never agree to it, but would prefer to die, they were burned at the stake in March 1421. Their property had long been confiscated, their loved ones were either dead or scattered, and now they had to pay the ultimate price. Within the next fifty years, the Jews who had lived in Tyrol, Styria, and Carinthia, were expelled as well, owing to a church trial in which some Jews were accused of ritual murder.[2]

Although there were occasional visits by Jewish merchants, and indeed a presence of some court Jews who handled finances for several emperors, it took over 200 years for another Jewish community to achieve legal status in Vienna, when the edict of 1624 entitled them to a ghetto with a considerable amount of self-rule. The taxes they had to pay for this privilege were horrendous, but they had little choice and therefore it was evidently worth it. In fact, that ghetto soon proved to be a haven for Polish Jews who fled their country on account of the fierce Chmielnicki pogroms of 1648. Outside of Vienna, Jews continued to live in small groups, always at the mercy of their aristocratic masters, often subjected to maltreatment, to be jeered at, to be persecuted, and finally, to be expelled.

In 1670 Emperor Leopold I (r.1658–1705), influenced by his Spanish wife and the bishop of Wiener Neustadt, banished the Jews once again. As he was constantly waging war and therefore heavily indebted to Jewish bankers, he felt that he could profit from the expulsion by not having to pay his debts. At the same time, he would be able to please his wife, the bishop, and his subjects by getting rid of the Jews once and for all. His decision was well received by the church and by the people, but the finances of the royal house nearly collapsed, forcing the emperor to ask some of the most "important" Jews to return and once again take over the banking system.

In the meantime, however, over fifty of the wealthiest families had been invited by Frederick Wilhelm von Hohenzollern to be the founders of a new Jewish community in Berlin, where most of them decided to stay even after Emperor Leopold I wanted them back in Austria. There were some, however, who followed his call, and one of the Jews who returned to Vienna was Samuel Oppenheimer, whose connections with other banking houses stretched far and wide. It was he who founded the third Jewish community in Vienna, one that would, in spite of occasional setbacks, endure until the early 1940s.

Notwithstanding the increasing importance of Jewish financiers and their influence at court, the great majority of the Jews had to suffer many ludicrous restrictions, one of which seems incredible: when praying, they had to keep their voices down, so as not to bother or disturb their Christian neighbors! Furthermore, they were forbidden to receive guests from out of town, although permission was occasionally granted, and they had to pay enormous taxes, all the while living in fear of expulsion, regardless of whether they were rich or poor.

By 1772, Vienna contained 594 "permanent" Jews. Others held permits allowing them to stay for five years, or even ten years. The fees for these permits were exorbitant. The Empress, Maria Theresa (r. 1740–1780), hated and distrusted her Jewish subjects; she refused to listen to her son and later coregent Joseph, who wanted to ease the life of these useful people.

It was only after the empress's death in November 1780, when Joseph II acceded to the throne as emperor, that he could do as he had wanted for so long. His first orders for dropping certain onerous Jew taxes concerned only the Jews in Bohemia, but his famous Edict of Tolerance, promulgated on January 2, 1782, vis-à-vis the Jews of Vienna, not only freed them from the personal Jew taxes but also encouraged them to increase their financial and economic activities and even permitted them to attend public schools and other institutions of learning. They could, if they wished, join the armed forces as well. In fact, by 1788, they were obligated to enlist in the military, as was everyone else.

For the most part and despite some lingering doubts, Joseph's Jewish subjects were relieved and happy, even though some of their former religious autonomy was severely curtailed. The emperor abolished their rabbinic courts, did away with their "Kehillot" (Jewish administrative agencies) and forced them to adopt German surnames and often even first names. He did not permit them to have Jewish books brought into the country, since he wanted to Germanize them as rapidly as possible. According to a well-written new analysis by Walter Grab,[3] Joseph II wanted "useful" citizens, but did not realize that his orders, coming from "above," would not be acceptable to the masses, no matter what their ethnicity. In addition, the Jews, despite the edict, were still not considered true citizens, since they were not permitted to own land.

Yet, the contrast between Emperor Joseph's behavior towards them and that of the late empress was such that the Jews felt far more secure and hoped that his reign would last for a long time.

Alas, it was not to be. He died in 1790, and no sooner had his brother Leopold II (r. 1790–1792) assumed the title of emperor, when the City

Council of Vienna asked that the Edict of Tolerance be revoked. Leopold II, however, was a very prudent man and did not act on this demand. Leaving the debated edict in place made it possible for Leopold's son Francis II (r.1792–1806) to further increase the taxes levied at Jews. At the same time, the new emperor ennobled several of his Jewish subjects, and it was now possible for wealthy Jews to live outside the ghetto. Their poorer brethren stayed inside the ghetto and reverted to relying on rabbinical authorities and ignoring the efforts of Germanization sought by Joseph II. Thus, once again, records of births and marriages were kept within the ghetto and there existed a proliferation of surnames often within the same family. The Jews preferred this kind of autonomy and were loath to part with it even in modern times.

The Napoleonic wars and the subsequent Congress of Vienna in 1815 led to many more privileges for Jews, since Prince Klemens von Metternich, whose word was law, relied on the advice of the prominent Jewish financier Salomon Rothschild. Jewish entrepreneurs brought wealth to the Austrian Empire and von Metternich was grateful.

Starting in 1811, Jews were permitted to buy houses and own land. In that same year, they also received authorization for a public synagogue. An unusual, elliptical temple located in Vienna's first district, at 4 Seitenstettengasse, was consecrated in 1826.[4] Wedged in between other houses, it was the only temple in Vienna not destroyed on November 10, 1938, when the other temples all over Austria and Germany were blown up and set afire.

In addition to the beautiful temple, orphanages and hospitals were built, financed chiefly by the newly minted Jewish aristocracy. By 1830 there were 1,600 Jews in Vienna; smaller numbers lived in other towns and many lived in Moravia and Bohemia, all considered Jews of Austria.

The revolution of 1848 gave the Jews much hope of being finally treated the same way as their Christian neighbors. Several Jews were elected to sit in the new Parliament, but by 1851, when the new absolutism engendered by Prince Felix Schwarzenberg alarmed some and pleased others, some of what they had hoped for did not come to fruition. On the other hand, as Marsha L. Rozenblit in *The Jews of Vienna, 1867–1914* points out, a growing influence of the *Israelitische Kultusgemeinde Wien* made itself felt. In 1852, for example, the Austrian government authorized the *Kultusgemeinde* to be the sole agent to manage the religious education and philanthropic needs of Vienna's Jews. In 1867 the powers of the *Kultusgemeinde* increased even more, all to the betterment of its members. Through the continued support of Vienna's wealthiest Jews, it was possible to indulge in all sorts of humanitarian efforts, such as a Burial Society, hospitals, and orphanages. There were also a number of charitable organizations that, for

example, helped poor brides obtain dowries and supplied poor Jewish children with clothing and food. All of this was paid for by the richest Jews, but was always under the administration of the *Kultusgemeinde*, which in turn was administered by a board consisting of these same Jews who supported the charitable institutions.

Furthermore, despite the conservative policies of Schwarzenberg, the young Emperor Francis Joseph I (r.1848–1916) treated his Jewish subjects with respect, and it was during his reign that Austria's Jews saw a "golden age" that was unequalled anywhere else.

"The Jews," to quote the eminent Austrian historian Friedrich Heer, "found unprecedented opportunities for their various talents."[5] They did indeed.

In every corner of that multinational, multiethnic Austria, in every crown land, no matter what language the indigenous population spoke, in every village, town, or city, wherever there were Jews, they revered the emperor, becoming his most loyal subjects and remaining so until the end of the monarchy itself. The upward mobility of the Jews during Francis Joseph's reign saw their rise in every field; at the same time, their contributions to Austrian culture and industry helped to make the capital the world's center for literature and music. Since the Jews were able to enter many professions, although sometimes at the price of having to accept baptism, they became highly visible and therefore, politically at least, quite vulnerable.

In 1867, when the emperor instituted liberalized programs and extended greater powers to Parliament, other changes were ushered in as well. Education and church were separated, great industrial expansion began, and the belief arose that in the long run, a policy of economic laissez-faire would provide the maximum of opportunities for everyone in the multicultural, multilingual, and multinational empire. These new policies, however, brought upheaval to a formerly more or less stable society. While there were not many changes in the lives of the aristocracy, peasants left the land and workers suddenly realized not only their own importance in the scheme of things but also their political impotence. For the first time, slums became a real problem in Vienna, and the difference in income among the general population was felt to be unfair. Although there were many poor Jews in Austria, by thrift and inclination they were somehow able to become part of the growing middle class at a faster rate than their Christian neighbors. Other Jews became wealthy and prominent, another sign of the changing times. It did not take long for politicians to exploit the always present anti-Semitism, and make it into a political, ethnocentric program.

At the time, the three main political parties consisted of Socialists, mainly workers; German Nationalists, a right-wing group; and the Christian Social Conservatives, considered the center. Both the German Nationalists and the Conservatives were at first not too concerned about the new liberalism, but were intent on a new, violent kind of nationalism for a German Austria, not a multinational one. Yet, many of them supported the monarchy, incongrous as it may seem.

Students at the various local universities were the first to see a solution to Austria's problems in a union with Germany. They admired the victories won by Germany at Koeniggraetz (1866) and Sedan (1870), and their slogan "*Heim ins Reich*" (return home to the Reich) was one that was used again and again until 1938 in Austria and 1939 in Czechoslovakia. (To be sure, after the end of World War II, when thousands of "German" Czechs were expelled from that country, their departure, too, was called "*Heim ins Reich*," albeit in a jeering manner, befitting the occasion.)

It is Walter Grab's belief, also shared by other political analysts, that the devastating depression of the nineteenth century, which lasted from 1873 to 1896, was the incubation period for the most rabid anti-Semitism since the Middle Ages.[6]

One of the nineteenth century leaders of Pan-German, intensely anti-Semitic students was Georg von Schoenerer. In 1887 he came up with a proposal to put Jews into ghettos and restrict them to certain occupations. *Von Schoenerer established a journal, Unverfaelschte Deutsche Worte* (True German Words), which was dull and expired quickly. After he was tried and found guilty of a brutal assault on a Jewish editor, his party, made up of virulent anti-Semites and Pan-Germans, fell apart. He resurrected it a decade later, in 1897, when he led several parades throughout Austria to protest the inclusion of the Czech language as one of three languages spoken in Austria. Von Schoenerer and his followers triumphed and it cost the empire dearly, for it signalled a time when mob action would influence parliamentary procedures.

In 1890 the Christian Social Party, founded by Karl Lueger, in addition to several social reforms also adopted anti-Semitism as an important platform. By that time, Vienna was a city of 1,364,548 people, of whom 118,495 (8.7 percent) were Jews.[7] Lueger's mudslinging attacks on Jews were well received by the large artisan class, which was the mainstay of his party. His utterances were such that Francis Joseph I, to his credit, refused to pronounce him mayor at first, but gave in later when Lueger toned down his language.

Heir to both von Schoenerer and Lueger was none other than Adolf Hitler. In his book *Mein Kampf*, he credited them for having the foresight to "recognize Jews for what they were."

After the disaster of World War I, with German Austria a republic forbidden by the Versailles Treaty to amalgamate with its neighbor, the parties in Austria continued very much as they had done before. In addition to many other diatribes against the Jewish minority, there arose the myth of "the stab in the back," making Jews responsible for the defeat suffered by both the German as well as the Austrian Empire, notwithstanding the fact that many Jews had given their lives on the field of honor.

Nevertheless, bowing to realities in Austria, a coalition with a Social Democrat as chancellor and a Christian Socialist as vice chancellor did its best to put the new, truncated country on an even keel. Fringe parties created disturbances, and although the Social Democrats held the country's communists in check, the Christian Socialists could not or would not control the hard-core, right-wing extremist group. In time, when the coalition fell apart, the Christian Socialists fused with the disenchanted right-wingers. In 1927 the situation came to a head. After a strike, there was an armed clash between Social Democrats and Christian Socialists over the acquittal of three right-wing nationalists following the murder of two Social Democrats. It was won by the Christian Socialists.

By this time, still another party had made its appearance. It was the Nazi Party, or as it was called in Austria, the Hitler Movement. With its policy of denouncing the peace treaty, parliamentary institutions, Marxism, and above all, Jews, it was built very much on the model of its German counterpart, the NSDAP (*Nationalsozialistiche Deutsche Arbeiter Partei* [National Socialist German Workers Party]). This Austrian Nazi Party called for blood and the first Jewish victim of prominence was Hugo Bettauer, the editor of a liberal magazine and author of the best-seller *Die Stadt ohne Juden* (The City without Jews).[8] Bettauer was shot in his office by the fanatical Nazi Otto Rothstock in 1925.

Despite the turmoil, during the coalition as well as during the rule of the Christian Socialists, great social progress had been made, with advantages for the common man surpassing all other countries. There was as well a cultural life second to none, owing in no small measure to the Jewish presence. As in the latter part of the monarchy, the Jews were represented in every sphere. Simultaneously, anti-Semitism could be found in every social class, and there were often bloody results.

Attacks on older Jews on their way home from the synagogue on Friday nights were all too frequent. Hakoah and Makkabi, the Jewish sports organizations, took it upon themselves to organize small groups that would usher the old Jews home safely. The upshot was that bloody fights broke out when young Nazis confronted young Jews, many of whom were quite

tough and did not shy away from such clashes. In the summer of 1936, at one such melee at the Cafe Augartenbruecke in the twentieth district, the Nazis shot and killed one of the Jews, who was a member of the Hakoah wrestling team. His colleague Max Temel, a well-known soccer player, used his brass knuckles to defend himself and felled the Nazi, who had attacked him with a piece of pipe. When it became clear that the Nazi would never again get up, everyone scattered, and the suddenly busy police arrested Temel. On the way to the station, he managed to break free; he hid in a friend's house until he could get out of Vienna and travel to Bogota, Colombia, where his older brother lived.[9] Cases like this became commonplace. With few exceptions, the police always sided with the Nazis and blamed the Jews.

The success of the Nazi Party in Germany in 1933 had resulted in a surge of power of the Austrian Nazi Party as well; they were able to enter Parliament and weaken the existing structure of government. The newly emerging leader, Engelbert Dollfuss, was a right-winger but also a loyal Austrian. In order to stem the existing economic depression, he asked for and received a League of Nations loan, but had to forswear a coalition with Germany for another twenty years. Trying to fulfill this obligation, he started to suppress the now vigorous Nazi Party, forbidding them to wear their brown uniforms and forcing their leaders to flee to Germany.

When, during a brawl, a Christian socialist was killed by some of the Nazis still in evidence, Dollfuss ordered the dissolution of the Nazi Party and had many of its members arrested. Others went underground and later took the "honorable" name of "illegals." At the same time, Dollfuss issued a decree dissolving all other parties in the country and formed one catch-all organization called Fatherland Front. The ensuing bloody uprising by the Socialists was squelched under the leadership of Prince Ernst Ruediger von Starhemberg, who then emerged as vice chancellor.

Dollfuss now tried to get some kind of working agreement with everyone, be they former Socialists, Centrists, or Nazis. He did not realize that the latter decided the time was ripe for their own putsch, in order to set up an all-Nazi government. Their leader, Theo Habicht, who had been expelled by Dollfuss earlier, had met with Hitler in Berlin on June 6, 1934, but since Hitler was busy "restructuring" the SA (*Sturm Abteilung* [Storm Division]), that is, getting rid of his former friends and supporters by murdering the most influential, he found little time to sanction an operation in Austria.

On July 25, 1934, a gang of Nazis in Vienna seized the chancellery, hoping to do away with all members of the government in one fell swoop. They could not find anyone from whom they could "wrest" the govern-

ment at first, but suddenly discovered Dollfuss, as he tried to slip out of the building where he had been the only person of substance. They killed him without mercy and showed no remorse at their subsequent trial and execution.

Kurt von Schuschnigg, minister of education, was appointed the new chancellor. Von Starhemberg came back from vacation to stand by his government in time of need, but despite the shockwaves felt all over Austria, the various factions did not come together. It seemed that aside from some dignified memorials to the slain man and a new rousing song (written by the Jew Hermann Leopoldi), which proclaimed Dollfuss's eternal leadership, little was accomplished. The new chancellor was in much the same position as had been the last one. At the same time, the German Reich was growing in strength and daring, making an eventual coalition even more attractive to Pan-Germans. Von Schuschnigg felt that he could forestall their intentions by reliance on Benito Mussolini, who had allegedly stood by Austria in July 1934, preventing Hitler from interfering in the Dollfuss affair. There was, however, no way that Italy would stand by Austria once again in view of the face that the *duce* had become dependent on Germany's might and military power as well as its diplomatic support during his invasion of Ethiopia.

It was during March 1936 that von Schuschnigg discovered this closeness of Mussolini and Hitler, when he was told by the former in no uncertain terms to come to an agreement with Germany. Von Schuschnigg reluctantly did so and was forced to accept several Nazis into his government. They, in turn, prepared the way for the triumphant entrance of Hitler into Austria and the subsequent *Anschluss*.

Not realized by the majority of observers, the *Anschluss* signalled the end of a Jewish community in Austria. Two-thirds of its members went into exile. One-third, however, fell victim to the "Final Solution." It is their story which will be told in all its aspects and in all its tragedy.

Spring and Summer 1938

In March 1938, among six million Austrians, there lived approximately 200,000 Jews, including converts and off-spring of mixed marriages. Among them lived my own family, numbering about sixty men, women, and children, answering to such names as Merlin, LeWinter, Hirschhorn, Wolfzahn, Spielberg, Ackner, Kisner, Peczenek, and Rintel. They were steeped in that charming mixture of Jewish and Viennese cultures, and most of the family members had strong ties to their country. Some were Orthodox Jews, others had become less so over the years, and some barely acknowledged the High Holidays. Among them there were businesspeople, white collar workers, teachers, physicians, and bon vivants, in other words, the middle class. A good number of them came from the former crown lands of the empire, but most of them were born and bred in Vienna. The men of my parents' generation and older had served in the emperor's forces; in fact, several were soldiers even before the Great War and had served in the reserves, as had my grandfather.

Wherever I went in Vienna, in almost every district, in addition to many friends, we had either close or distant relatives on both sides and it was a very good feeling. The fate of this particular family and some of these friends during the next seven years mirrored what happened to the rest of the country's Jews. Their tragic end or, in some cases, their miraculous survival, bring the awesome statistics to life, so that the Holocaust, as it occurred in Austria, will be seen from a personal side, rather than just be relegated to numbers. Of course, the documentation will also be included,

the correct dates and places will be given, but all of it will assume flesh and blood and above all, oceans of tears.

Friday, March 11, 1938, was a day like all the others of the last few weeks. Soon there would be a much touted election. The weather held a promise of spring. People went about their business. It was only in the evening of that fateful day when several events began to foreshadow what would become a catastrophe for Europe in general and the Jews in particular.

Who among Austrians of any denomination could ever forget the speech given by Chancellor Kurt von Schuschnigg over Radio Vienna that evening? He told his fellow citizens that he had bowed to the inevitable and that he had, in order to avoid bloodshed, surrendered Austria to Adolf Hitler's Germany, whose troops had already crossed the border and were now on their way to the capital. Von Schuschnigg's speech ended with a tearful *"Gott schuetze Oesterreich"* (may God save Austria) and then there was a scuffle, clearly indicating to all those who were listening that the Austrian Nazis pulled him away from the microphone.

In later years, when discussing that speech with other Austrian Jews, it seemed that they not only remembered what von Schuschnigg had said and how he had said it, but also their own apprehension; yet, not one of them, including the members of my own family, had any idea that this day, March 11, 1938, signalled the end of an enlightened Jewish presence in Austria, incomparable to any other in the world.

In addition to these momentous political events, my family was faced with personal tragedy. At just about the time of von Schuschnigg's involuntary exit, my grandfather, Abraham Merlin-LeWinter, who had been seriously ill for the last few days, lifted up his head, looked at his wife and at each of his six children, and slipped into a coma from which he never recovered. He died in the early morning hours of Sunday, March 13, while German military vehicles kept rumbling into the city.

Although his death had been expected, his four sons and two daughters were grief stricken. As they came to realize later, however, he was a truly fortunate Jew to die like this, just when the Nazis had entered Austria, while surrounded by his children, in his own bed, just ten days short of his sixty-eighth birthday.

His seven grandchildren had visited him on Friday, after school, for the last time. He was still conscious then, but he was lying there so still and his face was very pale, even though his beard was full and dark. Although he had been a tall man, it seemed to me that he had shrunk.

On the way home with Rosa Stiegelbauer, our housekeeper, my younger sister Rita, then seven, asked her whether "Opapa"—our name for him—

would to go heaven. Rosa, a devout Catholic, took the question quite seriously and replied that he would first have to be judged. She thought, however, that he had a good chance to go to the Jewish heaven since he had been a kind man, a good husband, an exemplary father and grandfather, an observant Jew, and had fought in the Great War for the emperor and fatherland.

It was our grandfather whom she thus described, but the same could have been said about many other Austrian Jews who would not be permitted to die in peace, surrounded by their loved ones, but would have to go through hell on this earth for no other reason than being Jews.

Of the six children around Abraham Merlin-LeWinter's deathbed, only the two youngest, Bernhard, born 1908, and Yvette, born 1910, survived the war. Nachman, the oldest, born 1896, died in one of the Polish extermination camps. The next in line, Pinkas (my father), born 1898, died in the concentration camp Buchenwald. Jacques, born 1904, and Antoinette, born 1905, died in Auschwitz.

Four of the seven grandchildren survived. The other three, Bernhard (born 1920, the son of Nachman), was murdered in Sabac, Yugoslavia. Henny (born 1930) and Arthur (born 1932), the children of Antoinette, were gassed in Auschwitz.

Grandfather's wife Bertha survived too. She was his second wife and had borne him Bernhard and Yvette. His first wife, Henny Rose, had died in 1907. The four older children who perished during the Holocaust were those whom she had borne.

My mother, Charlotte LeWinter, born 1898, also came from a large family. She was the youngest of eight children, two of whom lived in the United States, two in Poland, and the other four, including herself, in Vienna. Samuel and Joachim, the two brothers who lived in Poland, perished with their families during the Holocaust.

Samuel Mandel, the oldest, born in 1868 to Charlotte's father and his first wife, was murdered by his Ukrainian neighbors in June of 1941, a few days after the war between Germany and Russia had begun.

Joachim LeWinter, born 1884, a highly decorated officer in the Great War, was murdered at the Janowska camp near Lemberg. He and his family had dwelt in the ghetto there for a short time. His daughter Tusia, who had become a physician in Vienna, had chosen to go back to her parents in 1938 and thus perished with them.

The fact that mother's siblings Jack (born 1888) and Minna (born 1886) had left for America shortly after their father's death in 1906 proved to be fortuitous, for it was they who brought a part of the family to the United

States during World War II. Both of them used the name Mandel, rather than LeWinter.

Having lost her mother at the age of three and her father at the age of eight, my mother spent the next few years in a private orphanage in Wiener Neustadt. She could thus visit her older sister Bertha and brothers Hermann and Leon on weekends and holidays. They used the name LeWinter, as did Charlotte.

The two families, hers and that of my father, were distant relatives often bearing the same surname, as well as close friends. Charlotte and Pinkas, who were to be my parents, decided while in the third grade that they would marry one day. They did so on January 11, 1920.

Thus, when grandfather died, he was mourned not only by my father's side of the family, but by my mother's side as well. Having been considered the patriarch of both families, his death signalled the end of an era to everyone, not just to his sons and daughters.

The plebiscite in Vienna, which had been scheduled for Sunday, March 13, 1938, was called off shortly before von Schuschnigg's speech on Friday. Thus, when my grandfather died on that Sunday, the removal of his body by the Burial Society, the *Chevrah Kadishah*, became problematic, since all thoroughfares were clogged with German vehicles and it was not wise for Jews to be on the streets. Thus, contrary to the custom of burying a Jew on the day after his death, which would have been Monday, my orthodox grandfather was buried on Tuesday, March 15, 1938. On that day, the four sons who carried their father's coffin, took no notice of the insults hurled at them. They had prepared themselves to carry the coffin all the way to the Central Cemetery, but were lucky when the Burial Society arrived with a horse and wagon, which brought them to the fourth section (the Jewish part) of the Central Cemetery, where services were held. In one way or another, the majority of the adult family members managed to get there as well, and then came back to my grandparents' apartment. It was to be the last time that the family was together. Three of grandfather's sisters and one brother as well as their families were there along with his children and grandchildren, my mother's family, and what seemed to be a stream of people that would never end. In the dining room, the large table was set up like a buffet, with its contents being renewed again and again by the employees of my grandparents' restaurant. While everyone talked about the deceased, there was also talk about the latest political events; curiously, it was the younger generation's members who seemed doubtful about our future in Austria. The middle-aged people and the very old felt that "this, too, shall pass." My father, unfortunately, just forty at the time, shared the viewpoint of his elders, despite the ominous events occurring all around him.

Already since Saturday, March 12, Austrian mobs maltreated Jews wherever they could find them, looted stores and apartments without interference from the police, and forced old, bearded Jews to wash the streets with the fringes of their religious undergarments and sometimes their beards to remove the symbolic Austrian crosses painted there in preparation for the election. Their pent-up fury knew no bounds. The day was cold and windy, and Jewish matrons were made to clean the streets using their coats; others were given toothbrushes to do the job, and some orthodox women, wearing the proscribed wigs, were forced to take them off and use them to clean the sidewalks. As the Jews, fearful and appalled, bent over their task, they were kicked and beaten. Even the newly arriving German soldiers could not get over the ferocity of these anti-Semitic Austrians and the treatment they meted out to their momentary captives. In some cases, it was the Germans who stopped these mindless cruelties and saw to it that the Jews were no longer molested by sending them home.

My own parents experienced no such treatment. They spent all day at grandfather's deathbed, while Rosa Stiegelbauer took Rita and me to the Maerzpark on Huetteldorfer Strasse, even though it was chilly. While inside the park, we could see German trucks rolling towards the city's centrum. The soldiers on the trucks were greeted with flowers and the raised hands of the Hitler salute. People were already hoarse, yelling "*Heil Hitler*," and there was much joyous excitement swirling around us. Rosa seemed perplexed, but did not say much all day. Ilse Jank, my best friend for the last four years since we entered first grade, was there too. She came over to me, indicating that she had something important to tell me. "I cannot be your friend anymore," she said in a kind of gloating manner. "My father is a high-ranking member of the formerly illegal Nazi Party, and told me never to speak or play with Jewish children." With that, she turned away and ran to watch the passing trucks. I was more surprised than hurt just then. Her pronouncement had come so suddenly. But it was an omen for what was in store for Jewish children all over Austria in general, and for me in particular, the only Jewish child in my class.

On Sunday, March 13, in the first wave of arrests, even Baron Louis Rothschild was not exempt; in a show of aristocratic bearing, however, he made the six men who had come to arrest him wait until he had finished his lunch. He was interned at the Hotel Metropole, where he spent a whole year, but was eventually ransomed by his family and then left for England. Others were not so lucky.

On April 1, 1938, when the first transport of prisoners from Vienna left for the concentration camp at Dachau, there were sixty Jews among them.

They soon began to feel the effects of what Theodor Eicke, the commandant of Dachau, was so fond of reiterating: "Leniency is a sign of weakness!" That was what he preached and the Jews soon realized that there would be no leniency as far as they were concerned.

On the day of my grandfather's funeral, Tuesday, March 15, Hitler addressed his fellow Austrians from the balustrade of the *Hofburg*. From the very place where Habsburg emperors had once ruled, Hitler saw a sea of faces turned towards him, calling his name again and again, and forever giving lie to the idea that Austria was a victim. How they loved him! How happy they were! The same Hitler who had been a vagabond with artistic pretensions in that very same city of Vienna, where he was standing now, admired and beloved, promising the multitude that the German Reich would never again be torn asunder by anyone. His listeners were jubilant and when Vienna's Cardinal Theodor Innitzer visited Hitler that very day and gave thanks in church for the bloodless annexation, exhorting his flock to follow all orders willingly, their joy knew no bounds. Quoted by Guenter Lewy in *The Catholic Church and Nazi Germany*, Innitzer issued a widely publicized statement in which he praised the various accomplishments of the Nazis both in internal as well as in foreign policies. In addition, the cardinal, who had only a short time earlier opposed an *Anschluss* with Germany, wrote two letters to Josef Buerckl, at that time *Reichskommissar* and future *Gauleiter* (section chief) of Vienna, ending with the greeting of "*Heil Hitler.*" According to Lewy, this behavior was seen elsewhere as "blunt opportunism." For Innitzer's many Jewish friends, however, it seemed more like treason.[10]

On orders by the new government, the *Kultusgemeinde* was closed temporarily on March 18; only the most basic services were permitted. At the same time, for the next three weeks, there was much preparation for another plebiscite. On every corner there were mobile German soup kitchens for "poor" Austrians. On April 10 when the plebiscite finally took place, Hitler managed to get 99.71 percent of the vote.

The former editor of the *Neue Freie Presse* (New Free Press), defunct since the *Anschluss*, Theodor Meysels wrote in *Die Erste Woche* (The First Week) how the Germans had duped the Austrians as well as the world. While purporting to help the starving proletarians of the city, and publicizing pictures of the poor, hungry populace, they quietly absorbed the Austrian State Treasury of 240 million *Goldschillinge* which backed the Austrian currency and was later replaced by the Reichsmark.[11]

Meysels, an old friend of my father, had been one of the first to flee. Almost as soon as the Germans had taken over, there was a mad scramble

to reach the borders. Jews began to arrive in all neighboring and accessible countries such as Switzerland, Belgium, Italy, Poland, Hungary, Yugoslavia, and especially Czechoslovakia, entering both legally and illegally.

Among those making for the borders was Siegmund Wolfzahn, a cousin of my father. Already during the first week of the occupation, he and several of his friends, all avid skiers, took off for Austria's snowcapped Alps and at the 2,000 meter high Silvretta Mountain skied right into Switzerland. The Swiss gendarmes arrested the whole group in Klosters, and after having spent a month in a Chur jail, the young men were expelled to France rather than being sent back to their point of origin as was the case with many other arrivals.

Although Switzerland expelled most of the Austrian Jews who entered illegally, the records at the *Kultusgemeinde* still have the escapees listed as having gone to Switzerland, arriving at a total of 2,265. In reality, at least two-thirds of that number were expelled to France where the majority eventually perished.

Siegmund's brother Martin, upon hearing that his brother was in France, left Vienna for Germany and from there crossed the border. After a series of adventures, the two young men were reunited and when war was imminent, both enlisted in the French army.

In September 1939, as part of the Foreign Legion, the brothers were sent to Casablanca. However, their hopes to be part of a fighting force were soon dashed.[12] Not long after their arrival, Martin was interned in a labor camp and worked on building a railroad in the Sahara Desert. Siegmund was sent to Indochina, taken prisoner by the Japanese, and spent the latter part of the war in a camp. Some time after the war had ended, he made his way back to Casablanca, where he found his brother Martin alive and well, despite the hard work and the terrible conditions. Both brothers married and in the early 1950s made their way to the United States, where they met their mother and sister, who had by then left England, having survived the war there as a cook and maid, respectively, as did many Austrian Jews who were permitted to enter that country as servants.

A younger brother was able to make his way to Palestine, wading ashore at night so as to trick the British. Unfortunately, however, not all Jews who had the foresight to flee were that lucky; those who had left for countries that were eventually invaded by the Germans were especially vulnerable. Yet, anything seemed better than staying in inhospitable Austria.

Only a short time after the first onslaught of refugees, most of the borders were closed to further escapees, and owing to the unwillingness of these countries to permit other desperate Jews to immigrate, registration at the

foreign consulates and embassies seemed often pointless. Jews did so anyway. Endless lines formed and Jews could be seen waiting for permits and visas at the foreign embassies as well as at the Austrian offices where passports were issued and other necessary documents could be obtained. Some people were able to take part of their belongings into exile, but most often a veritable fortune remained behind, much to the pleasure of the authorities.

In the meantime, the jails were becoming overcrowded. On May 23, another transport was sent to Dachau, and among the prisoners were fifty Jews. Then, on the very next day police stations all over Austria received orders to the effect that every Jew who had at any time been in conflict with the law was to be arrested at once; enclosed with these orders were special forms to be used at the time of the Jews' apprehension. Predictably, a wave of arrests followed this order. Those taken into custody were at first held at the *Rossauerlaende* and from there were taken to Dachau.

On May 30, there was a transport of five hundred Jews; on June 2, there was a transport of six hundred Jews; on June 16, there was another transport of six hundred Jews; then, on July 15, for the time being the last in this series, there was one more transport of five hundred Jews. Thus, up to that day, 2,310 Jews from Austria had been sent to the Dachau concentration camp, where they remained until August. At that time, 2,200 were transferred to Buchenwald; the remaining 110 had died from various causes, the main reason being severe beatings.

Jewish artists, especially humorists, known to have made fun of the new regime, were among those arrested during that particular wave as well, having had run-ins with police at some time. One of them was the famous composer, sometime librettist and folk singer Hermann Leopoldi (real name Herschel Kohn) the very prototype of a Viennese, but a Jew, alas. He was the composer of the Dollfuss anthem, which had been mandatory in every school after that chancellor of Austria had been murdered by the Nazis in 1934. Together with the other Jewish inmates, Leopoldi, after spending three months in Dachau, was transferred to Buchenwald. At the request of one of the "kapos" (a professional criminal in charge of Jews), Leopoldi composed a song which was to become the very hymn of Buchenwald. The lyrics were written by Fritz Loehner-Beda, who had created most of Franz Lehar's libretti. The kapo won ten Reichsmark for the song; it was chosen to be the best in the camp's competition. The inmates had to learn it and sing it at every occasion, since the then commandant of Buchenwald, Arthur Roedl, was very, very fond of it.[13]

Buchenwald, as well as all other concentration camps, followed a similar system of administration. At the very top of the pyramid was the SS (*Schutz Staffel* [Safety Troups]), starting with the commandant, his deputy, and in larger camps, the physician. Then there was the *Rapportfuehrer*, whose main responsibility was to count the prisoners at roll call, also when they left for and returned from work. For female prisoners, there were the SS *Aufseherinnen*; these female supervisors were at times far more cruel than their male counterparts. There were, furthermore, the guards, both inside and outside the camps.

In addition, although prisoners themselves, there were the kapos, whose allegiance was to their masters and only very seldom to their fellow prisoners. Each prisoner wore a cloth label sewn to the left side of his chest. On the label was his number as well as a colored triangle.

The green triangle denoted the professional criminal, most often transferred to the concentration camps from German jails for crimes ranging from murder to petty larceny. Being kapos and very powerful, they were considered the elite. Most of the time, they ran the camps and were favored by the SS, who could always depend on them.

Next in line were the political prisoners, who sported a red triangle. Until 1939, this symbol was seen as a badge of honor; the wearer was clearly an enemy of the fascist regime and thus was trusted, especially by Jewish prisoners. After September 1939, however, prisoners brought to the camps from Eastern European countries were often automatically classified as political; in many cases their red triangles were misleading, for they could not be trusted as far as Jewish inmates were concerned.

Jehovah's Witnesses wore violet triangles. Their suffering in the camps could have been eased had they been willing to denounce Jehovah; very few did so. For the most part, knowing that they were steadfast and honest, even the SS trusted them and they were used as personal servants in the commandant's and deputy's private quarters.

Pink triangles were worn by homosexual prisoners. They were often abused and used for exactly the same thing that had led to their incarceration. Feelings about the "*175ers*" (paragraph 175 of Germany's criminal code outlawed homosexual behavior) were ambivalent; most of the other prisoners had little to do with them and they were shunned; their behavior patterns seemed strange at times, especially when they fought among themselves.

A black triangle denoted the "asocial" prisoner. Many of them deserved this description, since at first it was the pimps and whores who were made

to wear this sign. Later, however, the gypsies, too, were included in this category.

When the black triangle was combined with a yellow one, to form the Star of David, or just a yellow triangle by itself, the wearer was a Jew and therefore on the lowest rung of the ladder in camp hierarchy. No matter what the colors were or signified, the new arrivals had to learn the difference quickly, for often their very lives depended on knowing whose path not to cross.

In Vienna, after the *Kultusgemeinde* had been opened again for business on May 2, 1938, a succession of anti-Jewish laws was promulgated during that fateful summer.

Jews were forbidden to enter parks; even benches along the tree-lined streets were marked "*Nur fuer Arier*" (for Aryans only). Jews were forbidden to go to theaters, cinemas, or the opera; Jewish students had to leave the universities, the high schools, and even the elementary schools—although in Germany itself, the authorities waited with the expulsion from schools until the fall. Jewish businesses had to be handed over to Aryan comptrollers; some of those stayed on for a while, others left, some of the businesses were closed, others were sold for a pittance, with little or nothing going to the former owner; Jewish bank accounts were frozen; that meant that they were closed for all practical purposes, except for small sums doled out to the rightful owners. The Nuremberg laws, pertaining to marriages between Jews and gentiles, were extended to Austria and there were many surprises when people had to prove that they were Aryans. Jews in the outer districts and suburbs of Vienna had to vacate their apartments and move into the second or twentieth districts, where a majority of Jews had always lived. Now these Jews had to make room for boarders and very soon many families shared their domiciles. Eventually, Jews living in other Austrian cities and villages had to move to Vienna as well.

During that summer, our family suffered another loss. Mother's oldest brother, Hermann LeWinter, died of a massive coronary in July, at the age of fifty-eight, only a week or so after his sons had left the country. Alfred had gone to Sweden, and Bruno to Palestine. Uncle Hermann left a widow, Fanny LeWinter née Grossman, and two daughters, Margareth Ackner and Elizabeth LeWinter. My mother was heartbroken. As the family observed shivah, the seven-day mourning period, some of the visitors who came to pay their respects said their good-byes as well.

Although there were sporadic arrests during the summer, mainly due to Aryans denouncing Jews for real or invented deeds, or some skirmishes between the younger people, it was a quiet time and had two results: The

optimists thought it would get better, and the pessimists saw no future for themselves or any other Jews left in Austria. It was this latter group who, if they could, fled, and since they were in the majority, Vienna's Jewish community began to shrink at a predictable rate. My mother, seeing so many of her close friends and relatives leave, advised my father that we do the same. Just then, however, he felt rather safe: By going to court he had effected a postponement of our moving out of our apartment! The judge had granted him a year's time to stay in the fourteenth district, rather than having to move into the overcrowded second or twentieth districts. For an incurable optimist like my father, this small victory was a sign of better things to come.

Some of our neighbors were not at all happy to still see us come and go. The worst among them was a man who lived on our floor, the owner of a fine made-to-measure ladies garment store, educated and seemingly refined. He hated Jews in general and our family in particular and never left us in doubt about it. Long before Hitler came, whenever the radio brought programs featuring Jewish singers such as Joseph Schmidt or Richard Tauber, he would call out to his wife to turn off the radio so that he would not have to listen to those Jewish pigs. At that time, we could afford to ignore him; later, however, his diatribes became more and more threatening. We avoided confrontations and succeeded. We were told after the war that he had been mobilized in 1943 and had given his life to his beloved *Fuehrer* somewhere in Russia; his wife, a very subdued woman, tried to apologize for his behavior. My mother just looked at her and remained silent.

Despite my father's optimism, I remember that he was quite disturbed when Rita and I were expelled from our elementary school in May in a rather humiliating way. As each of us was the only Jewish child in our respective classes—she was in second and I was in fourth grade—the embarrassment of being singled out in the middle of the lesson and being told to leave at once was extremely painful. Although subsequent experiences in later years were horrendous and very often life threatening, neither my sister nor I ever forgot the naked joy and glee exhibited by our classmates and the arrogant demeanor of our teachers when we were told to leave.

The authorities in Germany proper waited until the fall of 1938 with the expulsion of Jewish students from their classes, but all over Austria the same degrading scene that we experienced was played out in every elementary or secondary school as early as May. It was obviously designed to make it clear to both Jewish and Aryan children that there was to be no further contact by the two groups. From an administrative point of view, it would have been much easier to wait until June, the end of the academic year, but

no, those Jewish children had to be reminded once and for all that they were unacceptable and unworthy to be with all the other children. These, in turn, could enjoy the feeling of superiority. It was clever, and few, if any, of the educators voiced a complaint. It might have been too late for that for if they, personally, were not comfortable with these policies, they would have been unwise to object, nor would their objections have helped.

In early July a solution to our problem to emigrate or not to emigrate seemed to present itself when Switzerland informed the *Kultusgemeinde* that they would accept one hundred Jewish children to come and spend a few weeks in Canton Appenzell. Both my sister and I were to go and my parents made plans to follow us. While they would cross the border illegally, they did not think that the Swiss authorities would turn them back, knowing that their children were already there.

To our consternation, after everything had been arranged, including the hiring of a guide who would take my parents across the border, the Swiss, via the *Kultusgemeinde*, informed us that only my sister would be permitted to enter, but not I, since I had passed my tenth birthday just six weeks earlier, on May 27, and was therefore deemed too old. Rita, not yet eight and very unhappy at the prospect of being on her own, left with the other children, among them our first cousin, Oswald LeWinter, then seven. All of the children were sent back to Vienna only three weeks later, since other parents had done exactly what my own parents had planned to do and had been arrested at the border and sent back. Despite high expectations and contrary to some stories, the children came back in a deplorable state. My parents and I waited for the train at the Westbahnhof Station and were shocked by the way all of the children looked. What was supposed to be a wonderful vacation had turned out to be a fiasco and despite the general hopelessness among the Austrian Jews, parents and children were happy to be reunited. Both my cousin Oswald and my sister Rita, even after the passage of six decades, shudder when they tell of the treatment they received at the children's home run by one Ruth Riesenfeld in Canton Appenzell, who exacted gratitude rather than giving love and understanding to the traumatized children. At no time was there an effort made to keep the children in Switzerland rather than send them back to a hostile environment.

This hateful and biased behavior of the outside world strengthened my father's resolve to wait and see. Prodded by my mother, however, he did write to her brother Jack and sister Minna in New York, asking them to send affidavits, which they did. He registered with the American Consulate and applied for an extension of his passport, all of which was done. The main reason for his acquiescence to my mother's advice was his unease about the

severe lessening of our means of support. All of his sources of revenue had dried up after the business had been Aryanized and some of his interests as silent partner had vanished. Aware of the fact that they would have to move out of the apartment by April 1, 1939, my parents started to sell some of the furniture; it was a realistic thing to do, but I could see that both of them were sad to part with the things they had so lovingly collected. The one who took it especially hard was Rosa Stiegelbauer. She cried over every piece that was carried away.

Waiting was not in my father's nature. Through some connections going back to his school days, he obtained a position where his job consisted of building and repairing bridges. He showed great aptitude and was soon assisting one of the architects; in a curious way, he seemed happy, especially when he received a coveted stamp on his identity card, which made him a *Wirtschafts-Wichtiger Jude* (a Jew important to the economy), and therefore thought to be a valuable commodity. His older brother Nachman, being head bookkeeper of a clothing firm, which now started to produce uniforms, received the same classification. Both brothers thus felt safe; both preferred the known to the unknown; both had served in the imperial forces of the Great War and therefore felt less vulnerable; and both were to pay a terrible price for their optimism and their never-ending affection for Austria.

Kristallnacht *November 1938* and the Family's Dispersal

Austria's shrunken Jewish community, lulled into complacency by a quiet summer, which was interrupted only by the disappointing results of the Evian Conference[14] held in July, received a rude awakening on November 10. Already during the night and on that day, all of Vienna's magnificent synagogues were totally destroyed, with the exception of the temple on Seitenstettengasse, which was wedged in between apartment houses and the building that housed the *Kultusgemeinde*.

The "reason" given for this drastic operation was the murder of the German diplomat Ernst vom Rath by one crazed Herschel Grynszpan in Paris. Grynszpan's parents had been deported to the East and he wanted to avenge them. In reality, this operation was carefully prepared beforehand; as a matter of fact, our family had proof of it although we did not understand it just then. It became clear to us once the nightmare had passed, never to be forgotten.

In early October 1938, at least five weeks before *Kristallnacht* (so called because of all the shards of glass), mother's niece Margareth telephoned and asked my father to please come over to her house at once. Her husband, Max Ackner, a wealthy jeweler who specialized in expensive watches, had just received a call from then *Gauleiter* of Vienna Odilo Globocnik, whose family he had helped while the latter was in jail during the 1930s. Without mentioning his name, Globocnik asked Max Ackner whether he recognized his voice. When the answer was affirmative, he said, "Listen Ackner, you've been good to me and my family when the chips were down. I am paying you back and we are quits. Get out of Austria at once. Your name is on a list

of people to be arrested in a couple of weeks. You might even get killed. Just get out." With that he hung up.

Luckily, Max believed him; despite everything, he felt Globocnik was an honest man. He decided to heed the warning and leave. His passport was in order and he had a visa for Switzerland that was still good. It had been his habit to go to that country at least once a year on business. After a tearful good-bye to his wife and seven-year-old son Joseph, he left his family in my father's care, so to speak, and departed for Switzerland, secure in the thought that they would follow him very soon.

Many years later, once the war was over and it became known that Globocnik had risen far higher than being merely a temporary *Gauleiter* of Vienna and had in fact turned into a veritable monster whose brutality vis-à-vis Jews was almost legendary, Max Ackner could only shake his head in wonder. That same man who sent thousands of Jews to their death without compunction or a second thought had taken the time to call and warn him of the impending disaster.

After Max had left, we did expect some arrests to occur based on what Globocnik had said, but no one could even imagine the wild excesses that were committed all over the German lands, including Austria, once that fateful day arrived.

Our own experiences on November 10, 1938, were typical. Five men, wearing the brown uniforms of the SA came to our apartment between 10 and 11 A.M. Among them was Rudolf Randa, the son of our grocery's proprietors. He proudly wore the insignia of the "illegal" party member and convinced his cohorts not to smash our valuables, but rather to pack them into two large oval laundry baskets standing in the foyer in preparation for the monthly wash day. They took paintings from the wall, among them two lovely oils by Pettenkofen, they took the Augarten porcelain statue of Prince Eugen on his horse (the only object I got back fifty-three years later after a long, protracted court battle and only after I pointed out that it was a numbered piece), they took crystal and silver, money and jewelry, going systematically through every drawer. When they got to my father's desk, they found his sword, his father's bayonet, and a valuable, engraved, seventeenth-century scimitar. Accusing him of being an assassin who was going to murder Aryans with these antiquated weapons, brandishing hand-cuffs, and screaming obscenities they wanted to arrest him immediately. It was Randa who convinced them that arresting my father was really not necessary. "Let's just take the weapons, and go," he said, "we have still other calls to make."

As they left, Randa managed to tell Rosa Stiegelbauer to get us out of the house as fast as possible. For the benefit of the others, however, he yelled at her that she should be ashamed working for Jews. Rosa was shaken and insisted that we leave immediately. We did so. As we reached the *Guertel*, a large thoroughfare, a Christian acquaintance of my father, who worked for the police, walked next to us for a minute or so and exhorted my father to take us to a safe place and get off the street.

Both of my parents were especially concerned about Margareth and little Joseph; they therefore decided that we would go to them and find out how they had fared until then. On the way to their apartment on Schoenborngasse in the eighth district, we saw wild excesses aimed at Jewish stores; windows being smashed and people looting, Jewish storekeepers being beaten and kicked while people laughed and applauded. The whole thing had a carnival atmosphere at least as far as the population was concerned; for us it was very frightening.

Arriving at the Ackner apartment, we were confronted by a group of uniformed men who ignored us; their leader was in a rage and screamed at Margareth, "*Juedin Ackner hinunter zur Juedin Popper!*" (Jewess Ackner go down to Jewess Popper)—which meant that the terrorized young woman and her son had to leave their ransacked apartment and join another Jewish woman in her apartment downstairs. My mother helped her niece to pack a small bag and the six of us traipsed downstairs to Mrs. Popper's, listening as the men sealed the apartment and left the house carrying paintings and filled suitcases and bags.

Mrs. Popper's apartment was also in shambles. After consoling her, the six of us left; it had been decided to go and see Aunt Fanny and Elizabeth, Margareth's mother and sister, respectively, who lived on Neustiftgasse in the seventh district. We walked in groups of two; many stores on Josefstaedterstrasse were still being plundered and shards of glass were everywhere.

A similar scene to the one at Margareth's apartment greeted us when we arrived at Neustiftgasse. The two women there were told to leave while the large apartment was being ransacked. It was, however, not sealed up and they were able to return there on the next day, together with Margareth and Joseph. In the meantime, Dr. Simon Adler, whose apartment and offices were on the ground floor, gave all of us shelter for the night. For some reason, he and his wife had not been harassed, but they were extremely agitated. To us they were absolutely charming and tried to make us comfortable, setting up makeshift beds on the leather sofas in the office, serving supper, commiserating with us, in short, perfect hosts despite the bizarre circum-

stances. Just as we were sitting down to have supper—it must have been about 5:00 o'clock by then—a radio message came through: The "operation" was over. For those of us who lived through it, however, it was not over by far.

When we settled down for the night, the adults spoke about the day's events for a long time; they were shaken and the consensus was that it would be wise for all of us to leave Austria. Even my optimistic father could not overcome his chagrin and heartache about the destruction of the synagogues. I remember hearing him say, "I can understand thieves, I can understand felons and robbers, and sometimes even killers . . . but I cannot, for the life of me, understand vandals."

After we had left our own apartment, Rosa cleaned up and went to visit one of her friends for the night. Despite Randa's "public" admonition, she remained with us until April 1939, when we were finally forced to give up our apartment. She had been with my parents since their marriage in January 1920. We received occasional postcards from her until our deportation in February 1942; thus we knew that in 1940 she had married the father of her two children and that they had gone back to her native Salzburg. When we returned we found out that she had died in 1944 at the age of forty-two of peritonitis.

On November 11, 1938, as we approached our house in the early afternoon, we found Mrs. Randa, Rudolf's mother, waiting for us. Unmindful of who might see her, she kissed my mother's hand and tearfully apologized for what had been done to the synagogues. According to her somewhat garbled account, Rudolf had known that my father was on some list prepared by the authorities to be arrested. So much for the spontaneous operation!

We had much to be thankful for; my father was safe—for the time being—thanks to the intervention of the "illegal" party member Rudolf Randa who had seen to it that we should leave the apartment for the night. He was to give his life for the *Fuehrer* at Stalingrad; his inconsolable parents were killed during an air raid in 1944.

The willful destruction of the synagogues, stores, and apartments in Austria was far worse than in Germany. On this day, November 10, 1938, later to be called *Reichskristallnacht*, approximately 8,000 Austrian Jews were taken into custody; they were mainly professionals, that is, physicians, lawyers, dentists, well-to-do businessmen, famous actors, writers, other artists, and newspaper employees.

Twelve hundred of the arrestees were released within the next few days, since they had visas to foreign countries. Another one thousand were sent

home after a few nights either because of benign neglect or bribery. All of them were told in no uncertain terms to get out of Austria; most of them did.

At the same time, a large transport of 4,600 Jews was sent to Dachau, while the remaining 1,200 arrestees were forced to spend the next few weeks in various makeshift jails, such as schools, former dance halls and barracks, and some empty stalls. They were crowded together, the toilet facilities were totally inadequate, and there was very little food. In addition, they were beaten and harassed. In the former convent school on Kenyongasse for example, twenty-seven Jews were killed outright and eighty-eight were critically injured. Although the majority of these 1,200 prisoners were eventually released, the fate of many could never be ascertained and they remain missing.

Among the 4,600 Jews who were sent to Dachau and from there some time later to Buchenwald, were my father's cousin, the physician Dr. Isadore Spielberg, and the latter's friend, the psychiatrist Dr. Bruno Bettelheim. According to eyewitnesses quoted by Guenter Kuehn and Wolfgang Weber in *Staerker Als Die Woelfe* (Stronger than Wolves), the convoy from Vienna arrived in Weimar in a deplorable state. As a result of hunger and frequent beatings, several men had gone out of their minds. From the station at Weimar they had to walk up the Ettersberg where the camp was located, with SS men deployed on each side of the steep road. These inhuman beasts used their truncheons to make the Jews walk faster. By the time they reached the gate that bore the inscription "*Jedem das Seine*" (to each his own), many of them were no longer capable of walking and died within the next few days, since the authorities did not permit the wounded and sick to receive aid of any kind.

Of the approximately 7,000 Austrian Jews who had come to Dachau and Buchenwald between March and November 1938, almost 5,000 were permitted to leave during the early spring and summer months of 1939, provided they could prove that they had a visa or permit to emigrate. Among them were Drs. Spielberg and Bettelheim. Both of them left for the United States in February. Upon arrival in the United States, Bettelheim became an instant expert on life in concentration camps, turning against the Jewish prisoners as it were and accusing them of "behavior changes and delusions of grandeur." His theories, as stated in his essay, "Individual and Mass Behavior in Extreme Situations," were patently untrue and ludicrous, to say the least. Although he spent only three months in captivity, he always claimed to have been in the camps for two years and insisted that he had kept his "ego" intact, in contrast to all those others, who, he asserted, dreamed of becoming world leaders and exhibited megalomaniac tenden-

cies. Owing to his skill in public relations, he pretended that it was Mrs. Eleanor Roosevelt, wife of the American president, and New York's Governor Herbert Lehman who got him out of Buchenwald. This assertion was not true either. After the war was over, when the truth became known and survivors were heard, most serious scholars and psychoanalysts discarded Bettelheim's claims and theories. Yet, even at this late date he is sometimes quoted. His obituary in the *New York Times* on March 14, 1990, perpetuated some of his claims, much to the chagrin of those who spent many years in various camps and, unlike him, had no way out.

My father's best friend, Leon Aptowitzer, was among the released prisoners too. He told my father that all of them had been sworn to secrecy about the goings-on in the camp, but just before he left for England, in early April 1939, he begged him to get out of Austria, based on his experiences and what he had seen first in Austrian jails, then in Dachau, and finally in Buchenwald. Aptowitzer taught me the Buchenwald Song, whose composer, Hermann Leopoldi, was among the released as well. When Leopoldi arrived in New York, he knelt down and kissed the ground. His subsequent compositions, of which he wrote both music and lyrics, reflected the New York of the early 1940s, the trials and tribulations of the Jewish exiles, and also the relief of living in a free country. His success depended on a German-speaking, middle European audience and he was enormously popular among the exiles. Since they did not have too much money, he eked out a precarious existence. Once the war was over, Hermann Leopoldi returned to Vienna—but neither he nor his beloved city would ever be the same.

The events of November 10 touched most of our family's members. Bernhard LeWinter, father's youngest brother, had a harrowing experience and a narrow escape. He, too, was on one of the Gestapo's lists, since he was a wealthy man for one so young. His elegant carpet store on Marc Aurel Strasse had been Aryanized during the summer, but he had to do some more work there from time to time. Becoming aware of danger, he went home to join his beautiful, pregnant wife Esther, née Goldhirsz, and when they heard a group of SA men enter their apartment, both of them hid in the pantry.

Their housekeeper Chana Reiter had to watch as the uniformed thugs, angry at my uncle's absence, despoiled priceless objects of art and filled several suitcases and satchels. She was forced to leave with them and the apartment was sealed. Late that night, however, the faithful and courageous woman who had been with Esther's family for over twenty years, came back, removed the seal, and freed them, enabling them to flee within the next few days. They went to Italy, where their son Abraham was born. With the help of Aunt Minna and Uncle Jack in Brooklyn, the small family was

able to emigrate to the United States in August 1939. The baby had been ill during the voyage and upon arrival in New York, died. Although they subsequently had two more sons, the pain of their firstborn's death stayed with them. Mr. Chana Reiter, their housekeeper, was killed in Riga, Latvia. She was part of a transport that left Vienna on December 3, 1941.

My grandparents' kosher restaurant in Vienna's sixteenth district was still open for business in November 1938, although in accordance with arrangements made by my grandmother, it was to be transferred to another owner by the end of the year.

Nelly Frommer, the restaurant's only waitress by then, was standing in the doorway when four storm troopers marched in on the morning of November 10. They knew tall, red-haired Nelly as did everyone else in the district, and told her brusquely to stand aside while they proceeded, in a rather methodical fashion, to break every chair, every table, the dishes, the glass vitrine with pastries displayed, and, of course, the bevelled windows. They also ripped out the phone.

The spacious kitchen in the back, where my grandmother was busy cooking on the large, old-fashioned stove, came next. For some inexplicable reason, probably because she was listening to the radio, grandmother had been unaware of the destruction in the dining rooms, and was therefore surprised to see them come in and create havoc. First the thugs broke the modern refrigerator that had been installed only two years earlier. It extended over a whole wall; they ripped out its doors, its trays, broke off all handles, and finally despoiled the food stored inside. They smashed the radio and then their leader, Alfred Slawik, whom all of us had known for years as a real bum, poured water over the range. As the fire went out, he asked grandmother with unconcealed glee whether she was satisfied. Although my usually unflappable grandmother was shaken to the core by this wanton destruction, she answered coolly: "The restaurant was sold, as is, to party member Hans Maurer. He is the one who might not be satisfied!"

While the four men were busy in the kitchen, bent upon the same destructive behavior they had exhibited in the dining rooms, Nelly had slipped out and ran to get Hans Maurer, who was married to Millie, one of the girls formerly employed part-time at the restaurant. He had indeed bought the place, inventory and all, and was to take over on New Year's Eve. He had given my grandmother a down payment and although it was not much, she did not register it as he did not want anyone to know about it. Maurer looked forward to being a restaurant owner, albeit no longer kosher. Now, however, after what the storm troopers had done, he would have to invest a fortune.

He arrived shortly and there was a very ugly scene, during which grandmother and Nelly prudently left. Maurer never opened the restaurant. It was eventually converted into several small stores and the lovely garden became just another yard between houses. While Maurer did not succeed as a businessman, he had rewards of another kind—he became an officer in the SS. We met him and Millie in late 1946, shortly before we were to leave Vienna for the United States. Both looked quite prosperous and asked us to give best regards to "all the family in America." We did not tell the Maurers that very few of the family had survived, nor did we tell them that Nelly, after being sent to do all kinds of forced labor on farms in Germany, was eventually deported to the East, together with her parents and her daughter. None of them ever returned.

When grandmother, out of breath, arrived at her apartment, she packed two small satchels, and then, together with Yvette, left during the night and hid for a few days at Nachman's house, where there had never even been a search. On November 18, the two women left for Belgium via Aachen.

Within just a few weeks, they were joined in Antwerp by Jacques LeWinter and his wife Regine, née Knoll, and by Antoinette (Toni) Kisner, her husband Jakob, and the children Henny and Arthur, all of whom had been severely harassed on November 10, had been locked out of their apartments and had finally made up their minds to leave.

Although life in exile proved to be difficult, that part of the family felt themselves to be extremely lucky to be finally free and together once more. With the help of the Jewish community in Antwerp, the American Joint Distribution Committee, and some occasional work the men could find, they started to breathe easier. According to the letters we received, Henny and Arthur even went to school and life assumed normalcy.

In Vienna, several weeks after the events of November 10, Margareth Ackner and her son Joseph left for Switzerland, full of hope to be reunited with Max. Unfortunately, the Swiss authorities had no intention of permitting entry, and after a few nights in a Swiss jail, despite pleas from the distraught husband and father and ample evidence of his hefty bank account, Margareth and Joseph were escorted across the border. They had no alternative but to take the train back to Vienna.

Once again, a family council was held and it was decided that Margareth, Joseph, Aunt Fanny, and Elizabeth should all leave together, but this time for Belgium. They left on February 24, 1939, taking only what they could carry and after establishing a foothold in Brussels, were joined there in March by Max, who had gladly left the safety of Switzerland to be reunited with his family. In January of 1940, Margareth presented her husband with

a little daughter, whom they named Hermine, after her grandfather. To quote Charles Dickens,[15] it was the best of times and it was certainly the worst of times for a Jewish baby to be born just then, in the European theater of war. Mother's brother Leon LeWinter, and his wife Regina, née Horowitz, left Vienna a short time later for New York. Their son Oswald, then eight, had gone ahead with a children's transport, one of the very few to be accepted in the United States.

Of her family, mother was now the only one left in Vienna, and on my father's side, besides his brother and family, only two elderly aunts and several cousins remained. Whereas before Hitler's entry into Austria we could find either a relative or a friend in almost every district in Vienna, that was now no longer the case. It seemed that all those who mattered most to us had left. Just like us, the other remaining Jews in Vienna must have felt a sense of isolation too. It was to become worse. Much worse.

Spring and Summer 1939

On March 15, 1939, Czechoslovakia became part of the German Reich, and thousands of Austrian Jews who had fled there after the Germans had marched into Austria only one year earlier were put to flight once more or had to stop running. Since very few of them could leave for a safer place, they had to remain in Czechoslovakia and thus most of them eventually fell victim to the Germans and suffered the same fate as did the indigenous Czech Jews. A few of the Austrian Jews returned to Vienna and rejoined their families to whom they had said good-bye only a few months earlier. Among the returnees was my mother's friend Wilma Taussig, who eventually ended up in the mass graves at Maly Trostinec near Minsk. In retrospect, it did not matter whether these exiles stayed in Czechoslovakia or returned to Austria; their fate was sealed. Most of them ended up in one of the camps in the East.

The records compiled by the *Kultusgemeinde* once the war was over showed that seven of the Jews who had fled to Czechoslovakia and had then been sent to various camps from there returned to Vienna. It is, of course, quite possible that a few others registered upon arrival, giving the names of the camps where they had been, but not indicating that they had been sent there from Czechoslovakia. Either way, there were very few survivors. Based on observations by Czech Jews, and several written accounts, over 3,500 Austrian Jews had fled to this neighboring country, and since none of the other, safer countries were willing to take in refugees, it is certain that the majority of Austrian Jews who had found a temporary haven in Czechoslovakia fell victim to the Nazi terror. The true number can never be

ascertained, since in many instances their original flight from Austria was never even recorded, owing to the fact that the *Kultusgemeinde* was closed during the time most of them had taken flight.

Based on his belief that exile at any of the neighboring countries was useless, Uncle Nachman and his wife Bertha had decided to stay, just as my parents had done. The developments in Czechoslovakia unfortunately seemed to prove them right. That same month, however, with the help of the ultraorthodox *Agudath Yisroel*'s good offices, Nachman and Bertha managed to get their two younger sons, Walter (15) and Leon (10), onto a children's transport bound for England. The boys left just after Passover.

Only six months later, when war broke out, Walter, not yet sixteen, was classified as an "enemy alien" and sent to Canada. He eventually settled in the United States.

Leon, after a short stay outside London, was sent to Dublin, Ireland, but moved back to London once the war was over. The two brothers saw each other for the first time since the war in 1960.

After the two boys left Vienna, their older brother Bernhard, who had just turned nineteen, left Vienna also to learn how to work the land at what was called "Hachsharah" on a farm in Lower Austria. As a member of the orthodox Zionist group Misrachi, he joined an illegal transport to Palestine, with his parents' blessing.

Detailed by Gabriele Anderl and Walter Manoschek in *Gescheiterte Flucht* (Shattered Flight), that so-called Kladovo transport was supposed to go to the Holy Land via Yugoslavia; unfortunately, it never left that country with the exception of a few chosen people who received bona fide certificates from the British. All others, after having spent some time in the small town of Kladovo, were brought to the town of Sabac, where a camp for them had been established. They were joined there by indigenous Yugoslav Jews as well as by a group of gypsies. There was hunger and sickness in the camp, and hopes of deliverance were extinguished as time went by.

In early October 1941, all the men, Jewish and gypsy, were led out of the camp and taken on a bloody march to the nearby village of Zasvica, where mass graves had been prepared. On October 13 and 14, in groups of fifty, all 910 men who had survived the march were killed by bullets in the neck, among them my first cousin Bernhard Hirschhorn, who had dropped the name Merlin while still in school. He is listed on the *Totenliste* (list of the dead) at Yad Vashem under that name and his correct birthdate is given as March 1, 1920.

In late October 1941, my uncle Nachman must have had a premonition. He spoke to my father about it and it was decided that on All Soul's Day,

he, my father, and I would go to the Central Cemetery to ask for the two men's parents' help. It was better to go on such a busy day, without the Yellow Star, which we had been wearing since September 1, 1941. I was carrying flowers. As is the Jewish custom, we left stones on the monuments, and it was only after the war that I collected these stones, still in their place, and brought them to the United States.

My uncle and aunt never found out that their tall, good looking, highly intelligent firstborn son had been so cruelly murdered, one of the first Austrian Jews to find his place in a mass grave on foreign soil. In May 1942, Nachman and Bertha Merlin-Hirschhorn were deported to Izbica, Poland. From there they were taken to one of the extermination camps in the neighborhood, either Sobibor or Belzec. Having been a decorated soldier in the Great War did not count, nor did the fact that these two gentle people had never harmed anyone in all their lives. Through the Red Cross, Leon, by then in Dublin, was informed that his parents had "moved" to Izbica.

On April 1, 1939, after saying a tearful good-bye to Rosa Stiegelbauer, we moved into the second district of Vienna, to Hollandstrasse 15, apartment 7. The owner of the apartment was Mrs. Taube Einhorn, a widow, whose son Moses and daughter Lotte had to give up their rooms to make space for us. The four of us moved into Lotte's room, which overlooked Krumbaumgasse and the Karmeliter Market; distant relatives of my father, Samuel and Malvina Degenstueck, got Moses's room, which overlooked a lovely, old-fashioned courtyard. The Degenstuecks' three daughters had been fortunate in obtaining teaching positions in South Africa, and so their parents, both in their fifties, were unencumbered.

My sister and I were enrolled at a day-care center for after-school activities, the *Piper Heim*, at that time located in the twentieth district, on Denisgasse. Later on, it was moved to the second district, Mohapelgasse 2, the former Tempelgasse, next to where a beautiful temple had once stood and was now nothing but rubble, owing to the vandalism perpetrated on *Kristallnacht*.

As for formal schooling, Rita was supposed to be part of the school at Sperlgasse 2, while I was supposed to go to the gymnasium at Castellezgasse 35. Either school presented problems, with frequent closings, and while my sister did not mind too much, I did, and I became what my father called a "gypsy" student, as did several of my friends. The formerly rigid educational structure had lessened and so we went to whatever school we could, be it at Stumpergasse in the sixth district, or at Albertgasse in the eighth district. The reason for the schools at Sperlgasse and Castellezgasse

being closed was that both of them were used as collection points for Jews being deported or for a variety of things, none of which made much sense.

I had a student card that entitled me to unlimited fares on the trams all over Vienna, and I could therefore enjoy the sort of freedom that seems incredible even after all these years. My sister, being two years younger and still in elementary school, did not share in the fun. Whenever the Sperlschule was closed, she was given lessons at home by Lotte Einhorn, who had studied to be a teacher.

While for the school year 1937–38 there had been 15,321 Jewish children enrolled in 492 schools, and in the following year, 1938–39, there were 10,690 Jewish children in 24 schools, by 1939–40 only 2,339 children were enrolled in 4 schools, with the numbers declining even further in the next two years. After that, there were none.

In those first few years after the *Anschluss*, the rapid decline in the number of Jewish children was due to forced emigration. According to statistics for foreign countries and their policies in regard to Jewish refugees from Austria up to age sixteen, compiled by Rosa Rachel Schwarz and quoted by Herbert Rosenkranz in *Verfolgung und Selbstbehauptung: Die Juden in Oesterreich 1938–1945* (Persecution and Identity: The Jews in Austria 1938–1945), the figures given for March 1938 to September 1939 are as follows: The United States had accepted 1,000 children (among them my cousin Oswald LeWinter), England had accepted 2,262 children (among them my cousins Walter and Leon), France had accepted 109 children (mainly paid for and housed by the French branch of the Rothschild family), Sweden had accepted 78 children, and Switzerland had accepted 5 children. All of these little fugitives came on their own. They were placed either in hastily set up homes or orphanages, or were housed with foster parents. Only a few were eventually joined by their parents. In addition to the children's transports, there were also those children who actually fled together with their parents and found new homes and hope in the receiving countries.

The children as well as the adults who had the good fortune to legally come to the United States, England, Sweden, or Switzerland survived the war intact—at least physically. The others, for the most part, did not.

During the summer of 1939, some of the Jews remaining in Vienna tried, if possible, to leave and many were successful for the time being. My father, too, made some half-hearted attempts toward leaving, but he felt that things would quiet down. He had made friends at work and his wages, although low, helped to pay most of the expenses. So as to contribute to the family's well-being, my mother utilized the sewing skills she had learned at the orphanage and made alterations on clothes. As she proved to be very skillful,

she had more customers than she could handle, both Jewish and Aryan, with the latter usually arriving after dark. She was thus in a position to help other less fortunate Jews, among them Mrs. Reiter, Bernhard LeWinter's former housekeeper.

Rita and I had made many new friends as well; it was at first an odd experience for us to be among Jews at all times, since previously we had always been the only Jewish children in our classes. Both of us were being groomed for membership in Zionist organizations; this was a part of the *Piper Heim*'s policy. We joined Betar, the revisionist fighters for a free Palestine, and felt very grown up. Actually, Betar was being outlawed and we were, ostensibly, part of the Barak group. Everyone, however, knew that this was only a camouflage. Our membership brought us in contact with the *Palaestina Amt* (the Palestine Bureau) where we were to learn a lot; it became a place both of us loved.

The deceptively quiet summer for us and for the world at large ended when a jubilant Joseph Goebbels, the minister of propaganda, announced the pact between Germany and the Soviet Union in August 1939. My father, usually so optimistic, prepared us by saying that war was imminent. He was right, of course, but he also said that the Western Allies would be triumphant against Hitler and perhaps even against Stalin, and both of them would have to capitulate. With hindsight, it is clear that he overestimated the Allies and underestimated the Germans. As for the Soviet Union, while they bought themselves time, they did not use that time advantageously to prepare for war but rather amassed more territory.

When the war against Poland started on September 1, 1939, the immediate effect in Vienna, besides general mobilization, was a crackdown on those Jews who, until then, had been more or less left alone and treated as Polish citizens from Austria's former crown lands. Most of them had lived in Austria all their lives and had in fact often been born there as, for example, the younger Einhorns with whom we lived.

Only a week after the war started, another wave of arrests began directed mainly against these Polish Jews no matter where they lived or what they did. Moses Einhorn tried to evade the Gestapo but was picked up one night when he had come home to take a bath. We were all witness to his arrest; listening to his mother's pleas falling on deaf ears and observing the brutal behavior of the thugs who had come for him filled all of us with great misgivings. While Moses was one of many, the difference was that we knew him and that made it harder to bear. As it turned out, not even older kids in orphanages or men in old-age homes were spared.

After spending several weeks in a Vienna sports arena, the Stadion, 1,048 males aged seventeen to eighty were brought directly to Buchenwald in open cattle cars without food or water and with a cold rain pelting them for almost the entire trip. According to Eugen Kogon's account in *The Theory and Practice of Hell*, their reception at the camp was extremely bloody and sadistic, leading to injuries and instant death. No wonder then that sixty of the Austrian Jews lost their minds during that very first night at the camp. By December 1939, only three months later, 394 were dead.

This transport to Buchenwald was the last one to arrive there or in Dachau directly from Vienna, with the exception of forty-one Jews who were sent there in October 1943. They had been living in Austria, shielded until then by their foreign passports.

Recapitulating the numbers between April 1938 and September 1939, a total of 7,958 Austrian Jews had been sent to Dachau or Buchenwald. Of the earlier arrivals, nearly 5,000 had been released in the spring and summer of 1939. The majority of the Jews still left at Buchenwald, including the lyricist Fritz Loehner-Beda, were sent to Auschwitz in the summer of 1942, leaving only skilled workers behind. Loehner-Beda was gassed on December 4, 1942, half-dead already from a beating he received for being unable to stand straight due to illness. Survivors reported how he mumbled the lyrics he had written for Lehar's music and how he had hoped to the last minute that Lehar would help him.

Moses, after a short stay in Auschwitz, ended up in Sachsenhausen where he was liberated. He made his home in Germany. When he read in one of the then popular publications that we had survived and were back in Vienna, he came to see us in order to find out what had happened to his mother and sister. All we could tell him was that the two of them had been ordered to report at the Sperlschule for the Litzmannstadt transport, which left on November 2, 1941. That was the last time we saw them. We could further tell him that ever since his arrest, his mother, a deeply religious woman, had prayed for his survival every day of her remaining years. Moses, tough and hardened after having spent six years in camps, broke down and cried. He vowed never to forgive and never to forget. In 1964 he came back to Vienna and died there a few years later, alone and unhappy, and for all practical purposes yet another victim of the Holocaust.

No sooner had that last transport for Buchenwald left Vienna when the ever inventive Adolf Eichmann, the man in charge of the deportation of Jews and head of that government section, had still another idea: He decided to use the newly conquered territories in Poland for the expulsion of Jews from Vienna as well as other places. Eventually, this idea would become

the nucleus of wholesale slaughter; at the time, it was just an ambitious attempt.

Eichmann selected Nisko, a small town in the Lublin district, situated on the River San, surrounded by marshland. He felt that this district was precisely the place where he would have able-bodied young Jewish men from Austria and Czechoslovakia build a *Judenreservat*, that is, a Jewish settlement for all the Jews still residing within the German Reich. Following his orders, Brunner I (Alois) and Brunner II (Anton)—no relation—with the help of the *Kultusgemeinde*, put two transports together. Leo, the husband of my mother's young friend Selma Breitner, née Glattstein, received orders to report at the school on Castellezgasse on October 19, and already on the next day, October 20, he was made part of 912 Jewish men who left Vienna for Nisko. They were followed by a second transport containing 672 Jewish men, which left Vienna on October 26. Among them was Willi Zauderer, husband of my father's first cousin, Anna Zauderer, née Peczenik.

Several weeks later, in a censored letter to his wife, Leo Breitner wrote that they had reached Nisko three days after leaving Vienna, that the River San was flooding the countryside, and that only a few of the men he came with were permitted to stay in Zarzecze near Nisko where barracks had been erected by Jews from Moravska Ostrava, who had arrived there a week earlier. To Selma's amazement, however, the letter had been posted at Lemberg (Lvov), which was located in the Russian sphere of influence ever since the pact between Russia and Germany.

Only much later did Selma and others like her find out that the newly arrived men from Vienna were chased by their Viennese transport guards and other such uniformed devils toward the direction of the Russian border. The luggage that the Jews had brought with them was left behind and although the majority of the men were young and strong and tried to run as fast as they could, a good number of them were killed along the road and robbed of their valuables by the indigenous gentiles. Those who made it to the border and beyond, as did Leo Breitner, were supported and helped by the Jewish communities in such cities as Lvov, Tarnopol, Stanislav, and others. Some of the men even found work.

Willi Zauderer was one of the unlucky members of the second transport. What happened to him was predictable under the circumstances. He had sustained a leg wound in the Great War while fighting at the Italian front and had suffered from a pronounced limp ever since. Owing to this affliction, he could not run at all and was clubbed to death by several enraged SS men. His wife was notified that he was shot while trying to flee! Willi's

friend Oscar Flaschner survived and told us the true story when we met in Vienna after the war.

For the time being, these transports were the only ones sent to the General Government and after several months had passed, the whole project was discontinued. There is speculation that this was because of a dearth of railroad cars, which would soon be needed for the drive against France, or, more likely, that the Russians complained about the sudden influx of Jews.

The majority of the Austrian Jews who had fled to the Russian side eventually fell victim to the Germans once the war against the Soviet Union had begun. Those who had been deported to Siberia by the Soviets during 1940 had a better chance of survival, but even they could not withstand the harsh conditions in Siberia. One such man was Leo Breitner. He was among those deported to Siberia and died there in the winter of 1941–42, at the age of thirty-eight. Selma received a letter to that effect in 1945, written and posted by Moses Margulies, a friend of her husband. Margulies died on the way back to Vienna.

Of the Austrian Jews who had been permitted to remain at Zarzecze near Nisko, the 198 still alive when spring 1940 finally arrived were permitted to return to Vienna on April 16, 1940. All of them were in a deplorable state. During the next two years they were sent to other camps in the East where they perished. The Czech Jews who had come to Nisko were sent home as well and for the most part ended up in Theresienstadt. Only the barracks at Nisko and Zarzecze remained behind, but they did not go to waste. They were later used for Polish Jews, who enlarged these camps before they, too, were sent to the death camps in the vicinity.

Of the 1,584 Austrian Jews who had been sent to Nisko, 70 survived the war in Karaganda, among them Oscar Flaschner. These survivors came back to Vienna and with them came one of the Czech Jews who had been in Nisko with them. One other Jew came back; he had survived the war in Romania but also had been in Nisko for a short time. The high rate of survival was no doubt due to the fact that most of the men were young and strong.

Despite the Nisko fiasco, Eichmann did not give up on his idea of "resettlement." He just had to wait a while.

Case Yellow:
The War against France

In May 1940 the Germans captured Belgium and the majority of the Austrian Jews who had found a haven there, including the members of my family, were forced to flee once more.

After a series of hardships and a few weeks of living precariously in occupied Paris, they managed to reach the south of France. Grandmother, Yvette, the Ackners, Aunt Fanny, and Elizabeth arrived in Toulouse on July 3, 1940, and lived there for several months. Yvette and Elizabeth, both thirty, became engaged, Yvette to a Jakob Schapira and Elizabeth to Willi Szapiro. Both young men were Jews from Austria. Years later, Elizabeth told me that Willi had been one of the few Jews at the time who correctly interpreted Hitler's intentions. He foresaw the destruction of his people, and vowed that he would not go down without a fight. Willi Szapiro was executed in France in February 1944 for underground activities, but there has never been a ceremony to honor this courageous Jew from Austria.

Jacques LeWinter and his wife Regine went from Belgium to Marseilles. While still in Belgium, Jacques had received the coveted visa for the United States but did not take advantage of it. He decided to wait until his wife would be permitted to leave with him. As she was born in Kolomea and thus had the unfavorable Polish quota, their dreams were not to be realized, for the United States never relaxed its stringent regulations. In the meantime, they lived from what she could earn as a seamstress and from the odd jobs he did in a factory on the outskirts of Marseilles.

In January of 1941, Max Ackner was arrested during a roundup of foreigners. He was brought to Camp Gurs. Within a few days, owing to the

zeal of the *Garde Mobile*, he was joined there not only by his wife and children, but also by Aunt Fanny, his mother-in-law, Elizabeth, his sister-in-law, as well as by my grandmother Bertha LeWinter and her daughter Yvette. As all of them had shared the same large apartment, the police had taken them to Gurs as a group.

Conditions at the camp were deplorable, but since Max Ackner still had money, he was able to bribe the guards into letting the family go on outings, get better food, and ease their lives.

Other Jews, who had been brought to the camp directly from Germany, were in dire straits, and so were some prisoners interned at Gurs for having fought in Spain. An excellent article by Hanne Liebmann, entitled, "A Deportation to the West before Wannsee: A Page of History Rarely Told," in the Jewish magazine *Together*, describes the situation in Gurs when the French were still in charge. The fact that they guarded and administered the camp proved to be lucky for the Ackners, however.

It was Elizabeth's fiancé, Willi, who voiced his forebodings. He did not like the camp situation at all and convinced Elizabeth, her mother, and finally the Ackners to seek a way out. By the end of February 1941, wheeling the baby carriage with little Hermine in it, holding Joseph by the hand, the six of them went for their usual walk but did not return in the evening. With the help of Willi Szapiro, Elizabeth had been able to rent a small house in Saint Cezèrt; curiously, no one bothered them, for the house abutted a convent and the good sisters soon made friends with the family. Most of them came to appreciate Aunt Fanny's cooking.

The Kisners, after fleeing Belgium, felt extremely insecure and decided to split up to minimize the danger they sensed. Both children were settled in a Jewish orphanage near Montpellier, and the parents lived near Montauban, but not together. In a long letter Toni managed to send to us in early summer 1941, she gave us news of the family and made fun of having dates with her own husband, quoting the famous Strauss operetta "*Die Fledermaus*." She related that he worked as a lumberjack and that she helped out on a farm. As for their children, Henny and Arthur, they visited them often. She wrote in her letter that both were very good and a great joy. Aunt Toni made veiled references to the anti-Semitism she encountered among many French people, but also praised those who were helpful to her family.

Susan Zucotti, in *The Holocaust, the French, and the Jews*, described the anti-Jewish measures by the Vichy government, and the administrators' efforts to please the Germans, doing even more than expected of them. Zucotti's careful study thus explains the immediate concerns expressed in my aunt's letter. It bore no return address and was mailed to our old address

from Munich. Our former mailman had written the street and number in the second district on the envelope and it had been en route for several weeks before it finally reached us. I remember my parents' relief as well as their agitation when they read it.

After the Ackners had left Camp Gurs, my grandmother felt not only deserted, but very uneasy as well. Conditions were steadily deteriorating and thus, in her usual forceful manner, she managed to bribe a guard and left one night in May 1941 together with a very unwilling Yvette who did not want to desert her fiancé. He, on the other hand, could and would not leave his aged parents. All three of them died at Auschwitz two years later.

My feisty grandmother, however, was insistent and together with her unhappy daughter, who never looked at another man for the rest of her life, crossed the forbidding Pyrenees. Upon arrival on Spanish soil, the two women were brought to Zaragoza and incarcerated, but they were not turned back as was sometimes the case. After spending a few weeks in jail, they were expelled to Portugal, where they lived for several months, with my grandmother working as a cook and Yvette as a chambermaid at a hotel in Lisbon. In October 1941, Bernhard, who had been very active on their behalf in New York, managed to get them the coveted visas with the help of a kindhearted congressman. Grandmother and Yvette left for New York in late December 1941 on the *Qanza,* a Portuguese vessel, and were finally reunited with Bernhard.

In August 1941, Max Ackner, his wife Margareth, and their children received visas for the United States and, after paying the proper exit taxes, obtained the *visa de sortie de France* (exit permits) on September 6, 1941. They did have to wait for permission to go to Portugal. Without it, the Spanish consul would not grant them a transit visa. On October 22, they received both documents and started on their journey. After spending a few weeks in Lisbon where they met grandmother and Yvette, they were able to board the USS *Essex*, arriving in New York City on December 8, 1941, one day after Japan had attacked the United States.

Before leaving Saint Cezert, Max Ackner gave his mother-in-law some of the jewelry he still possessed in the hope that it would help her and Elizabeth to weather the time when he would not be there. His generosity may have saved their lives; they sold the pieces one by one, with the help of the good sisters next door. In addition, they had the wages Elizabeth earned doing odd jobs. In a letter dated November 1943, addressed to Margareth Ackner and sons Alfred and Bruno LeWinter, Aunt Fanny exhibited doubts about her chances of seeing all of them again. She asked them and Max to take care of Elizabeth and she exhorted her two sons to

say the *Kaddish* for her. She begged all of them to care for each other, to be good to each other, and never to forget her.

Notwithstanding her doubts, Aunt Fanny as well as Elizabeth did survive the subsequent time of war. Both of them went into hiding whenever danger seemed imminent. Warned by the sisters next door, they found temporary help at a small convent in the hilly section of Haute Garonne. They came back to Saint Cezert, where they lived until January 1947, when they could finally make their way to the United States. The strain of those years had evidently been too much for Aunt Fanny; she died only a year later of a massive coronary attack.

My mother, my sister, and I had come to the United States in March 1947, and when talking to my mother on the very day of our arrival, Aunt Fanny said that she considered herself to be a very lucky woman, since all four children of hers had come through the war with little damage to show for, as did so many others. Her early death, therefore, may have been a blessing, for she never knew that her two sons, Alfred in Sweden, and Bruno in Israel, were to die within weeks of each other in the early 1950s.

Elizabeth, after a suitable period of mourning for Willi Szapiro, married a concentration-camp survivor and they had two children. She, too, died young, at age sixty-seven, like her mother, but Margareth lived to be eighty-two, surviving Max by twelve years.

Fate was not kind to either Jacques and Regine LeWinter, nor to the Kisners. Of them, only Jakob Kisner survived, a broken man who shunned people and never spoke another German word to the end of his days, making only one exception when he told my mother the whole sad story in 1960, in Israel, where she had gone to see him.

The records compiled by Serge Klarsfeld in *Memorial to the Jews Deported from France 1942–1944*, and detailed reports of these events told by friends after the war, showed that Jacques LeWinter was the first among the family in France to fall victim to the Germans and the Vichy government's policies. He was arrested in early summer 1942 and incarcerated in the camp at Les Milles in Vichy France. From there he was transferred to the Drancy camp, near Paris, which was under German occupation. On August 17, 1942, Jacques left with convoy 20 for Auschwitz. Besides him, there were sixty-three other Austrian Jews aboard the train, but there may have been more of them since many members of the convoy were classified as either stateless or of undetermined nationality. That was true for subsequent transports as well.

Convoy 20, numbering 997 persons of whom more than half were children, arrived at Auschwitz two days later, on August 19. Sixty-five men

and thirty-four women were given numbers and permitted to enter the camp. All others were gassed. In 1945, only three men were still alive but Jacques was not among them. The visa from the United States had gone unused and had not saved this charming, talented man after all. He had waited too long and had thus become another statistic.

Toni Kisner, née LeWinter, was the next one of the family in France to go to her death. She left with convoy 31, on September 11, 1942, also from Drancy, having been brought there from Montauban. On September 3, just as her husband and his fellow lumberjacks passed the farm where Toni had worked, Jakob had seen the *Garde Mobile*, the French police well-known for their collaboration with the Germans, arrest her. As they brought her out to the waiting vehicle on which there were already other potential victims, she noticed her husband and warned him with her expressive eyes not to be so foolish as to join her. No doubt she was thinking of their two children.

On September 5, Toni managed to write a note addressed to Bernhard LeWinter in New York City. The letter must have been posted by a guard. In it she wrote: "My dears, I am on the way to my father-in-law . . . [old Arje Kisner of Tarnopol had passed away in 1931] . . . take care of my children! I do not know where Jacques is . . . I hope he writes to you. I beg you, contact my children, try to keep them with you. I am healthy. Gratefully yours, Toni. P.S. The address of the committee which will inform you of the children's whereabouts is Union O.S.E. 12bis Jules Ferry, Montpellier, Haute Garonne, France" (translated from the German by Gertrude Schneider).

From this hastily written letter it is clear that Toni not only knew that she was going to her death but also that she was going to Poland. In Jacques Adler's book *The Jews of Paris and the Final Solution*, he maintains throughout that despite some evidence to the contrary, the Jews believed in a "mythical" place in the East where they would work. Looking at Toni Kisner's last message, however, seems to make short shrift of this assumption. Her letter clearly indicated that she fully expected to die in the East; as she was not in a position to actually "know" the awful truth, we must conclude that even at that early date, the rumors were convincing enough for her. And if she was that wise, then there must have been many others who were just as devoid of hope. There was, however, absolutely nothing they could do.

Toni was careful not to reveal the children's address, but just that of the committee. Moreover, she was unaware of her brother Jacques's fate. Bernhard, living in Brooklyn, received the letter in October 1942. There

was no way, no way at all, in which he could fulfill his sister's last wish to save her children.

Convoy 31 numbered 999 Jews, including 69 Austrians. At first, 1,069 people were supposed to leave, then 1,037, but in the end, although the report said 1,000, there were only 999. Along the way, in Kosel, a small town about an hour before the ultimate destination, several young men were taken off the train and the convoy continued on its way. Upon arrival at Auschwitz, two men and seventy-eight women were selected to go into the camp. The others, including black-haired, dark-eyed, vivacious and clever Antoinette Kisner, called Toni, were gassed. According to Klarsfeld's research, thirteen men of the Kosel group survived the war.

Regine LeWinter, whose given name was Rebecca, was safe for another few months. Then, on June 23, 1943, after having spent several weeks at Drancy, she was made part of convoy 55, by none other than a fellow Austrian, *Hauptsturmfuehrer* Alois Brunner, who had come to Drancy with a contingent of Austrian SS to see how things were progressing and improve upon them. Regine was one of twenty-four Austrian Jews on this convoy of 1,002, which included 160 children under the age of eighteen. They arrived at Auschwitz on June 25. Some 283 men and 217 women were selected for work; the other 502 Jews were gassed. By 1945, forty-two men and forty-four women had survived, but Regine was not among them.

Alois Brunner, on the other hand, after a spectacular career as a trusted aide to Eichmann and known for his efficiency and inordinate hatred of Jews, resides in sympathetic Syria. He is an old man by now, but he had a good life and does not feel sorry for anything he did. On the contrary, he is even now very proud of himself.

Throughout this time, with the Jewish population of France being decimated, Jakob Kisner was still employed as a lumberjack. The big, blond, blue-eyed man was well liked by the other workers and ever since his wife's deportation had been trying to get his children to another, safer place. As he told my mother in 1960, he asked several of his local acquaintances to take the children into their homes. Both Henny and Arthur were blond and blue-eyed like him and like Toni's late mother Henny Rose. They spoke excellent French and Jakob Kisner felt that they could safely be taken in by a kind soul, since they neither looked nor sounded Jewish. He also told my mother that he had a premonition of his children's doom ever since Toni had been taken away. At one point, he contemplated taking them out of the home and moving somewhere else, but was persuaded by the home's administrators that this would be foolish.

All his schemes came to nothing. On April 29, 1944, when it seemed that the liberation of France was imminent, Henny and Arthur, together with all the other children of the home as well as many adult Jews, were made part of convoy 72. Among the adults was the famous poet Yitzhak Katznelson who had written earlier, while interned at Camp Vittel " . . . the sun, rising over a town in Poland, or in Lithuania, will never again greet an old Jew murmuring psalms at the window, or another man on his way to the synagogue."

These prophetic words, translated from the Yiddish, serve as the foreword to the chapter on the deportations from Drancy to Auschwitz in the book *The Last of the Just* by André Schwarz-Bart.

Of the 1,004 Jews in convoy 72, 174 children were under eighteen, including Henny and Arthur. The two of them were also part of the nineteen Austrians. Upon arrival at Auschwitz, forty-eight men and fifty-two women were selected for work. All others were gassed. In 1945 it turned out that twelve men and thirty-eight women had survived the ordeal, but Henny and Arthur Kisner died the same way as had their mother two years earlier, in the gas chambers of Auschwitz.

For all practical purposes, Jakob Kisner's soul died with them. As for his mortal shell, he died in 1961 shortly after his meeting with my mother. To the end of his life he felt that he should have given himself up after he found the children gone, so that he could have shared the fate of his family. Burdened by a tremendous sense of guilt, he died a broken man, neither forgiving himself nor the Germans or their French helpers.

Altogether, among the convoys from France that brought Jews of every nationality to Auschwitz and other extermination camps during 1942, 1943, and 1944, there were, according to Klarsfeld's book, over 2,217 Austrian Jews among the deportees. After an exhaustive study of every list in the book, I came up with a minimum of 2,783 deported Austrian Jews, since I added those who were listed as stateless but who were born in Austrian cities. I further included family members of people whose cities of origin were listed as Polish, Hungarian, Romanian, and other parts of the former Austrian empire, while their spouses and children were listed as having been born in Vienna. Even so, there were many more Austrian Jewish victims, since the lists compiled in 1943 and 1944 gave no indication where the people about to be deported originally came from. Furthermore, based on the experience of my own family members, many Austrian Jews who had fled to Belgium made their way to France and were caught in that country, and thus, together with their German counterparts, constituted the largest group of refugees in occupied France as well as Vichy France.

According to the records at the *Kultusgemeinde*, in the *Loewenherz Bericht* of November 10, 1941, as of that date 1,650 Austrian Jews had left for France in 1938 and 1939, and 4,270 Austrian Jews had left for Belgium during that time period, a total of almost 6,000. No allowances are made for Austrian Jews expelled from Switzerland or Luxemburg who were therefore left vulnerable. After the war had ended, eighteen returned from France, including some who had fought in the Spanish Civil War, thirty-one from Belgium, and one from Luxemburg. These returnees to Austria had survived a number of camps, including Auschwitz, and had been deported to these camps from either France or Belgium.

In addition to the deportees from France, there were approximately ninety-five Austrian Jews who died in the camps on French soil, and there were, among the Jews executed in France, eighteen Austrian Jews, including Willi Szapiro, Elizabeth LeWinter's fiancé. The recorded total of Austrian Jews falling victim to the German policies, therefore comes to 2,896, but Jonny Moser says in *Dimension des Voelkermordes*, that by combining France and Belgium, the estimated total of those who perished was 4,840. Even this figure may be on the low side, judging from Austria's records pertaining to restitution of confiscated Jewish property.

The flight of all these victims from Austria had, in the end, been of little avail. They suffered the indignities of exile, they eked out a living hoping for the war to end, but sadly, Hitler's hordes caught up with them and they became part of the Final Solution as did most of those other Jews who fled to countries which were incorporated into the Third Reich as well as those Austrian Jews, who, like myself, had stayed in Vienna.

A Quiet Year in Vienna: 1940

By the advent of 1940, more than half of Vienna's Jewish inhabitants had left the city that had meant so much to them.

As has been stated, at the time there were only 2,339 children going to school, but since these children by now had only three schools to go to, classes were very crowded. On the other hand, owing to the devotion of our teachers, I can say in retrospect that the education we received was superb. Both teachers and students alike seemed to feel that they had to make up for all the chicaneries of life experienced by either group, and prophetically, for what was yet to come. Strictly speaking, it made no sense for Jewish children in the Vienna of 1940 to learn anything, for learning presumes a future, and there was no future for us. Yet, between the officials of the *Kultusgemeinde* and the various institutions where we spent our time, plans had been made and realized, all in an endeavor not to let our minds go to waste.

Students were grouped not only by age, but also by ability. For some subjects, all the students of a particular class had to be in attendance. These core subjects consisted of German grammar and literature, geography, history, mathematics, biology, music, and handicrafts. Other classes, such as languages, special writing, world literature, as well as advanced subject matter, were not really mandatory and therefore much smaller and far more selective. Nevertheless, even these classes were often crowded, although not as badly as the regular ones. For instance, in my sister's fourth grade class there were sixty-four children, while in my second form of gymnasium, there were fifty-two. Yet, the discipline was superb and not a sound would be heard once the teacher started to explain the day's lesson.

One special event in the spring of 1940 was of great interest to the whole school, but especially so to my sister's and my classes. Her teacher, Miss Elizabeth Kohn, married my mathematics teacher, Dr. Egon Boehmer! I remember that all of us were somehow scandalized. We did not consider teachers "regular" people who got married while in office, as it were. As Dr. Boehmer was also a supervisor at the *Piper Heim*, to which we went after classes let out, there was a party held for them and their students were invited. We had a great time and wished them the best of luck. Evidently, our wishes did not come true. Luck in those days went just so far and no further.

I came across their names in the *Totenbuch Theresienstadt* (Book of the dead in Theresienstadt), and found that Egon and Elizabeth had been sent to Theresienstadt on October 10, 1942. On June 15, 1943, at the age of thirty-eight, Elizabeth gave birth to a little boy, whom they named Dan Eli. But then, on October 1, 1944, Dr. Egon Boehmer, aged forty-three, was sent to Auschwitz. Elizabeth, together with little Dan Eli, followed him on October 12. Their luck had run out. All three of them perished.

In 1940, besides school, there were not too many places where Jewish children could go. Since the classes in the schools still open to us were staggered so as to accommodate more children, we had a lot of time on our hands and thus, being part of the *Piper Heim* was a stroke of luck for my sister and myself. Not only were we able to socialize with other children there, but we learned songs and folk dancing, and we put on plays; our lives were not drab at all.

In addition, and with far reaching consequences, we were also a part of the Palestine Bureau (which we called *Palamt*), on Marc Aurel Strasse 5, and we spent time there learning Hebrew, how to march and follow commands given in that language, to love Eretz Israel, and to realize that having our very own country was the only hope for us. It did not matter to which of the various organizations one belonged, whether Zionist or Revisionist, all that mattered was that we were oppressed but proud Jews, and children at that.

Our leaders at the *Palamt* were Professor Leo Kulka, Aron Menczer, Barry Kandelmann, Kiki Neumann, Miriam Neumann, Martin Vogel, among others. All of them served as role models, especially Aron, and all of them expected us to succeed in whatever we attempted.

During the summers of 1940 and 1941, it was our youth leaders who took us to the Central Cemetery where they combined an unused area for graves to create a small swimming pool for us, since we were forbidden to enter parks or use the pools in the city. Notwithstanding the somber surroundings of the nearby burial grounds, we frolicked in the pool and managed to have a good time.

Only about two city blocks away from the *Palamt*, on Morzin Platz, was one of Eichmann's offices, as well as that of his legal expert, Dr. Rudolf Lange and that of Alois Brunner. At times our youth leaders told us that all these people "next door" wanted the Jews to leave Austria, but the question was always how and where. It was thus made clear to us that we were not wanted anywhere, which served to emphasize that we had to have our own country.

Aron Menczer was in charge of one of the farms where boys and girls older than myself (in May 1940 I celebrated my twelfth birthday) learned how to be farmers so that they could help build the Jewish state. Without a "capitalist's certificate," however, one had to go there illegally. Quite a number succeeded; too many, alas, did not.

According to the records of the *Kultusgemeinde*, 9,195 Austrian Jews made it to Palestine, but based on actuarial studies by Albert Sternfeld, the author of *Betrifft Oesterreich: Von Oesterreich Betroffen* (In Regard to and Regarded by Austria), there were about 4,000 more than that. The *Kultusgemeinde* could not know where people had ended up, especially if they had first gone to another country. The number of Austrian Jews living in Israel and claiming restitution amounted to about 13,500; among the claimants were Jews who had first gone to England, as had Sternfeld, or Italy, or Yugoslavia, or the United States. There were, furthermore, concentration camp survivors among the claimants who had gone to Israel after the war.

In the Austria of 1940, some Jews were still able to leave. Many times we came to school finding some of our friends gone. It seemed that most of the children we knew were quite well informed about outside events. That may have been due to the fact that there was little room left for grown-ups to discuss politics and other serious matters privately because of the closeness we were all subjected to in our apartments. What was on everyone's mind during that summer of 1940 were the events in Belgium and France. My parents' friends were not too optimistic about an early end to this war and since most of the men had served in the Great War, their opinions were based on experience. Only my father remained optimistic.

Generally, my sister and I did not spend too much time at home. Mother still made alterations and was quite busy, father was building and/or repairing bridges, Lotte Einhorn worked part-time in a Jewish day-care center for very small children while her mother kept house and spent the rest of the time praying. After Moses was arrested and sent to Buchenwald, the two women were forced to take in another boarder. Her name was Antonia Weitz. She was a widow with a son in England. Having brought with her many good books, this lovely lady let me read every one of them.

Malvina and Samuel Degenstueck, who lived in Moses's former room, managed to keep themselves occupied in a way that was greatly admired by all of us. They had started out on a very interesting and adventurous business. As Samuel had been an officer in the Great War and had been stationed in Yugoslavia for several years, he knew that country as he liked to say "like the back of his hand." Now, with himself as a guide and Malvina taking care of all other matters such as security and money, he took Jews who had nowhere else to go across the border into Yugoslavia. Of the approximately 1,700 Austrian Jews then listed by the *Kultusgemeinde* as having gone to Yugoslavia, the Degenstuecks had taken at least 200 more of them as far as Zagreb. Efficient and daring, Samuel came to know several of the border guards, they in turn came to know him, and he managed to smuggle quite a number of people over the border in this way.

Both he and Malvina thought that they would eventually join all those whom they had helped to escape; alas, it was not to be. One of their clients, despite having promised not to do so, had come back to Vienna in order to take his girlfriend across the border on his own. They were caught and when questioned he succumbed to the threats used by the Gestapo. Once they made him talk, he implicated the Degenstuecks. They were arrested in November 1940 and after spending several months in a Vienna jail, were sent to Opole via Pulawy with the second and last transport to that dismal little town on February 26, 1941. We had one letter from them in which they complained about the price of food. After that letter, despite a package sent by my mother, we never heard from them again. Earlier though, before the Degenstuecks' luck ran out, we were lulled into a false security. For the greater part of 1940, it seemed that conditions for Vienna's Jews had somehow become more stable. Still, in my father's letters to his brother Bernhard in the United States, he urges the latter to get us out. If he had apprehensions, as the letters seem to imply, he gave no sign of them to us. With the exception of the problems we had with shopping, being permitted to go to stores only between the hours of 11 A.M. and 4 P.M., I remember that year as a quiet one, interrupted only by occasional letters from relatives and their experiences in exile. We found out that Yvette had become engaged in Paris, to a Jakob Schapira. My father, in a letter to Bernhard dated October 27, 1940, joked that "we now had four Jacobs in the family: Jacques LeWinter, Jakob Kisner, Jacob Merlin called Bubi, and last but not least Jakob Schapira."

In that same letter he told his brother that he led the Yom Kippur prayers and was very honored to be chosen. He added that their father Abraham Merlin-LeWinter would have had great joy to hear his "unbelieving" son pray so well and so fervently, hoping that God would send much-needed

help to the Jewish people. Although the letter was censored, nothing was crossed out. (After Bernhard's death in 1982, his wife Esther found these letters in his desk and gave them to me.)

All I can remember of that holiest of days was the heat and the many men gathered in the former dining room of the Einhorns, listening to my father's prayers and joining in the familiar melodies, while the women prayed separately, in the foyer.

After the holidays, life resumed its rhythm. School in the morning, several hours at the Palestine Bureau, and then, after that, the *Piper Heim*. As soon as we got there each day, virtually famished, we were given a good, hearty lunch, and later in the afternoon a snack of some kind. There were two cooks and three women helpers and the man in charge of the kitchen and other supplies was Mr. Karl Epstein, who used to chase us out of there. He and my father's cousin Laura Brender were engaged. She had been divorced in 1935 (the only such case in our family) and had a daughter Lili, one year my senior. I was extremely fond of Lili and we spent much time together. Laura worked as a secretary in the *Kultusgemeinde* and therefore, with Mr. Epstein an employee of the *Kultusgemeinde* as well, all three of them seemed quite safe for the time being.

Echoes of war notwithstanding, Vienna during the Christmas season of 1940 still had much charm all its own. As Jews we had never been a part of the religious aspect of Christmas, and now of course even less so than ever before, but the general sense of expectation and excitement affected everyone. In an adventurous spirit, Lili wanted to go and see a new film, a thing strictly forbidden for Jews. I said I could not go with her, for my parents would never forgive me and, anyway, I was supposed to be part of a Chanukah pageant at the *Palamt* and had to go to rehearsal. Although somewhat disappointed, she laughingly pulled my braids and said that I was just too good and not much fun. With that, she went off to the Nestroy Kino. Just that evening, the local police entered the movie house and checked everyone's identity card. Lili's card had a big "J" for *Jude* (Jew) on it and there was no help for her. She was taken into custody, her mother was called to come to the jail and bring some clothes and toiletries, and it seemed that their luck had run out. Laura's position was of no help, Epstein could not do a thing either, and thus, just because she wanted to see a movie, beautiful thirteen-year-old Lili Brender and her mother Laura Brender, née Merlin, were shipped to Opole via Pulawy on February 15, 1941, the first transport to that town, when still another effort was made to send Austrian Jews to Poland.

Leaving just then was heartrending for Laura as she left behind not only the man she loved, but also her aged mother Chaja Merlin and her brother Jacob, called Bubi.

Laura and Lili wrote to us from Opole via Pulawy just once; Aunt Chaja received two letters and then nothing else. From one of the few survivors of that transport, Nelly Adler, we found out that Laura had died of typhoid fever several months after their arrival, and that Lili was later taken away with a transport to one of the death camps in the vicinity.

Jacob (Bubi) Merlin was sent to Modliborzyce on March 5, 1941, having to leave his aged mother all alone. For that reason and also because of the conditions at that poverty-stricken village, he made his way back to Vienna on foot, as did several others. It took him almost three months to reach the city, but during that time, his mother, then seventy-seven, was transferred from her apartment to the Jewish old-age home in the ninth district on Seegasse. Bubi was now in a quandary, for he had counted on joining her in their apartment once he reached the city. Having nowhere to hide, he came to our house. After the first shock, my father made it possible for him to stay in our foyer for several nights and then found him a place where he could stay intermittently at our old house with Christian friends, Emma and Eduard Jonke.

From time to time he visited his mother and for safety's sake, both of them made believe that he was a former neighbor. In September 1942 when he came to see Chaja on one of his sporadic visits, he learned that she had been deported to Theresienstadt. Acting peculiarly, he was picked up by police and sent to Mauthausen, where he was killed in 1943.

At Christmastime 1941, these good people Emma and Eduard Jonke, who were childless, came up with a plan. They made an offer to my parents to take Rita as their own and move to a house they had outside of Vienna, near the Semmering, a very pretty resort town. They had found someone who would make up false papers showing that she was their niece from Hungary. My parents could not bring themselves to be separated from my sister, and Rita, too, became hysterical when she heard about it. Not having accepted this generous offer proved to be fortuitous. Eduard Jonke, whom we called Uncle Eddy, contracted an infection and died in late summer of 1942. Emma collapsed at his funeral and died a week later. My sister would thus have been doomed. As it turned out, she survived the deportation to the East. Nevertheless, when mother, Rita, and I returned to Vienna and found these good people gone forever, we cried bitter tears for them and for all of us.

War with Russia
and Transports to Poland

The year 1940 had ended on a sour note. All of us were distraught by the fate of Laura and her daughter and by the Degenstuecks. Until her deportation in February, Laura was free and came to see us several times. She was worried about her aged mother and her desperation, especially when she talked about the occasional visits with her remorseful child, left us with deep sorrow.

In a letter dated January 24, 1941, written by my father to his brother Bernhard in America, he did not mention this calamity at all, but reported that their nephew Bernhard, Nachman's son, was in Yugoslavia. As to Nachman, my father wrote that he was now working at the iron works, in a job that severely taxed his strength but which again afforded him some protection.

Upbeat as usual, my father wrote of having been informed by the American Consul that all the papers needed for our immigration into the United States were now complete and that it was just a question of time. Father's remark in the letter that "Americans had crusts of ice around their hearts" turned out to be prophetic, for the consulate never called us in for a final check, and thus, completed papers notwithstanding, our time ran out and we were eventually deported. Many other Austrian Jews suffered the same fate, with their visas remaining unused forever.

According to the statistics compiled by the *Kultusgemeinde*, on January 1, 1941, there were 53,604 Jews still living in Austria. Almost three-fourths had either fled or had been taken into custody, but that was clearly not enough for the people in charge of Jewish policies, especially Eichmann,

and thus, in February 1941, the transports to Poland started once again. In charge were Alois and Anton Brunner.

Starting on February 1, the gymnasium at Castellezgasse was used mainly as a collection point and classes were suspended for almost two months. In a fit of pique, I went back to the gymnasium at Albertgasse and received permission from its director, Dr. Alex Goldstein, to attend classes there once again. I stayed at that school until the end of the academic year, which meant that despite all the obstacles, I had at least three years of gymnasium to my credit. I was to enjoy one-half of a year more of schooling before deportation, but in a different setting, at the *Piper Heim* itself.

On February 15, 1941, the first transport of Austrian Jews in this series left for Opole via Pulawy, including Laura and Lili Brender. In *Die Juden-verfolgung in Oesterreich 1938–1945* (The Persecution of Jews in Austria 1938–1945), Moser wrote that the transport contained 996 Jews. Herbert Rosenkranz, on the other hand, in *Verfolgung und Selbstbehauptung*, quoted the transport leader reporting a total of 1,034 Jews. The transport list itself, compiled by the Gestapo, showed 1,005 Jews. This dilemma was due to the two Brunners' habit of adding Jews at the last minute, Jews who went unrecorded in the general chaos, and while the figures of transports always hovered around the magic number of 1,000, it is extremely difficult to give an exact number.

Four days later, on February 19, 1941, 1,003 Jews left for Kielce, where they joined the existing ghetto, already overcrowded with Polish Jews and Jews who had been sent there from Czechoslovakia.

One week later, on February 26, 1941, another transport left for Opole via Pulawy. Among the 1,002 Jews were Samuel and Malvina Degenstueck.

On March 5, 1941, 1,000 Jews left for Modliborzyce, including father's cousin Jacob Merlin, called Bubi, who must have been added at the last minute; he is not on the list. There were also, among the 1,000 listed, a large number of Austrian Jews who had come to Vienna from the Burgenland.

The last transport in this series left for Lagow-Opatow on March 12, containing 1,001 Jews, making a total of over 5,000.

The people of each transport were brought from the school in vans to the Aspang Station, and although passenger cars for the journey to the East were provided, each deportee's experience depended on the accompanying personnel, especially the leader. If he was halfway decent, the same number of people were put into each car, there was drinking water along the way, and most important, there was heat. If, however, the leader, that is, the commanding officer, either did not care or wanted to show the others what a great Jew-hater he was, the journey became a nightmare. There was

overcrowding in some cars and overflowing toilets. Very often there was thirst since in those early days the Jews were forbidden to fetch water at the various railway stations. The willful behavior of the commanders and the whole harrowing trip served as a preparation of what was to come.

In every one of the villages or small towns to which they were brought, the Austrian Jews were added to the existing Jewish communities sharing whatever meager food was available and, thus, in many cases, there was literal starvation. No wonder then that the death rate among the newcomers was extremely high and that diseases were rampant.

A report dated April 11, 1941, "Opole ueber Pulawy," and addressed to the *Kultusgemeinde* in Vienna, stated that twenty-three people (fifteen women and eight men) died between February 28 and March 22; the oldest person was eighty-two years old, and the youngest person was fifty-seven years old. The report was signed by Heinrich J. Birnbach, president of the evacuated Viennese Jews; it arrived in Vienna on April 16, 1941, and has been preserved at the Central Archives for the History of the Jewish People in Jerusalem.

While the very old people were the first to die, once diseases became commonplace, the younger people succumbed as well, since there was little, if any, medication.

The Jews still in Vienna, including members of my own family, received letters that acquainted us with the realities of forced resettlement, and we became terribly agitated and concerned. We were totally unable to help, except for sending small food packages that more often than not were lost or stolen along the way.

A letter from one of the deportees was published in *Lebenszeichen aus Piaski: Briefe Deportierter aus dem District Lublin 1940–1943* (Messages from Piaski: Letters of Deportees from the Lublin District 1940–1943) edited by Gertrude Luckner and Else Rosenfeld; the letter indicated how good-hearted and helpful these poor Polish Jews were when confronted with the added burden of totally impoverished foreign Jews.

A small number of the deportees tried to come back to Vienna illegally. Some of them survived as so-called "U-Boats" by being hidden by Christians, but most of them were caught eventually as happened with Bubi, my father's cousin. After a stay in jail, they were usually deported. Very few survived, but there were occasional miracles, as for example the incredible saga of a girl from Rechnitz, a town in Austria's Burgenland.

Attached to my own transport to Riga in February 1942 was a group of about twenty Jews, men and women, kept separate from us, who had been deported once before and were now being deported once again. Not one of

them appeared on our actual transport list. Among them was Elizabeth Holzer, called Elsa, born in 1928, who together with her parents had been sent to Modliborzyce on March 5, 1941. Her parents, both ill and realizing the hopelessness of the situation, helped Elsa to scale a fence and bade her to join a group of Austrian Jews who were just about to leave. After a while, the group split up along the way and finally just Elsa and an older woman she met, Mrs. Anna Schreckinger, made their way south until they reached Vienna. By then it was warm enough for the two of them to sleep outdoors, hidden in parks, staying with acquaintances only to clean themselves and eat, and always trying to stay one step ahead of the police. With the advent of cold weather, sometime in October 1941, both of them were caught and landed in jail, where they were separated.

Just before boarding the train to Riga on February 6, 1942, we saw an Austrian police officer bringing an emaciated girl to the station, where she was added to the group of people standing at the other end of our car. We found out later that Mrs. Schreckinger was among them. With stern words to my father, Alois Brunner, our transport commander, warned that none of us was to speak or have anything to do with those "criminals" who were then put into our car; they were separated from our compartment by the toilets located in the middle of the car. It was only in the ghetto, at a much later time, when Elsa and my sister became friends, that I found out what had happened to them earlier and where they had been. My father had known all along.

Of the more than 2,000 Austrian Jews who had been sent to Opole via Pulawy in two transports, fifteen were still alive in the summer of 1945, when the war was finally over. One had been hidden by Christian friends in Vienna after she had walked back from Opole, thirteen had gone through a variety of concentration and labor camps, and one, who had fled to Russia in the summer of 1941, came back from Karaganda.

Of the more than 1,000 Austrian Jews who had been added to the Kielce ghetto, ten returned. Among them was Otto Glattstein, Selma Breitner's brother, who had been the ghetto elder there. He had not been deported from Vienna, however, but had been sent to Kielce with a transport from Czechoslovakia, to where he had fled in 1938. The other nine survivors had gone through Auschwitz and Ravensbrueck after the ghetto's liquidation.

There were only four survivors of the Modliborzyce transport. One of them left Modliborzyce just one week after his arrival there and survived the war as a U-Boat. Another one tried to do the same thing, lived as a U-Boat for over a year, but was caught and, miraculously, sent to Theresienstadt rather than to one of the extermination camps. Another survived the

concentration camp at Flossenburg, and the fourth one was Elsa Holzer, the girl from Rechnitz, who also survived the ghetto and the concentration camp Kaiserwald in Riga, as well as the fearsome extermination camp Stutthof.

Only three women and one man survived Lagow-Opatow. They lived with Polish farmers in the Lublin district and worked as farmhands until the war ended. Altogether, of the more than 5,000 Austrian Jews sent away with this second wave—Nisko was considered the first such wave—thirty-three survived the ordeal.

In Vienna, after the Degenstuecks had been deported and whatever they had left behind confiscated, the room in which they had lived now became home for a newly married couple, Alice (called Lizzy) and Fritz Brunn. She was Barry Kandelmann's sister, *the* Barry Kandelmann of the *Palamt*, and we were properly impressed whenever he visited. At that time, Fritz Brunn ran errands for several Jewish lawyers still in office; they worked on litigation cases and other problems engendered by Jews who had either fled or had been deported. Fritz was very talented and always in a good mood. He had a marvelous singing voice, could play several instruments, and seemed to know every Viennese song ever written.

In June 1941 the principals of the three schools still open for Jewish children announced that all those who had finished the third form of gymnasium or high school would be split up into groups and that their further instruction would either cease altogether or be given at various other sites. In my own case, it would be at the *Piper Heim*, albeit only in the afternoons. We were twelve girls, including myself. My very best friend was Martha Zieg. In late June, when we came to the home with our report cards, having finished the third form, our teacher of dance and gym, Dr. Gertrude Neumann, had arranged a lovely party for us. She had written a poem reflecting on each girl's character, and we each received charm bracelets for good luck; henceforth, Dr. Neumann would function as our homeroom teacher as well.

Dr. Egon Boehmer was to be the homeroom teacher for the fourteen boys in my form ordered to take instruction at the *Piper Heim*; in addition he taught mathematics as he always had done. Several other teachers came to the *Piper Heim* as well. Professor Gollerstepper taught German, literature, and history, his sister taught religion, and Professor Singer taught science.

Since our formal schooling took place after lunch, our mornings were spent helping take care of the small children in the nursery school and kindergarten located on the ground floor of our building at Mohapelgasse 2. The man after whom the school was named, Israel Piper, held the post of director and together with his charming wife saw to it that even though we

ostensibly "worked" during the morning hours, we were also given language lessons, particularly in English by Dr. Paul Stagel, a most devoted educator and scholar. He was the only one of my many male teachers to return to Vienna in 1945, having survived the Theresienstadt ghetto. Recognizing his excellence, the city of Vienna gave him a post as principal in one of Vienna's schools during the late 1940s; perhaps it was a restitution of sorts.

None of the boys in our class—called simply *"Die Vierte"* (the fourth)—survived. Of the twelve girls, besides myself only Vera Korkus came back. She survived Theresienstadt and Auschwitz, while I survived Riga and Stutthof. We met only once thereafter, in 1952 in New York, and talked about those bitter years. Of the younger children, who still used the *Piper Heim* as an after-school center, only my sister came back; none of the others survived the deportation to the East.

Sunday, June 22, 1941, was my mother's forty-third birthday. Even in these difficult times, we were going to have a traditional birthday party for her; my father had procured silk stockings and a shawl; notwithstanding ration cards, Rita and I bought chocolates for her; Mrs. Einhorn had baked a nutcake and Lotte Einhorn gave her a book of Heinrich Heine's poems. That book was one of the few that we managed to keep, even in the Riga ghetto, until we were transferred to the Kaiserwald concentration camp. Mrs. Weitz had knitted gloves for mother to be used the next winter, and from the Brunns she received a blue flannel robe. Unfortunately, both these lovely gifts were in our luggage, which we never saw again once we disembarked from our train in Riga. Luckily, the book of poems was among the items in my mother's large purse.

The very best present, or so we thought, was the electrifying news that Germany and Russia were at war as of this day! My father was jubilant about the "second front." He predicted that all of our troubles would be over within six weeks; several guests who had come to celebrate Mama's birthday agreed with his assessment and so we went to sleep that Sunday night with the certainty of having weathered the worst. Everything would be much better from now on. How wrong we were to hope! How we overestimated Russia's ability to withstand the German forces! How naive we were not to realize that the war against Russia would actually be the death knell of six million Jews alone, and so many other people as well! How could we envision that the *Einsatzgruppen*, those agents of destruction, had been formed even before the attack on Russia, and that Hitler had given Heinrich Himmler full powers to eliminate us? How could anyone have known? As early as May 30, 1941, certain of final victory, the German

Foreign Ministry had made plans to divide the Soviet Union into four parts, complete with borders and *Reichskommissars*, but we knew none of this.

There was, at first, no communication from the frontlines and we went on with our lives, in blissful ignorance, not realizing that the dreaded *Einsatzkommandos* were hard at work in the East, following in the footsteps of the invading army and killing without mercy.

In fact, while we were still hoping, the Austrian *Hauptscharfuehrer* Felix Landau, a *Blutordenstraeger* (bearer of the order of the blood), kept a war diary in which he noted his murderous activities during the month of July 1941. While in Drohobycz, Poland, Landau went to see "a batch of Jews to be shot the next day, on July 15." He noted that most of them were Viennese Jews, "still dreaming of Vienna," who had fled to Poland after the *Anschluss*, but had now been caught in the Nazi net. His entry for the fifteenth, where he discussed the actual murder of his fellow Austrians, was a comment on "the incredible courage of the victims," but he added that their death left him completely unmoved. Landau's diary was published in 1991, as part of the book *Those Were the Days: the Holocaust as Seen by the Perpetrators and Bystanders*, by Ernst Klee, Willi Dressen, and Volker Riess. The callous young diarist, born in 1910 in Vienna, had been adopted by a man his mother married in 1911, and that man was in fact a Jew, who died in 1919. Felix Landau, bearing his adoptive father's name, joined the NSDAP in 1931 and was a participant in the Dollfuss affair of 1934. Afterward, he left Austria for Germany and during the war served with the SD (*Sicherheits Dienst*, Security Service) for several years. In addition to participating in a number of massacres, he was in charge of organizing Jewish labor in his section. Although arrested by U.S. forces in 1946, in Linz, Felix Landau was able to escape from the Glasenbach prison camp, but was found several years later, living under a false name. In 1963, a Stuttgart court sentenced him to life in prison.

As we had done the year before, we used the fourth section of Vienna's Jewish cemetery as a sort of playground, and for the few remaining children, the summer of 1941 had moments of great beauty.

On July 18 we celebrated my father's birthday, just days before Hermann Goering wrote a note to Reinhard Heydrich asking him to submit the plans for the "*Endloesung der Judenfrage*," the "Final Solution of the Jewish Question," thus coining a phrase that would forever remain a stain on Germany's honor.

There is no way to describe our desolation when the news of the German victories in the East began to circulate in the media. It seemed that nothing and no one could or would stop the German advance. Any hopes we may

still have had for an end to this cruel war were dashed every time the newspaper headlines proclaimed still another German victory at the Eastern front.

Starting September 1, 1941, every Jew living within the German lands had to wear a six-pointed yellow star affixed to the left side of his or her chest. Ours said "*Jude*," (Jew) in pseudo-Hebrew lettering and if any Jew was found without the star, he or she had to face a stiff jail sentence, which usually culminated in being sent away with the next transport scheduled.

On the very first day of our wearing the yellow star, my sister Rita and I were accosted and beaten up at the corner of Hollandstrasse and Sperlgasse by a bunch of rowdy boys our age. There were seven of them. It was the lady in charge of the Anker Bakery who came out of the store, chased them away, and consoled us. Other adults just passed by and did not interfere.

That same day, in one of the rooms at the *Palamt* that we were still able to use, Aron Menczer made an unexpected appearance. He had come to Vienna to see the dentist, but he wanted to talk to us about the yellow star and told us not to regard it as a badge of shame but of honor. He went back to the farm and we never saw him again.

By November 10, 1941, according to a report by Josef Loewenherz, president of the *Kultusgemeinde*, 130,146 Jews had fled Austria. To that figure, the "other" kind of Jews must be added, Jews not part of the *Kultusgemeinde*, but still part of the oppressed. They, too, had fled, building new lives in safer places. Taking their numbers into consideration, the final count would show that more than two-thirds of Austria's Jewish community would suffer exile and hardship, but would be safe from Hitler's Final Solution.

Transports to Litzmannstadt

After a hiatus of six months, efforts to get rid of Austria's Jews once and for all were resumed. It was said that this was due to the lack of available apartments in Vienna and among the records presented at the International Military Tribunal, there was a letter, dated December 3, 1940, which in fact emphasized that the Jews of Vienna were to be deported precisely because of a need for their apartments. That excuse was as good as any other. The real reason was that the people responsible for our destruction simply saw it as an ongoing job they were committed to. What is more, most of them liked it, be it for personal enrichment, for deeply ingrained anti-Semitism, or because it gave those common men a feeling of unprecedented power.

This time, the destination of the transports would be Lodz, the "Manchester of Poland," called Litzmannstadt by the Germans. The collection point for this new series of transports and for subsequent series was mainly the Sperlschule augmented by a small building at Malzgasse 16. Anton Brunner preferred the Sperlschule and made it his headquarters. Jews were held at the school for several days, but sometimes these days stretched into weeks until such a date when a transport would leave, after which more Jews would then be brought to the collection point.

The system of apprehending Jews varied. Some of them received their orders by letter, commanding them to report at the school on specified days, others were picked up in their homes by Austrian police, some were brought to the school or directly to the train station from the jails in which they were held for minor infractions—lately mainly for being caught not wearing the yellow star. When these "perpetrators" were brought to the school, they were

housed in the basement and were registered on the transport lists, as were the Brenders and the Degenstuecks for Opole. When they were brought from jail directly to the station, however, they were usually not on the lists, as was the case with Elsa Holzer and the other nineteen on the transport of February 6, 1942, to Riga.

Still others were "collected" en masse. In that case, police, supported by SS, simply closed off a street at both ends. After that, certain employees of the *Kultusgemeinde*, called *Ordners*, fanned out into the houses on both sides of the street, telling the Jews living in specified apartments to pack one suitcase each and be ready in an hour. After this all-too-short time had passed, a cursory check by an SS official took place and everyone had to assemble downstairs and the trek to the school began, watched over carefully by the police and the SS. Upon arrival at the school, people were registered, their names were entered on lists, and they were assigned to former classrooms, where mattresses were laying around helter skelter. Chaos reigned until everyone found himself or herself a space, the mattress surrounded by the suitcase and hand-luggage brought from home. It was, and I am sure it was meant to be, a dismal experience. Personal hygiene was almost impossible, facilities at the school were hopelessly inadequate for so many people at once, food was scarce, people were perched either on their mattresses or luggage, looking extremely uncomfortable and unhappy. In a way, one had a foretaste of what was yet to come.

After several days of this treatment, the hour of judgment arrived. One was "commissioned," which was an interesting euphemism for ceasing to be an Austrian citizen and being turned into an expendable commodity. In charge of this judgment was Anton Brunner. Identity cards, birth certificates, marriage certificates, diplomas, and citizenship papers were all taken away, sometimes even torn up and discarded. One had ceased to be a person. Items of value, such as money and jewelry, had to be handed to Brunner's assistants. With that, one was told the day of departure, sometimes even the place to where the transport would be going, and Brunner then barked a gruff "Dismissed."

From time to time, although rarely, the flow of this administrative exercise was interrupted when someone begged to either stay or go with an ill relative, or when someone who should never have been brought to the school in the first place, having an Aryan husband or a wife, asked to be released. It was they who would experience the cold and ever-present rage of Anton Brunner. Often he did exactly the opposite of what he should have done had he followed the laws that spelled out the treatment to be given to certain groups. He had no mercy, he had no understanding, it seemed that

for him it was not just a job but a terrible passion, and there was no one who could have or would have helped his victims. If, at times, a higher ranking official overruled him, a rather rare event, as was the case with Mr. Aufrich-tig, the owner of our last apartment, Brunner eventually got even. The hapless person would simply be added to another transport, and could not be found in time, never to be heard from again. Yet, at his trial in 1946, Anton Brunner proclaimed his innocence and averred that "he had only done his duty."

Our landlady, Mrs. Taube Einhorn and her daughter Lotte received the dreaded deportation letter in the mail, and just one day later, Mrs. Toni Weitz did also. All three of them were to report on October 9. We helped them pack one suitcase each, as specified in the notice, and on the appointed day, my father and Fritz Brunn took the women to the Sperlschule, just a few blocks from our house.

There were five transports of Austrian Jews sent to Lodz. The first one left on October 15 and contained 1,005 persons, the second one left on October 19 and contained 1,003 persons, the third one left on October 23 and contained 991 persons, the fourth one left October 28 and contained 998 persons, and the fifth and last one in this series left on November 2 and also contained 998 persons, making a total of 4,995.

Mrs. Antonia (Toni) Weitz left with the first transport on October 15 and was listed as living on Siegfried Strasse 99 in the Lodz ghetto. Her age was given as fifty-four, and that was correct. In fact, the handwritten lists that were compiled in the ghetto in early February 1942 on orders of the Council of Elders were for the most part very thorough, but difficult to read. They are a part of the *Archiwum Miejskie* (City Archives) in Lodz.

Mrs. Taube Einhorn left with the second transport on October 19 and was listed as living on Hohensteiner Strasse 9/7a in the Lodz ghetto. Her age was given as sixty-seven, and that was correct. Lotte, however, was not listed on the original transport list, nor was she listed as living in the Lodz ghetto. The archives at the *Kultusgemeinde* in Vienna do not have an entry for her either, indicating that she did not leave with a later transport. It must be assumed, therefore, that Lotte Einhorn's ultimate fate will never be known; it would have been unthinkable for her to have left her mother and run away. Had she died at the school, the records would have shown this, unless Anton Brunner decided not to report her death or perhaps the report was lost in the general chaos. As far as we knew, she had gone to Lodz, and the mystery became known only when I began the research for this book.

My best friend Martha Zieg and her parents also left with the second transport. While the ghetto records listed their dates of birth, their address

was left out, but I remember that they lived on Rembrandt Strasse in the ghetto, since I did receive one postcard from Martha in January 1942 shortly before I, together with my family, was deported as well. On October 17, just two days before that second transport was to leave, Martha discovered that she still had one of my books. Perhaps because she was such a charming and lovable child, she received permission to leave the school, accompanied by one of the *Ordners*, and brought the book to my house. We said a tearful good-bye and she asked that we would let her sister Adele, who lived in England, know that they had gone to Lodz. It was almost as if she knew that they would not return. Sad to say, we never found Adele Zieg, although we did write to England after the war was over.

Father's aunt, Ernestine Peczenik, a widow, together with her daughter Anna Zauderer, also a widow, left for Lodz with the third transport on October 23. Aunt Ernestine was sixty-seven at the time, and Anna was forty-nine. Anna's husband, Willi, had been sent to Nisko two years earlier and had been murdered upon his arrival there. Ever since the two women found out about his death, they wore black and rarely went out. Now, according to the ghetto records, they had been assigned to separate apartments and did not even retain the comfort of each other's presence.

Conditions at the Lodz ghetto were catastrophic. The immediate and dreadful shock experienced by the Western Jews when they were confronted by this stark contrast of what they had been used to until then was horrifying. By early February, 296 of the people who had arrived three months earlier with those five transports from Austria had died of "natural" causes, which, in reality, meant that they had simply starved to death or that they had committed suicide. The Lodz ghetto, in contrast to other ghettos in the East, was totally isolated from the outside world; it was, therefore, impossible to smuggle food into the ghetto, as was done in most other ghettos, and the result was starvation. At one point, the Lodz ghetto contained 160,000 Jews, mainly from Lodz and surrounding towns and villages. The arrival of Jews from the Reich only increased the overcrowded and unsanitary conditions. Furthermore, it was a working ghetto, filled with shops and factories, where food rations were based on productivity. Thus, the enigmatic ghetto elder Chaim Rumkowski, who dreamt of saving those who could and would work, felt that he had to sacrifice the old, the sick, and the children, in order to do so.

Realizing that their diminished rations would mean their doom, some Viennese Jews wrote a letter to Rumkowski in January in which they begged him to heed their cause and have mercy. This petition was quoted in an article written by Lucjan Dobroszycki, entitled, "Wiener Juden im Ghetto

Lodz" (Viennese Jews in the Lodz Ghetto). In fact, the original petition rests in the Jewish historical archives in Warsaw. Dobroszycki points out that there were many more Austrian Jews in the ghetto than the 5,000 who had come directly from Vienna. A very large transport from Czechoslovakia, numbering 5,000 Jews, contained perhaps 2,000 Austrian Jews who had fled to that country in 1938. He comments that even though the ghetto was inured to death, the many suicides committed by Austrian Jews made an impression. As the majority of the deportees were rather old, they could not be used as workers in the ghetto's many factories. Little by little, they bartered the few things they had been able to keep in order to augment their insufficient rations. When they had nothing left to barter and were dependent on the collective soup kitchens, hunger took its toll and they succumbed.

Younger people among the deportees were always able to find work in the various industries of the ghetto, but even if they did get some addition to their meager rations, the work sapped their strength, they could not deal with the cold, and diseases took hold of them so that in spite of their youth, they too were doomed.

The Germans, however, were not willing to wait for them to die in this way. They wanted to eliminate the "useless eaters," as they thought of them, with greater efficiency, and for that task they had chosen a village only 60 kilometers west of Lodz called Kulmhof in German and Chelmno in Polish. A large castle in that village would serve as a collection point, the actual killing would take place in gas vans built by the Saurer Werke of Austria and Berlin, and the burial site would be the forested land around and near the village. Operations at Kulmhof began shortly after Christmas 1941. In addition to the German officials, such as administrators, drivers, and guards, there were also a number of Polish prisoners and several Jews who served mainly as personnel for unloading the gas vans and burying the victims. Later on, the Jews would have the task of exhuming and burning the corpses.

People in the ghetto were told that they were being resettled to another camp and were to take their luggage along. They were brought to Kulmhof in trains, spent some time in the castle and sometimes in the town's church, and then were herded into the gas vans, most of the time already stark naked. Their clothing and luggage were, for the most part, transferred to Pabianice, a small village where Jewish labor details were busy sorting the items according to value. Pictures of these workers amid the enormous mountains of clothing and other paraphernalia were taken by the director of the ghetto's finance administration, Walter Genewein, a Nazi Party member from Salzburg, Austria. His superior, the head of the Economic Division and Food Distribution, was Joseph Haemmerle, from Vorarlberg, Austria.

When Genewein returned home to Salzburg after the ghetto's liquidation, he took the pictures, most of which were in color, with him. Thus, the photos taken upon the arrival of Austrian Jews in Lodz as well as of their leaving for Kulmhof, in addition to the workforce in Pabianice, taken by a fellow Austrian, were silent witnesses to a shameful chapter of history.

In addition to the 296 Austrian Jews who had died in the three months after their arrival in the ghetto, another 788 died there during 1942, and the records showed that 3,274 Austrian Jews had been "resettled." The German word on these documents was "*Aussiedlung*," truly an ingenious euphemism for murder.

Thus, by November 1942, according to the records of the Lodz ghetto administration, there were 621 Austrian Jews still alive. Approximately twenty had been sent to outside commandos earlier but were never heard from again. They may have been part of either the Kulmhof or the Pabianice commandos.

During the summer of 1942, three Polish Jews from the Lodz ghetto were brought to Riga. The official who brought them had a very high position and kept them at the place in the city where he had his office.[16] On weekends the three were permitted to come into the Riga ghetto together with German Jews who worked at the same place, called *Baugruppe Giesler* (Construction Group Giesler). Moses Tellmann and Abraham Goldmann were tailors; Mayer Wiltzkowsky was a tool and die maker. From them, the ghetto inmates found out about conditions in the Lodz ghetto, which, according to their reports, were so much worse than in Riga. They were aware of the fact that the resettlements from the Lodz ghetto ended up in Chelmno; they also knew about the gas vans. All three had lost their families by then. Tellmann and Goldmann survived. Wiltzkowsky, blond and blue-eyed, was apprehended while walking freely on one of the city's streets and was later shot at Zentralka, Riga's main jail.

In August 1944, when the Lodz ghetto was dissolved, the majority of the inmates were taken to Auschwitz where selections were held and most of them were gassed. Those chosen for work were sent to various concentration and labor camps, including Stutthof, Dachau, Ravensbrueck, Buchenwald, Bergen Belsen, Mauthausen, Gleiwitz, and Czenstochow.

Several thousand were not even considered "worthy" of being taken to Auschwitz. Thus, although the death factory at Kulmhof had been shut down since March 1943, it was reopened to dispose of these old and infirm Jews. They were killed while evidence of the earlier killings was still being obliterated in the usual way. Pyres were built and the exhumed corpses were burned. Their ashes were scattered into the nearby rivers. Upon completion,

the Jewish workers, who had labored on this gruesome task, were thrown onto the pyres so that there would be no witnesses.

Working with the actual deportation lists and comparing them with the records compiled by the *Kultusgemeinde* in Vienna once the war had ended, I found that there were eight survivors of the first transport, two survivors of the second transport, three survivors of the third transport, two survivors of the fourth transport, and three survivors of the fifth and final transport. Thus, of the 4,995 Austrian Jews sent to Litzmannstadt in the fall of 1941, a total of eighteen survived the ordeal of the ghetto as well as of several other camps.

Three more survivors of the Lodz ghetto were treated as returnees, even though they had not gone to the ghetto with any of the Vienna transports. The two men and one woman had come to the Lodz ghetto with the transport from Bruenn. In fact, the woman was by then married to one of the Viennese deportees who was on the transport list.

Among the survivors of the first transport to Lodz was Sofie Rosenkranz (born 1901). At the time of her deportation from Vienna, she was forced to leave her daughter Felicia, then seventeen, behind.The young girl moved in with her paternal grandmother, Dora Rosenkranz, and both of them were deported to the Riga ghetto on January 11, 1942. Seventy-three-year-old Dora was murdered shortly after their arrival. Felicia, a stunning beauty, survived the ghetto and subsequent concentration camps, returning to Vienna on June 3, 1945. She was lodged at the former *Piper Heim*, together with the few of us who had returned by then. Only one day later, Sofie arrived in Vienna and was sent to the same house. It was late afternoon and we were sitting and talking on the second floor of the building. As she ascended the stairs, accompanied by the superintendent's wife, there was a kind of hush. The quiet was broken by Felicia's voice crying "Mama, Mama," and the older woman, beautiful like her daughter, running up the last few steps, laughing and crying as well, saying "I knew it, I knew it, I told myself to go on, I knew I would find you again." As mother and daughter embraced, we all were witness to what can only be called a miracle, and it touched us deeply. For most of the returnees, however, there would be no such miracles. Just sorrow.

Transports to Riga, Latvia

Shortly after the last of the Litzmannstadt transports had left Vienna, my family and the Brunns were informed that we had to move out of apartment 7 at 15 Hollandstrasse, since the former owner, Mrs. Taube Einhorn, was no longer there. We faced problems, for it was hard to get lodging for a family of four. Jews were being pushed together more than ever, but finally my parents were able to find a room at a rather nice apartment at Lilienbrunngasse 9.

The two bedrooms were occupied, but we were given the wood-paneled dining room, lined with four leather couches. The only thing that disturbed us, especially at first, was the fact that the tenants who lived in the bedrooms had to walk through the dining room when they wanted to go to the bathroom or the kitchen, or just out. Yet, with the specter of deportation hanging over every Jew in Vienna, discomforts of this kind were not taken that seriously. It was the cold that was hard on us; the winter had started early and there was little firewood. Although our moving date was only November 22, I remember the fierce north wind and the cold quite clearly.

The owner of the apartment was Mr. Fritz Aufrichtig, a widower, of whom it was said that his daughter was married to a very influential gentile. This turned out to be the case. Aufrichtig, a gruff man, obviously had been very wealthy at one time. The furniture in his apartment attested to that. He used one of the bedrooms; the other one was shared by two elderly ladies, one of whom was a very distant relative of my father. In fact, it was she who managed to get us into that apartment. A former maid's room next door was shared by the Brunns and Fritz's mother, Ida Brunn. They had taken her in

despite the lack of space, since, she, too, had lost her room in the apartment when the people had been deported.

My father still worked with the architect, but mother could not do alterations any longer; there was simply not enough space in the new domicile. She therefore was busy selling chocolates on the Black Market; her source of bonbons and other such goodies was an old friend who had been the owner of a chocolate factory in Wiener Neustadt. Some of his employees saw to it that he would not be without wares to sell.

Fritz Brunn was lucky. He had gotten a job in one of the food stores for Jews and was in charge of eggs and dairy products. He always brought something home for everyone, even if it was only an egg, and made all of us feel better with his optimism and good humor. Just a few days into January, Fritz told me to come to the store; small pastries filled with nuts (*Nusskipferl*), slightly stale but still a treat, would go on sale the next day; he had put some aside for my family. I came to the store on Zirkusgasse in late afternoon and he gave me a bag containing twelve of them. Both he and I were careful not to be observed.

On the way home, I met my uncle Nachman, coming from work, tired and worn out. Both of us were very happy to see each other and despite the cold, we talked for a few minutes. On an impulse, I gave him four of the pastries. He was very touched. Putting his hand on my head, he blessed me. I have never forgotten how good I felt just then. When I told my parents what I had done, I could see that they were pleased. Of course, we did not realize that this was the last time I would ever see my uncle, of whom I was very fond. He was the only person I ever met who knew all of Friedrich von Schiller's poems by heart.

In the fall of 1941, according to the records of the *Kultusgemeinde*, there were only 377 elementary school children, and 505 high school children of the Jewish faith left in Vienna. The fall transports had in effect closed the Sperlschule; the Albert Gymnasium was likewise out of bounds, and therefore these children, if they and their parents so desired, had only three places to go to where instructions of one sort or another were still given. One was the Girls' Home on Haasgasse, the other was the Palestine Bureau, and the third was the *Piper Heim*. Most of the children I knew liked to go to school. The designated rooms in each of these three places were much warmer than our respective homes and there was some food for us at the *Piper Heim*. The various subjects still taught were stimulating, and it was good to be with other kids. Despite these uncertain times and the loss of so many of our friends who had already been deported, we were happy, as children, and only children, can manage to be under great adversity.

Many of us were preparing for two big Chanukah productions, one to be held at the *Palamt* at the beginning of December, and one to be held at the *Piper Heim* by the end of December. The star in both productions was Bertha Wieselthier, a classmate of mine. Born in 1928, she had taken singing and dancing lessons as soon as she could talk and walk, and not only was she blessed with enormous talent, but also with a beauty that was absolutely breathtaking. Her little sister Evi, then just four and in nursery school, was also very beautiful. Both girls were watched over by their very attentive widowed mother, Frieda Wieselthier, who once told my parents that she hoped her children's beauty and talent would one day work in their favor. It was not to be.

On the eagerly awaited Sunday, December 7, 1941, the big hall at the *Palamt* was filled to capacity and we were not disappointed. Bertha was in almost every scene—some biblical, come comical—interspersed with many songs, but her greatest moment of triumph came when she played the role of the "*Dreydel*," the traditional Chanukah toy that is spun and deter- mines gains or losses of either money, nuts, or raisins. Bertha's slim body was encased in a silver-colored box, with a Hebrew letter pasted on each of its four sides. On her head she had a matching, silver-colored pointed hat, and she stood perfectly still on the darkened stage as the floodlight first showed her lovely face, then travelled over the box and those perfect legs sticking out from it clad in silver tap shoes. Finally, as everybody applauded, Professor Kulka came out onto the stage and made believe that he was looking for something. Suddenly, he "discovered" her, went over and touched the pointed hat. As the music started, at first slowly and then faster and faster, Bertha twirled and whirled, tap dancing her heart out, until finally, as the music slowed, she came to a stop, toppled over gracefully, and the audience went wild.

After the show, when we got dressed (I had been in the Menorah ballet, playing one of the candles and then singing a song of how Jews braved the worst times and would do so now), Bertha said to me, "You know, that was the happiest day of my life." She also said that she looked forward to another performance, somewhat different, on Sunday, December 21, at the *Piper Heim.*

The fact that this happy day for her and for her friends was also the day that brought the United States into the war seemed a good omen. Again, as once before when Germany went to war against Russia, we hoped that this time our prayers would be answered. But the U.S. forces were busy in the Pacific theater of war, headlines in the German newspapers during the coming weeks spoke of America's defeat by the Japanese, and the deporta-

tions had quietly started anew. This time, interrupted by just one transport to Minsk on November 28, the destination was to be Riga, Latvia.

During the second and third week in December, several streets in the second district were closed off, and Bertha, together with her mother and sister, was among those taken to the Sperlschule where she had been a student in earlier years. Thus, when the great performance at the *Piper Heim* took place, all the parts that had been Bertha's were given to the "lucky" ones, and the show went on. Dr. Egon Boehmer, the announcer, and Dr. Gertrude Neumann, our dance instructor, kept us on our toes. We danced, we sang, we entertained, and we received much applause. It was a very successful production, overshadowed only by Bertha's absence. Mercifully, neither we nor the grown-ups could imagine that many of the *Piper Heim*'s former students had either already been murdered or would be murdered shortly, or that the missing star of the show, Bertha Wieselthier, whom we tried unsuccessfully to replace, would soon lie in a mass grave in the Bikernieku Forest in Riga.

The first transport intended for Riga had left Vienna on November 23, 1941, and although the Gestapo transport lists still say "Riga," it had gone to Kovno, Lithuania, instead. The 995 Jews arrived there on November 26 and were all murdered on November 29, together with a transport that had come from Breslau. The massacre took place at Fort IX, and was described in a letter written by *Standartenfuehrer* Karl Jaeger to his superior, *Brigadefuehrer* Dr. Franz Walter Stahlecker. These were the very first Austrian Jews to be murdered as a group without a selection. It was only the beginning.

The next transport to leave for Riga on December 3 actually arrived there. It contained 1,042 people. The new arrivals were made part of a totally inadequate camp near Riga, in the village of Jumpramuize, which the Germans called Jungfernhof and which eventually became a model farm. The newly arrived Austrian Jews met Jews from Nuremberg and Stuttgart at Jungfernhof and were joined on the next day by a transport from Hamburg.

The next transport from Vienna, of which the Wieselthiers were a part, left on January 11, 1942, and arrived in Riga on January 15. After having spent almost four weeks at the Sperlschule, the deportees most likely felt that anything would be better than staying there. Worse was to come. Upon arrival, they were divided into two groups. Approximately 700 went to Jungfernhof and the other 300 went to what was called the German ghetto. There was also a Latvian ghetto, divided from the German ghetto by barbed wire. It contained the remnants of Riga's Jews, about 4,500. Over 25,000 had been murdered in the nearby Rumbula Forest in two large "operations," one on November 29 and the other on December 8, 1941.

At the Skirotava Station in Riga, where their transport was divided, many families were separated; if anyone had the temerity to ask if they could stay together, they were told that they would be reunited very soon. The approximately 700 people who arrived at Jungfernhof, including the Wieselthiers, found essentially the same catastrophic disorder, chaos, cold, hunger, dirt, and desperation as had been encountered by the previous transport, of whom quite a number had already died. The other 300, when reaching the ghetto, located in the oldest and most dilapidated section of Riga called *Moskauer Vorstadt* (Moscow suburb), were confronted by a similar horror, except that they were driven into houses after the long and difficult walk, unlike those at Jungfernhof who had to sleep in dilapidated barns or in sheds.

The German ghetto was divided into groups based on origin. The newcomers found six established groups made up of Jews who had come within the last few weeks. They were the Cologne group, the Cassel group, the Duesseldorf group, the Bielefeld group, and the Prague group. Eventually, there would be ten such groups in the German ghetto. Each group numbered approximately 1,000 people, and since the new arrivals from Vienna numbered only 300, they were not deemed enough to have their own group. The day after their arrival, they were all added to the Prague group, but on the next day, when a transport from Berlin arrived, leading to the formation of the Berlin group, half of the Viennese Jews were added to it, while the other half stayed with the Prague group.

Among the latter were two sisters, Olly Adler and Gerda Hacker. Their father had been ordered to go to Jungfernhof upon arrival. Olly, whose husband had been an inmate of Buchenwald ever since 1939, was one of the most beautiful women in the ghetto. Blond, blue-eyed, tall, and slim, she made heads turn even when totally bundled up against the cold. The commandant of the ghetto, *Obersturmfuehrer* Kurt Krause, noticed her when she was part of a work detail, called *Kommando*, sent out to remove snow from Riga's streets. He asked her some questions about her former profession and when she told him that she had learned to be a beautician, he created the ghetto's one and only beauty parlor and it was all hers!

It is not too hard to imagine what the price for this privilege was, but Olly cannot be judged by conventional mores. She had a younger sister for whom she felt responsible, and she wanted whatever was best for both of them at that time and in that place. Krause was obviously smitten with the blond beauty. The idea of *Rassenschande* (racial shame), a crime in German eyes against the purity of race, did not concern him. He was, after all, master over life and death and far more powerful than can be imagined, comparable only

to a medieval king. His word was law. It was rumored that he had other girlfriends in the ghetto, but he spent quite a lot of time at the "beauty parlor."

In January 1943, Krause left the ghetto on different assignment. Some time later he became the commandant of Salaspils, another camp in the vicinity, which by that time had become a camp for Russians and Latvians, having been built by Jews in earlier times. In October 1943, Krause came to the ghetto in order to attend the funeral of the Jewish group elder Guenther Fleischel. One month later, he was present at the ghetto's liquidation. He is supposed to have been killed during a skirmish with partisans in Poland.

Shortly after Fleischel's funeral, the sisters Adler and Hacker were taken to the newly erected concentration camp Kaiserwald in a suburb of Riga. Hans Hannes, one of the German criminal prisoners in charge of the Jews, fell in love with Olly. This time, a very jealous female SS guard, the *Aufseherin* Eva Kowa, reported this affair to commandant *Obersturmbannfuehrer* Albert Sauer, who promptly sent Olly to Riga's main jail, *Zentralka*. She was there for several months and was shot just a few weeks before the Germans evacuated Riga in October 1944. After Olly was taken away from Kaiserwald, Gerda Hacker got occasional handouts of food from a very contrite and remorseful Hannes. He was very careful about it so that his new lover, Eva Kowa, should not vent her anger at yet another helpless Jewess. In September 1944, Gerda was part of the second and last transport from Riga to reach the extermination and concentration camp Stutthof. She did not survive the following winter.

In Frederick Forsythe's lurid novel, *The Odessa file*, in addition to many other inaccuracies, he reports Olly coming from Munich, helping other Jews, and being the lover of the Austrian *Obersturmfuehrer* Eduard Roschmann, the subsequent commandant of the Riga ghetto, whom he calls "the Butcher of Riga." Roschmann's fame actually rests on his work as head of *Kommando* Stuetzpunkt, which exhumed and burned the bodies in Latvia's killing fields. Forsythe could have stuck to the truth. It was indeed stranger than fiction.

On January 26, 1942, another transport left Vienna for Riga, containing 1,200 Jews. Although the train at the Aspang Station in Vienna had been ready to leave in early afternoon, there was a delay; it was found that one of the cars had a broken window and so the whole transport had to wait until a glazier came to fix it. Julius Rubin, one of the few children who would eventually survive, sat next to the broken window and watched as the glazier worked. Suddenly the man looked up and told him gleefully: "*Wo ihr hinkommt, werdet ihr Alle erschossen!*" (At the place you are going to, all of you will be shot). Having said that, the glazier went away, leaving behind a rather stunned boy, whose mother was finally able to

calm him down. Mr. Rubin, who now lives in New York City, says that whenever he hears an Austrian's assertion that he or she did not know what happened to the Jews, he thinks of the glazier.

This time, all of those transported were permitted to walk into the ghetto, and at last, the ghetto had a Vienna group. Krause appointed Emil Loebl group elder; his assistant was to be Manfred Lemberger. Else Sekules was put in charge of forming *Kommandos*. A few of the original 300 Viennese Jews were added to the new group, but most of them stayed with groups Prague and Berlin, even though another transport had arrived from Berlin, increasing the size of that group to over 2,000.

On Thursday, February 5, the members of groups Berlin and Vienna, all of whom lived on Berliner Strasse, the former Mazu Kalna Iela, were kept in the ghetto and had to undergo a selection; in charge was *Obersturm-fuehrer* Gerhard Maywald, who let it be known that those chosen by him, as they filed by, would be taken to a fish cannery at a place called Duenamuende. They would work inside and conditions would be more favorable than in the ghetto. Maywald's superior, *Sturmbannfuehrer* Dr. Rudolf Lange, was absent from Riga at the time. He had not as yet returned from Berlin, where he had been invited to attend the Wannsee Conference.

In early spring of 1977, at his trial in Hamburg, Gerhard Maywald said that he had invented the story about the fish canneries in Duenamuende in order to quiet the victims; he felt that it was "decent" of him to send them to their deaths with illusions. When, for example, the Viennese Anna Sauerquell told him that she was a nurse by profession, Maywald seemed glad and told her that she could go along to Duenamuende, since the people would be very much in need of a nurse. But when her son Kurt, tall and good-looking like his mother, wanted to go with her, Maywald did not permit it.

Kurt was heartbroken and, using the houses as shields, ran up Berliner Strasse to see the people being loaded into vans. To his horror he noticed how they were actually pushed and thrown into the vans, and he was perhaps the only person in the ghetto to guess what was about to happen. Attending the trial in 1977 as plaintiff, he did not get much satisfaction. For Maywald's participation in the selection he was sentenced to four years in jail, but since he had already served some time while on trial, he was soon released.

The "*Aktion*" of February 5, 1942, was localized in that it only concerned groups Vienna and Berlin. The latter was made up of many older people and Maywald selected over 1,000 of them for Duenamuende. Of the Viennese, he selected about 400. Not one person, no matter how clever, could imagine any danger, for quite often, when he asked and found that at least one member of a family worked, he would send the whole family back

to their apartment. Furthermore, the Baltic Sea was known for its variety and abundance of fish and, thus, being sent to a cannery seemed logical.

Riga's river is the Daugava (Duena in German). On very old maps one can find a little hamlet called Duenamuende, just where the Duena flows into the Baltic Sea. But that was not the place where the 1,500 Jews from Berlin and Vienna were sent. Instead, they were brought to the Bikernieku Forest and murdered on February 5 and 6. The terrible truth was known not only to their murderers, both German and Latvian, but also to several members of the ghetto's Jewish police. They had been taken to the forest three days earlier and had to dig several large mass graves. Threatened with dire consequences for themselves and their families, they kept silent. Kurt Sauerquell kept silent too. When voicing his suspicions, he met nothing but disbelief. In retrospect, it seems clear that in order to keep their sanity, the inmates of the ghetto preferred to be ignorant.

At the Wannsee Conference, Dr. Lange, the real expert, was an unqualified success. He was promoted to *Obersturmbannfuehrer* and returned to Riga where he continued his work for the remainder of the Germans' presence there. He was next posted at the fortress Posen, and on February 10, 1945, was advanced to *Standartenfuehrer*. He is said to have found his end during the fierce battles there, but there were no witnesses.

The inmates of the ghetto had been told that, with the arrival of a transport from Dortmund on January 30, the ghetto was now complete, with the localized *Aktion* on February 5 pointing in that direction. Yet there was to be one more transport permitted to enter—or at least part of a transport. That was my own.

Taking Leave of Vienna

On Sunday, February 1, 1942, just as we were getting up, there was a knock on the door. Jewish employees of the *Kultusgemeinde*, called *Ordners*, had come to tell us that we had one hour to get ready for "resettlement." Police and SS had closed off Lilienbrunngasse, and now it was our turn. An hour or so later, during which we ate our last breakfast as free people and then packed one suitcase each, SS *Untersturmfuehrer* Alfred Slawik arrived at our apartment. My father showed him his I.D. card, which certified that he was "important to the economy."[17] Slawik was not impressed but said that the officials at the Sperlschule would decide what was to be done with us. He said the same thing to Mr. Aufrichtig, whose daughter actually got him out of the Sperlschule after a few days.

For us, however, there was no mercy. On Wednesday, February 4, Anton Brunner (Brunner II), the commissar, tore up our I.D. cards and passports, and as we stood in front of him, he told my father that he could now do some real work in the East. As of this moment, we had ceased to be Austrian citizens.

Our transport, containing 999 "registered" Jews and approximately 20 others not listed, left on Friday, February 6, and the transport leader was none other than the almighty Alois Brunner (Brunner I). Just before leaving, in early afternoon, after young Elizabeth Holzer had been brought to the train and had been added to the twenty or so "criminals" in the second half of our car, an ambulance arrived and a weak old man was taken onto car two of the train, still in his pajamas, carrying no luggage. It was the well-known financier Siegmund Bosel; just forty-eight hours later, after a

night of torture during which the unfortunate Bosel was chained to our car, Alois Brunner wearied of the game and shot him. Although Bosel was brought to the train almost at the last minute, his name is on the transport list. That was not always true of last minute additions. Very often people were added to have exactly one thousand passengers per train, or at the whim of either Brunner.

Our train reached Riga's Skirotava Station on Tuesday, February 10. Alois Brunner was greeted warmly by a tall, impeccably dressed SS officer, and introduced to the latter's aide. They were, respectively, Dr. Rudolf Lange and Gerhard Maywald, and it took years to find out that there was a connection between Lange and Brunner. They had known each other in Vienna, during 1938, 1939, and 1940, when both assisted Eichmann. Now Alois Brunner had come to see "how things were done in the East," accompanying a transport not expected in the ghetto!

As we stood freezing in front of the train, Lange addressed us as "Ladies and Gentlemen," and informed us that it was quite far to the ghetto, about 6 kilometers, that the temperature was 42 degrees below zero, and that he would therefore advise those who thought walking would be a hardship and strenuous to avail themselves of taking the buses waiting nearby. He added that the people who opted for the buses would be able to prepare a place in the ghetto for those of their friends and relatives who decided to walk. Almost 700 of the newly arrived Viennese Jews chose to ride in the blue buses, which were in plain sight. There was also an odd-looking, large van; as was realized much, much later, this was a gas van, or S-van, S for Saurer Werke, of the type used at Kulmhof. But we did not know this then and even after living in the ghetto, when we should have realized the truth, the rumors that made the rounds were just too awful to be believed.

My sister, then eleven, wanted to go on the bus, but my father would not permit it. When she started whining, he slapped her. (This was so out of character, that my mother did not speak to him the whole time it took us to walk to the ghetto.) Lange, who had evidently noticed the scene, gave my sister a stern look and told her that children should always listen to their parents. After we had started walking, Lange's behavior changed. We were no more "Ladies and Gentlemen," but rather were sent on our way by being called *"Ihr bloedes Volk, kommt 'mal her"* (you stupid people, come here at once).

Several hours later, after walking on the icy streets of Riga, prodded mercilessly by the rifle butts of the Latvian SS, we finally reached the ghetto. When searching for those who had chosen to ride the buses, we were told by people who had been in the ghetto for some time already that no

buses had arrived as yet, but that the new arrivals might have been taken to one of the other camps in the vicinity. As our transport had brought many young people whose parents had taken the buses, the ensuing alarm and desperation were heartbreaking. It was at this point that my mother turned to my father and apologized for her stubborn silence on the way.

There must have been several reasons for my father's unusual caution and behavior. One was the death of Bosel; that terrible night had affected my father enormously and had obviously taught him a lesson. Secondly, during the trip, my father, despite orders to the contrary, talked to some of the "criminals" who were in the second part of our car. They told him that all of them had been deported before and had illegally returned to Vienna, where they were jailed for a time. Then, as we arrived at the Skirotava Station, he chanced to watch those twenty Jews and noticed that all of them, without exception, chose to walk rather than take the buses. Feeling sure that people who had perhaps been in a similar situation before would know how to act, he had evidently copied their actions.

Curiously, but understandably, with so much stress to cope with upon arrival and so little time to speak about private thoughts, we never discussed what actually happened at the station and why he was so adamant in insisting that we all walk together. Since he did not survive, I never had a chance to ask him for an explanation and I do not think anyone else asked him either. Lange, who came to the ghetto from time to time, once saw my father and evidently recognized him, for he asked whether the family was all right and still together! And that from a man whose very presence in the ghetto brought panic. On later occasions, during his visits to the ghetto, it became clear that he hated and despised us, in addition to thinking of us as stupid. After all, we were so gullible, and he had duped us with such ease!

Ours was the last transport permitted to enter the ghetto and all because Alois Brunner was shown by his friend Rudolf Lange how easy it was to trick those Viennese Jews; in effect, we had performed our own selection!

During 1942 and 1943, many other transports of Jews from the Reich were brought to Riga and thousands were murdered there. Sometimes the records indicate Riga, sometimes they are marked "*nach dem Osten*" (to the East), but sometimes they are clearly meant to go to other places and are so labeled. But things were not always what they seemed. Another transport to Riga was to have left Vienna on March 23, 1942. Document 12501/41 of the Vienna Police is proof of that. All the names of the Austrian policemen attached to that transport are listed; they were to be commanded by Lieutenants Johann Peter II, and Johann Fahrnecker, and had in fact already been paid for taking the Jews from Vienna to Riga. Yet, that transport

never left Vienna—at least not for Latvia. Just then there was evidently too much going on in the forests around Riga.

First of all, there had been an *Aktion* in the ghetto on March 15 where the same ploy was used as before: People were going to a fish cannery, there would be more food, easier work, and better living conditions. To dupe the people even more, the group elder of Vienna, Emil Loebl, would be the camp elder at Duenamuende and was therefore joining the transport, together with his daughter Inge. Her feet had been amputated after their arrival in the ghetto. She and her father had travelled the four days from Vienna to Riga in an unheated car. Having kept her shoes on, she suffered from extreme frostbite that turned gangrenous.

As in every one of the transports, it was sheer luck to be in a heated car. There was absolutely no way that one could know beforehand which one would be warm. I visited Inge several days before the *Aktion*; she had been a classmate of my cousin Lili Brender and I therefore felt close to her. I cannot forget how she spoke about her hopes to be in a camp "where she would be able to do work while sitting."

Of the approximately 1,400 Austrian Jews contained in groups Vienna, Berlin, and Prague, over 300 were sent away on that day. Left behind were 1,100, with about 1,000 in the Vienna group and the remainder in the two other groups.

Following the *Aktion*, groups Vienna, Berlin, and Hanover were combined under one elder, a Jew from Hanover, Guenther Fleischel, with each group keeping its own administration consisting of a labor office, health service, police department, and school. Professor Manfred Lemberger, the former deputy of Loebl, was put in charge of our school as supervisor, while "Tante Mary" Korvill was our teacher.

But there was still more work to be done in the forest: On March 26 a final selection took place at Camp Jungfernhof, located even nearer to the forest. There had been several small operations since its creation, but this last one reduced the number of German Jews to 450, of whom approximately 60 had come there from Vienna in December 1941. In fall 1942, several women were transferred to the ghetto; their labor at that model farm was no longer required. In summer 1943 the camp was abolished altogether and with the exception of about fifty skilled artisans, the inmates were sent to Camp Kaiserwald.

In Vienna, therefore, after having waited a few days, the transport meant for Riga eventually left on April 9 and went to Izbica instead. Since Izbica was not as far as Riga, the policemen had to return some of the money they had received earlier! Likewise, transports meant for other locations in the

East ended up in Riga. Jews who worked at the *Kommandos*, where luggage was sorted and processed, reported finding suitcases from all over Europe, including Austria, with addresses prominently displayed as each deportee had been ordered to do before leaving. That was still another way of duping the unwary—who never ever saw their luggage again—even if they did survive that first crisis of arrival and were permitted to go either to the Riga ghetto or to one of the camps in the vicinity rather than straight into the forest.

There was a whole industry set up in Riga that took care of all this loot brought by the deportees. Places both inside and outside the ghetto were kept busy for a long time. Ida Brunn, Fritz's mother, worked at the *Gewerbebetrieb* in the ghetto, where mainly clothing was processed, starting with the week after March 15, 1942, and ending in the summer of 1943. Before working there, Mrs. Brunn had been part of a *Kommando* that searched the vacant houses around the ghetto, from where the Latvian Jews had been taken to their death, and which had remained vacant, as a sort of *cordon sanitaire*.

We spent the very first night of our arrival in such a house, and saw food that was frozen, still on the table, clothing thrown all about, and slippers right next to the bed. It was clear that the former inhabitants had left in a great hurry, and it was only our own precarious situation and the many fears we had for ourselves that prevented us from speculating on their fate. Yet, deep within our hearts, we must have known the truth.

After that one night in the ghostly house, we were given a kitchen at Berliner Strasse 13, which we shared with the three Brunns until the aforementioned big *Aktion* of March 15. After that the three Brunns stayed in the kitchen and we moved into the small apartment next door where we remained until we were transported to the concentration camp Kaiserwald on September 25, 1943.

When we had reached the ghetto, Alice Brunn was visibly pregnant. She carried the child to term and entered the ghetto's hospital on June 1. The physician in charge told her that her boy was stillborn, but she knew it was a lie—she had heard the baby cry. It was *Kommandant* Krause who killed the boy by injection; he always did that, since there were quite a few among the *Reichsjuden* who arrived at the ghetto pregnant. Later, only abortions were performed. In fact, there were signs posted inside all the houses proclaiming that sex was forbidden. Since families lived together, punishment was forthcoming only when there was evidence like pregnancy. So as to circumvent such punishment, which took the form of twenty-five blows with a whip for the male and sterilization for the female—without anesthe-

sia—the Jewish authorities opened a secret clinic in the ghetto in January 1943, about which the SS knew nothing. When Alice Brunn, however, became pregnant again in September 1942 and went to the hospital in the first week of December, the little clinic was not yet established. She was sterilized and Fritz was flogged.

Fritz worked at an army installation in the city, where in the spring of 1943 he broke his right ankle. It did not heal properly and he could walk only with a cane. As he was not able to leave the ghetto for work, he was assigned to clean the backyards and cesspools. On November 2, 1943, when the ghetto was liquidated, he and his mother were taken to Auschwitz. Alice had gone to work at the *Armeebekleidungsamt* (Army supply depot) as usual, and when she came home in the evening, she found her loved ones gone.

The last time I saw her was in Stutthof, in early September 1944. She had volunteered to go to a neighboring farm to bring in the harvest. I wanted to go with her, being all by myself; my father had been taken to Buchenwald and my mother and sister to the labor camp Sophienwalde. The farmer, however, did not want to take me along. I was too small, too skinny, I wore glasses, and he did not think I could do the work. Once the harvest was over, at some time after I had left that dreadful camp, Alice returned to Stutthof and died there during the typhoid epidemic of November and December 1944.

Other neighbors at Berliner Strasse 13 were the Hoffenreichs, two brothers, Gabriel and Karl, and a sister Hermine. Gabriel, the older brother, came to the ghetto only on weekends. He and another member of the Vienna group, Hans Stiassny, worked for a *Kommando* called *SS-Einsatz*, where the precious metals, jewelry, and other valuables were collected and sorted, all taken either from the suitcases or, more likely, from the purses held by the women and the pockets of the men on their way to the forest. Many times, despite the danger involved, Gabriel was able to smuggle a piece of jewelry into the ghetto, which one of his siblings would then barter for food at his or her place of work. Although this was extremely dangerous, it had to be done for it was the only way to survive.

Gabriel told my father about the unbelievable amount of jewelry he and Hans had to sort out. Since there were many such *Kommandos* in the city of Riga, it stands to reason that others told such stories too, and thus, in a way, the inmates of the ghetto lost some of their naïveté. Even the most optimistic persons among us knew that the earth in the forest was drenched in Jewish blood and that no one was safe. Yet, we still continued to hope.

In late August 1942, Gabriel was very depressed. He had, by pure chance, found a pocket watch belonging to his uncle Sigmund whom he had thought to be safe in Vienna. There was no way to find out what had happened at the time and it took almost five decades to unravel the mystery. On July 29, 1943, Karoline and Sigmund Hoffenreich had arrived in Theresienstadt. Sigmund's watch was either taken from him or he had sold it, for it came to Riga carried by someone who was part of a transport arriving on August 22, having left Theresienstadt on August 20. The two elder Hoffenreichs were not on that transport. They died in the ghetto of Theresienstadt in 1943, but our neighbors were never to know that, since none of the three survived.

In the article *"Das Schicksal der Theresienstaedter Osttransporte im Sommer und Herbst 1942"* (The Fate of Transports to the East from Theresienstadt in Summer and Autumn 1942), published in *Judaica Bohemiae*, Miroslav Karny reported that this transport was taken straight to the forest and that there were no survivors. In June of that year, the *Sonderkommandos* in Riga had received an additional gas van from Kulmhof, so that there were now at least two of these vehicles in operation. The older one had been a Saurer product, but this new one, according to a quote by Alfred Streim in the article *"Zum Beispiel: Die Verbrechen der Einsatzgruppen in der Sowjetunion"* (For Instance: The Crimes of the Task Forces in the Soviet Union), in *NS-Prozesse* (National Socialist Trials) was manufactured by the Gaubschat Firm of Berlin-Neukoelln. Altogether, Gaubschat produced thirty such vehicles. Streim's article is based on his research of Nazi crimes in the Soviet Union, and Latvia was a part of it.

The *Hoehere Polizei Fuehrer* in Riga, Friedrich Jeckeln, related at his trial there during the winter 1945–46 that many transports kept coming to Riga until 1943. He also admitted that most of the people in these transports, which had come there from Germany, France, Holland, Czechoslovakia, Austria, and other countries, were brought to Salaspils and then liquidated. By his own estimate, which was based on the reports given to him by Rudolf Lange, between 60,000 and 90,000 foreign Jews, of whom no more than about 800 survived, came to Riga starting in November 1941. There is no reason to doubt the veracity of his testimony.

Our existence was fraught with dangers in both ghettos of Riga, but life did go on, especially so in the German part. Although the Vienna group, very much like the Prague group, was not held in high esteem in that very German ghetto, it was always the Viennese who put on shows and organized concerts and cabarets, mainly on Sunday afternoons when people did not have to go to work. Once the weather got better, these "shows" were given

outdoors on a large area formed by the backyards of several houses, whose fronts faced Berliner and Moskauer Strassen. People from the other groups came to hear the Viennese perform and so did Latvian Jews who had to get a special permission slip. The German SS came and so did the commandant. Once he brought a guest: Anton Brunner!

Here he was, standing together with his host, listening to the familiar tunes! At the time of his visit, the last Sunday in May 1942, there were no more than one thousand of us left, and at his trial in Vienna in spring 1946, a number of survivors from Riga remembered his visit to the ghetto; they easily disproved his assertion that he had "only" sent us away, but had had no idea where we went or what had happened to us. For that and for the unspeakable sadism exhibited by him in the Sperlschule, he was convicted and hanged on May 24, 1946. That was one of the few cases in Austria where justice prevailed.

When comparing the survival chances of the Riga transports with those of the transports to Litzmannstadt and to Minsk, the differences were such, that it becomes apparent how "lucky" the inmates of the German ghetto in Riga actually were. Being able to govern themselves, as it were, the Jews from the Reich survived in far greater numbers in Riga than did their counterparts in the other two ghettos. In Lodz, they were simply added to the existing structure and for a variety of reasons—be it old age or administrative policy—were among the first to go to their death in nearby Chelmno. Even in Minsk, where there was at first an attempt to keep the *Reichsjuden* ghetto totally separate from the Russian Jews, it became apparent that the Jews from Germany, Vienna, and Czechoslovakia were but a small minority that was soon expendable. Furthermore, Minsk did not have the same status as Riga had, which was considered a *Frontleitstelle* (Regional War Office), that is, a supply depot where the German army, navy, and air force had their respective headquarters. Thus, Riga was seen as more important to the war effort and therefore more deserving of Jewish slave labor. That it was the Jews from the Reich who were chosen to be just that, was simply a fluke. When the Latvian Jews were murdered en masse, their very absence led to a hue and cry, leaving only the new arrivals to fill their former positions. Last but not least, it may also have been a matter of decisions made by higher SS officials in Riga, who correctly figured out that with the demise of *all* the Jews in their care, they would have nothing to do anymore and would—perish the thought—be sent to the frontlines.

The enigma of survival chances in Riga rather than at other killing centers will never be fully answered, but one thing becomes clear is that despite deprivations such as hunger, cold, inadequate health care, backbreaking

labor, and constant fear of being sent to the nearby forest, many more would and could have survived had they not been selected for annihilation for no other reason than being Jewish.

The Riga ghetto existed until November 2, 1943. Already during the summer of that year, many of the inmates were sent to work at the peat bogs of Latvia and then, after a short stay in the almost empty ghetto, to the new concentration camp in the fashionable section of Meza Parks, in German Kaiserwald. Others, like my own family, went to Kaiserwald directly from the ghetto. If we had thought our life there had been a hard one and at times unbearably so, we now realized that by comparison it had not been that bad at all. While families lived together, they could communicate, they could embrace each other, they could sustain each other, and when they closed the doors at night, they could have a little privacy.

At Kaiserwald, on the other hand, men and women were separated, lived in barracks, slept on bunk beds, and whenever the women wanted to speak to their men, they had to do so at the barbed wire that divided the two sections, and they often incurred a beating while doing so.

Although Kaiserwald was the main camp, most of the people who were registered there were sent to outside installations where they not only worked but also had their quarters. My family was not among those; we were part of the Kaiserwald inmates who went to work in the morning and came back at night. Our *Kommando* was the *Feldbekleidungsamt der Luftwaffe* (Supply depot for the air force). My father had been working there ever since he had returned to the ghetto from Camp Salaspils on June 2, 1942. He was in charge of bookkeeping for the clothing depot and we considered ourselves extremely lucky to be together, supervised by halfway decent air force personnel. We even received a bowl of good soup each day; with hunger being a much greater problem than in the ghetto, this too was seen as luck.

At the time of the ghetto's liquidation, almost 3,000 Jews (mostly the elderly, the sick, and children with their parents or other relatives) were sent to faraway Auschwitz, rather than to the forest. Once again, there was too much going on in the forest since an attempt was being made to remove all evidence of mass murder. *Kommando* 1005, called *Stuetzpunkt* in Riga and made up of Jewish men, exhumed the bodies of the victims who had been murdered during the last three years. After burning the decayed corpses, their ashes were scattered. The job, however, was never finished. When the Russians liberated Riga in October 1944, they found thousands of bodies in untidy mass graves, as well as barrels of fuel that were still intact.

Meanwhile, the harsh conditions at Kaiserwald and satellite camps took their toll and although the returnees from the peat-bog *Kommandos* bolstered our numbers, the camps were visibly shrinking. People got ill and died either in their bunks or at sick bay, where they were helped to die faster by the ever present medic Heinz Wiesner.[18]

New waves of Jews came to Kaiserwald: They came from Vilno, Libau, Siauliai, Kaunas, Daugavpils, and from wherever ghettos were being liquidated or reduced in numbers. Then, in May 1944, women came from Hungary and Slovakia via Auschwitz, and that name entered our vocabulary even though they did not seem to make themselves clear. Among the Hungarians were a few Austrian teenagers who had left Vienna with their parents in 1939; according to their garbled accounts, these parents "went through the chimney." What chimney? What were they talking about in those few instances when we could speak to them? Although they all looked much better than we did, having been safe until very recently, the death rate among them was great. They just gave up; for us it had come gradually, but they could not cope with all the deprivations, especially those who were sent to the labor camps at Dundagaand Poperwalen.

By midsummer it was clear that the war would soon be over, for we could hear the rolling thunder of heavy artillery in the distance. On July 27, to our horror, there was a selection in Kaiserwald itself and at each satellite camp. At this time, the men had to run across a square to show how fit they were, and Heinz Wiesner looked very closely at each and every female walking past him. In the satellite camps, he made them take their striped clothing off and thus, the selection there was more thorough and more devastating. At least 4,000 Jews were taken to the forest and killed there, just when it seemed that freedom was around the corner.

The others, like us, were taken to the concentration and extermination camp Stutthof, 35 kilometers east of Danzig, across the Baltic Sea in two large transports. Ours left on August 6, 1944, and the second one left on September 27. There was, in addition, an overland transport of Jews that left from Libau. Upon arrival of the Soviet forces in Riga on October 14, according to Dr. Bernhard Press in *Judenmord in Lettland 1941–1945* (Murder of Jews in Latvia 1941–1945), they found 152 Jews in Riga and other cities who had gone into hiding rather than be taken across the sea. Among them was one Viennese woman, Regina Schwarz. Having fled from her satellite *Kommando* Meteor after her husband had been selected for liquidation, she found a place of refuge with a very decent Latvian man, Janis Lipke. It took her several years to come back to Vienna where she remarried and lived for many years.

The boat in which we made the journey was the *Bremerhafen*; it was manned by Austrian sailors, who did their best to make our lives even more miserable than necessary. They must have known that they would have to account for their misdeeds one day, but it did not seem to matter. Their behavior vis-à-vis us was absolutely brutal. The *Bremerhafen* brought us to Danzig and we had to wait almost a day for the barges that would bring us to Stutthof. It was in that meadow, with men on one side and women on the other side of a little brook, that we said good-bye to father. He was, as ever, the optimist, but our forthcoming separation depressed even him.

On August 9 we arrived at Stutthof and were received with a hail of blows to our heads and faces from the Polish prisoners in charge there. The camp was worse than anything until now and the small gas chamber worked overtime. There was also an ever-present stench from the ditches next to the newly erected Jewish camp. It seemed that the crematorium could not deal with so many bodies, and so they buried the victims in ditches and burned them. We suddenly understood what the Hungarian girls had meant when they said "through the chimney."

On August 13 a large transport of men left for Buchenwald, among them my father. Before leaving, he managed to send us a note, delivered by a Russian prisoner who brought our food. The note said, "*Behuetet Einander. Kopf hoch, nicht aufgeben, es dauert nicht mehr lange. Wir treffen uns in Wien!*" (Take care of each other. Keep up your spirits, don't give up, it won't take long anymore. We'll meet again in Vienna!).

From Buchenwald, together with 1,600 men, many of whom had come with him, father was sent to Bochum, one of the worst places of work among the many satellite camps of Buchenwald. In March 1945, 1,250 men were sent back to the camp. Due to the lack of food and warm quarters coupled with hard work and senseless beatings, 350 had died during the past six months. Once the emaciated scarecrows reached the main camp, they deteriorated still further and most of them were sent to Dachau on what turned out to be "death trains."

Of those 1,250 Jews, 45 survived, but my father Pinkas Hirschhorn, the last living child of Henny Rose, was not among them. He died in a closed cattle car left on a siding next to the camp. When the Americans opened the sealed doors, only one youngster, Oskar Tycho, was still alive. He told us, months later, that my father had exhorted everyone to hold out, that their liberation was imminent, and that no one should give up. He also told us that father's body, according to what he heard the American physician say, was still warm when the cattle car was opened.

In Stutthof, on August 24, 1944, my mother and sister were made part of a transport leaving for the labor camp Sophienwalde. Of the 500 women chosen, two-thirds were Hungarian and the others a mixture of Austrian, Czech, German, Latvian, and Polish Jews. Despite entreaties to the Germans and Poles in charge, my mother could not get permission for me to go along. There were others in the same situation. Nothing could be done, and I was suddenly all alone.

Of the people I had known from Vienna, only Selma Breitner and Lizzy Brunn were still with me, but they soon left with farmers to bring in the harvest. I was not deemed fit for work and my situation was hopeless. Others, emaciated and helpless like me, were plentiful. After roll call, we would sit in the sand in front of the barracks and talk. In that way, I began talking to a Viennese woman who had come to Stutthof via Auschwitz and Theresienstadt. When I started to ask some questions, she told me an almost unbelievable story about one Aron Menczer, whom she called a hero. It was the same Aron who had been one of the leaders and role models at the *Palamt*, where I had known and admired him so long ago. It seemed that Aron, a youth leader in Theresienstadt as well, had been the only one who could handle a large transport of children who had come from Poland to Theresienstadt. They lived totally separated from the rest of the ghetto, in a section called "Kreta." She told me that everyone talked about them and said they were to be exchanged for German prisoners, but that the deal fell through and they were sent to Auschwitz, with Aron volunteering to go along, together with his staff. She said that rumors were rampant when it was known that Eichmann, who had known Aron in Vienna, told him to stay in Theresienstadt. Aron, on the other hand, had replied that the children knew and trusted him, and that it was therefore his duty to share their fate. Listening to her there in Stutthof, sitting on the sand and feeling very sorry for myself, I shed tears for Aron and for all of us.

Years later, when I checked her story, I found that in August 1943, over 1,200 children from Bialystock, separated from their doomed parents at the Treblinka death camp, had indeed been brought to Theresienstadt and had been put in quarantine, where Aron, who spoke Yiddish and could calm them down, together with a staff of fifty-two teachers and nurses, took care of them. The children became hysterical when they were taken to the showers at the ghetto and screamed something about "gas." People did not or could not understand what they meant. It seemed that only Aron exerted some calming influence over them, but it is doubtful whether he understood their fears either, although he was soon to find out what had traumatized them.

This particular transport was part of one of Eichmann's schemes. He wanted to exchange the children for German prisoners of war held by the Allies. When, after several months, nothing came of his plans, he ordered the children, who had never been entered on the Theresienstadt roster, to be sent to Auschwitz. There is only the registrar's cryptic notation that on October 5, 1943, transport DN, containing fifty-three persons, left for Auschwitz. The 1,200 children are not mentioned. When the transport arrived at Auschwitz on October 7, the children and their caretakers, including Aron, were gassed.

On September 16, 1944, my luck changed, and I left Stutthof for the labor camp Sophienwalde in the capacity of an expert roofer! My resourceful mother had invented this profession for me and had been able to convince the commandant at her camp to have the authorities at Stutthof send me there! Thus, we were reunited and I had the miraculous chance of surviving, even though, as the Nazi Empire fell to pieces around us, we still had to face another winter.

The hunger was incredible. The work we had to do sapped the last of our strength. There was a typhoid epidemic. And then, the very last plague, there came the death marches, from camp to camp, during which so many of the holdouts lost the battle. Those who could walk no farther were shot. Others froze to death during the bitter cold nights when the columns rested. And many, who were indeed liberated, died shortly afterward, not having the strength to recuperate from those punishing last few weeks.

Not too many of the Austrian Jews who had been sent to Latvia during the winter of 1941–42 lived to see liberation, even though their chances had been better than those who had been sent to any of the other sites of murder.

Of the first transport that left Vienna for Riga on December 3, 1941, and was taken to Camp Jungfernhof, thirteen Jews survived—five men and eight women.

The following transport of January 11, 1942, of which 700 were taken to Jungfernhof, with 300 entering the Riga ghetto and being divided between groups Prague and Berlin, had twenty-seven survivors—nine men and eighteen women.

The transport of January 26, 1942, which became the basis for the Vienna group and had entered the ghetto intact, had twenty-eight survivors—twelve men and sixteen women.

Of the last transport, my own, which left Vienna on February 6, 1942, and of which almost 700 chose the buses, thirty people survived—five men and twenty-five women, among them my mother, my sister, and I.

There are five more survivors, one man and four women, who are not on any of the lists, but who were in the ghetto, having been added to transports without being registered. Thus, the total of survivors for the four Riga transports comes to 103. It is the second largest group after Theresienstadt.

Actually, I should have added young Elizabeth Holzer to the survivors, but I already listed her earlier as one of the four who came back from Modliborzyce. She survived Riga, Stutthof, and the death march, but never bothered to go back to Vienna or her native Rechnitz once the war was over. She knew quite well that she would not find anyone from her family. After she had recuperated in a Czech hospital, she went to England and became a nurse. Many years later, when she decided to settle in the United States, we saw each other and could only marvel at how much human beings were able to withstand and still remain human.

Transports to Minsk

The first transport bound for Minsk left Vienna on November 28, 1941, only five days after a transport meant for Riga had gone instead to Kovno. It was to be the only transport from Vienna to reach the Minsk ghetto itself; all subsequent Minsk transports from Vienna ended up at the killing grounds of Maly Trostinec, several kilometers distant from the ghetto. This first transport contained 999 Jews and upon their arrival in Minsk they were immediately initiated into the brutal treatment so typical for the behavior of the SS in the East in general, and for Minsk in particular.

Theirs had been a long journey; the Viennese had been en route for eight days according to Heinz Rosenberg, the author of *Jahre des Schreckens* (Years of Terror), who had come to Minsk from Hamburg a few weeks earlier. Upon arrival, it was found that there were large amounts of edibles in their luggage. The SS guards walking next to the straggling Jews forced them to carry their luggage into the ghetto and then commanded the administration to confiscate everything. The Viennese, most of whom were older people, were devastated. Realizing their desperate straits, Rosenberg felt that the Jewish administrators should have given back the food rather than add it to the entire ghetto's rations. He was dismissed by his fellow Hamburgers for insubordination and was sent to work outside the ghetto in the city of Minsk. This judgment against him was to actually save his life, since at least three of the German Jewish administrations, including that first one, were summarily executed.

The newly arrived Jews from Vienna found Jews from various cities of the Reich already living in the ghetto and among them, curiously enough,

a number of Viennese Jews who had come with a transport from Bruenn (Brno), Czechoslovakia. According to the records of the *Juedische Kultusgemeinde Bruenn* (Office for Jewish Affairs at Bruenn), cited by Miroslav Karny in the previously mentioned *Judaica Bohemiac XXIV*, the transport contained mainly the poor Jews from Bruenn, supported solely by the local *Kultusgemeinde*. Austrian Jews, who had fled to Bruenn after Hitler entered their country, were in that same miserable economic state and had therefore been made part of that particular transport.

The German ghetto was made up of two parts connected by a corridor that was located in the Russian Jews' ghetto. The two ghettos of the Reich were called Sonderghetto (special ghetto) I and II. Sonderghetto I contained the Hamburg, Frankfurt, Duesseldorf, and Berlin camps, and Sonderghetto II contained the Bremen, Bruenn, and Vienna camps. Altogether, these two special ghettos held nearly 7,500 Jews from the Reich. Their meager sustenance was prepared in a communal kitchen that was located in the Hamburg camp. From there it was delivered to the other camps in large containers.

Hunger in the Minsk ghetto was a terrible scourge. According to Karl Loewenstein in *Minsk: Im Lager der Deutschen Juden* (Minsk: In the Camp of the German Jews), at first only 1,425 of the foreign Jews went to work outside the ghetto, and it was only they who could augment the communal food. For the majority, there was therefore little hope.

Comparing the Minsk ghetto to the Riga ghetto, it should be remembered that in the latter at least 75 percent of the inmates went to work outside. Furthermore, in Riga the Jews from the Reich were in the majority, while here in Minsk they were a very distinct minority, notwithstanding the fact that thousands of the Russian Jews had been killed and were still being killed in Minsk and its surroundings since the war had started. In fact, the latest batch, numbering several thousand, had been liquidated just before the arrival of the Jews from Hamburg, who had the sad duty of cleaning up the evidence of the massacre.

The two Sonderghettos contained several large buildings and many small huts; the latter afforded more privacy. Owing to the way the ghetto was laid out, however, it never became a cohesive unit. In addition, there was always the intrusive presence of the SS, and not a day passed by without an "inspection" of one sort or another. Each such inspection produced victims.

Loewenstein described one especially bloodthirsty SS man, *Oberscharfuehrer* Helmut Schmiedel, an Austrian, whose forays into the ghetto engendered panic and always ended in someone's death. Loewenstein commented that Schmiedel, "in order to enjoy his breakfast, had to kill a

few Jews." And he did so. Yet, that same Schmiedel, whenever he met some of the Austrian Jews, would give them cigarettes.

In their description of the conditions in Minsk, both Rosenberg and Loewenstein emphasized that the Austrian SS men were almost as terrible as the Latvian auxiliary police present to help with the wholesale murder of thousands. An addition to the officers' staff in the spring of 1942, owing to his expertise with *Reichsjuden*, was *Sturmbannfuehrer* Gerhard Maywald. Transferred to Minsk from Riga, Maywald remained in Minsk for six months during which some of the worst massacres occurred. Although tried for his crimes in Riga, for which he got four years, he has so far not been tried for his activities in Minsk. This may perhaps be due to the fact that while there were a number of witnesses who had survived the rigors of Riga, there were almost no surviving witnesses from Minsk.

For the Jews of the Sonderghettos who went out to work, life was extremely hard. Conditions at places where they were employed were fraught with dangers. As a matter of fact, it mattered little whether they were *Reichsjuden* or indigenous Jews; all of them were subject to sudden whims of their SS overlords.

While at first, according to Loewenstein, only 20 percent of the *Reichsjuden* were sent out to work, eventually all of them, with the exception of the very old, the sick, and the small children, were used for cleaning the streets of snow and the railroad tracks of ice. They also had to unload railroad cars carrying weapons and building materials. If lucky, they worked inside several large factory buildings, sorting and repairing the clothes that had been in their own suitcases and those of others who never reached the ghetto. As at other such "collection centers," the very best pieces were then sent back to Germany labeled "for our German liberators from the grateful Russian people."

The winter of 1941–42 was brutally cold, the coldest on records since 1928. Many of the Jewish women who cleared the rails of ice during the night so that traffic would be unimpeded during the day froze to death when lack of strength, due to hunger, made them rest for just a little while and fall asleep next to the shed that held the tools.

Paul Kohl in his *Ich wundere mich dass ich noch lebe: Sowietische Augenzeugen berichten* (I Am Surprised that I Am Still Alive: Report by Soviet Eyewitnesses), presented documentation of how the Latvian *Sonderkommandos* helped the Germans during the massacres; both Rosenberg and Loewenstein reported also on the Latvians' frequent incursions into the ghetto, which always proved to be catastrophic. (Latvian auxiliary forces

were used in many other concentration and extermination camps throughout the war years and were feared by inmates.)

Loewenstein, whose survival was one of the Holocaust's true miracles, had been a naval officer and aide to the German crown prince from 1910 to 1918. With the help of *Gebietskommissar* Kube, Lowenstein was the only Jew to leave the Minsk ghetto in one of the trains that had brought Jews from Vienna to Minsk. Six months after his own arrival from Berlin, Loewenstein left for Vienna, and after an audience there at the former Rothschild Hospital with Alois Brunner, by that time a *Hauptsturmfuehrer*, Loewenstein was sent to Theresienstadt, where, for a short time, he served as chief of the Jewish police. He had served in the same capacity in the Minsk ghetto as well.

Although there were quite a number of Belorussians who collaborated with the Germans and were even allowed to live among them at the Maly Trostinec farm complex, for the most part the population of Minsk hated the invaders. Many joined the partisans and made their transient homes in the nearby forests. Skirmishes with the SS and the *Wehrmacht* were common. The Jews in both ghettos, separated from each other and the outside world by barbed-wire fences, enjoyed hearing about the partisans' exploits; whatever was accomplished in harming their tormentors was greeted with delight.

There were many attempts at escape from the ghetto, especially from the Russian part, but it was extremely difficult for Jews to be accepted by Russian partisans and thus, the Jews tried to create their own special units. Most often these attempts ended in disaster, but from time to time there was help from sympathetic civilians, or, as in another miracle, from a German *Hauptmann*.

In the German magazine *Neue Zeit*, David Gai wrote a love story "Liebe im Ghetto" (Love in the Ghetto). It mentioned a girl from Hamburg, Ilse Stein. A friend of Heinz Rosenberg sent the magazine to Rosenberg in New York knowing that Ilse had been a friend of his. Gai had written that she now lives in Rostov on the Don, and Rosenberg, upon calling her, found out that she had been saved by one *Hauptmann* Erwin Schulz, who was in charge of her work detail, because he fell in love with her. They were on the phone for an hour and Ilse told Heinz that Schulz had joined her and her two sisters as well as twenty-two Russian Jews in the escape that brought them to a partisan unit near the village of Russakowitschi. Schulz became an aide to the Russian army. Ilse, together with her sisters, was sent to Birobidshan. She never saw Schulz again. One sister died; Ilse and the

youngest sister survived, all thanks to a German captain whose love was stronger than duty.[19]

As the story became known in Belorussia, it was made part of World War II literature in a book by Jossif Gerassimow entitled *The Escape*. Other survivors of the group, the Russian Jewesses Jelisaweta Gutkowitsch and Raissa Gitlina, are in touch with the former Ilse Stein and they bless the memory of Erwin Schulz, as well as that of all good people everywhere.

Most escapees, however, were soon caught and brought back to the ghetto where a "show" was organized during which their fellow inmates had to watch the indignity of their hanging. Yet, the handful of Austrian Jews who did survive their deportation to Minsk owed their survival to having fled from their *Kommandos*.

As the months went by, the population of the ghetto dwindled. The Russian ghetto, according to Kohl, had started with 85,000 and now, in January 1942, there were perhaps 30,000 of them still alive.

Between November 1941 and January 1942, there had been several small operations reducing the numbers still further. It was during January that Heinz Rosenberg first learned of the existence of gas vans; he saw them during one of those small surprise operations in the adjoining Russian ghetto. According to him, only about 100 persons could be pushed into those vans and the others who had been selected for annihilation had to wait in the bitter cold, until the vans returned after about an hour. To him that meant that not far from the ghetto, thirty or so minutes, there had to be mass graves where the victims were unloaded. He was correct in his assumption. In fact, there were several sites of mass graves and killing centers in and around Minsk where Russian prisoners of war were entrusted with unloading the vehicles and disrobing the victims before burying them in the previously prepared pits.

The biggest killing center was located in Maly Trostinec, which was made up of two parts. On one side of a small river was a very large farm where much work was done. It had sheds and barns for the Russian prisoners and Jewish workers to sleep in, and there were several buildings where the Germans had administrative offices to augment those in Minsk proper. There were also living quarters for the Russian collaborators, Latvian auxiliary forces, and low-ranking Germans.

The other, sinister part of Maly Trostinec was across the river and extended far into the forest. It was the last stop for thousands of Jews, for it was here where the gas vans emptied their cargo, and it was here where mass shootings of transports, which exceeded the capacity of the gas vans, were carried out.

In addition to the Maly Trostinec site, there was the Blahovtschina Forest east of Minsk; there was a smaller killing site on the Mogilew Chaussee, called *Gut* (estate) 16; there was the ghetto, where thousands lay buried; and there was also the courtyard of the Minsk jail, where two Jewish dentists were forced to pull out gold teeth and fillings from victims who were brought there to die.

At his trial in Jerusalem it was related that Adolf Eichmann had witnessed the killing of 5,000 Jews in Minsk. When questioned about his reaction, he said, "I went weak in my knees and left soon."

The death squads were always kept busy. Starting in May 1942, when the transports arrived with greater frequency, there was much work to be done. The victims were brought to a large meadow from the railway station and were then loaded into gas vans, disguised as caravans such as gypsies used. Others were loaded into regular vans and everyone, alive or dead by then, was taken to the prepared pits.

Among the transports from the Reich were nine additional transports from Vienna. They left for Minsk on May 6, May 20, May 27, June 2, June 9, August 17, August 31, September 14, and October 5, with each of them containing about 1,000 Jews, except for the last one, which contained only 549. Although the Jews had left Vienna in regular railroad cars, once they reached the town of Volkovysk, located 35 kilometers east of the Polish border, they were transferred to cattle cars.

Of the Jews who had left on May 6 and arrived May 11 at the Minsk railroad station, eighty-one were selected for work on the farm at Maly Trostinec. Among them were Johann Noskes, just twenty at the time, and Julie Hochbaum, age thirty-eight. They were destined to be the only two survivors of this transport. Julie fled as soon as she had made contact with like-minded Russian Jews and ended up in Karaganda, from where she returned to Austria once the war was over.

It is thanks to Noskes that much of the Maly Trostinec setup was discovered. When he came back to Vienna after the war, he related that at the time of his arrival there were about 600 Jewish and 300 Russian prisoners at the farm. As new transports kept arriving, those Jews who had in the meantime fallen ill or were weakened by the harsh conditions, were "taken away" and replaced by newcomers. He and other prisoners were told that there was a second farm in the vicinity. Eventually they found out that under the code name Estate 16, located on the Mogilew Chaussee, a country road, there was another site abounding with ditches, where thousands and thousands were killed, interred, and later exhumed and burned. He survived because he was lucky, because he was strong, and mainly because he was

made part of a transport leaving Minsk for Poland in September 1943, together with Heinz Rosenberg. In the course of an odyssey during which they went to many other camps, they even stopped in Treblinka but were let go.

There were no survivors of the transport that left Vienna on May 20, but there was one survivor of the next one, which had left on May 27. Marie Mack, age thirty-five, after having worked on the farm for over a year, was made part of a transport numbering 1,000 Russian and German Jews, which, in the month of September, left Minsk for Lublin. After spending several weeks at Majdanek, she was sent off to other camps and came back to Vienna once the war was over.

The two June transports from Vienna did not yield survivors. During July, although there was no direct transport from Austria, there was one transport that came from Theresienstadt which contained Austrian Jews. There was also a transport from Cologne. In addition to the killing of these Jews, there was also a big *Aktion* in the ghetto that month. The man in charge of the pits, *Unterscharfuehrer* Johann Arlt, member of the *Waffen SS* and leader of *Gruppe* Arlt, described the *Aktion* in his reports dated July 28 and 29. He related that over 6,000 Jews from the Russian ghetto and over 3,000 from the German ghetto were brought to the pits and taken care of. In fact, he referred to the Jews as "pieces." In his own report, *Gebietskommissar* Kube spoke of 10,000 Jews as having been liquidated in those two days.

According to Heinz Rosenberg, whose *Kommando* was not permitted to come home to the ghetto until one day after the *Aktion*, almost all the Viennese Jews still alive until then were selected for the pits. Since there were only about 2,500 *Reichsjuden* left, all of them were concentrated in the German Special Ghetto I. As for the Russian ghetto, after all these small operations and now this big one, there were no more than about 7,000 of them left.

Of the transport that left Vienna on August 17, there was one survivor. Hans Schuller, nineteen years old at the time, escaped from the train shortly before it reached Volkovysk and thus never came to Minsk. Since the arrivals were not counted at either station, he was not reported as missing. He spent the following years roaming the vast forests and his luck held. After the war, he returned to Vienna.

There were no survivors of the next two transports, which left Vienna on August 31 and September 14 respectively, but there are three survivors of the last and final Austrian transport to Minsk, which left Vienna on October 5. A father, Isaak Gruenberg, and his two daughters, Edith and Lotte Gruenberg, survived and theirs is an incredible story and yet another miracle.

When the five Gruenbergs, father, mother, and three daughters, arrived at the railroad station in Minsk on October 9, 1942, the SS man in charge permitted all five of them to go to the farm for work. Isaak was a plasterer, and there was much for him to do at the farm; since Mrs. Hanni Gruenberg was a seamstress, she was put to work repairing clothes taken out of the suitcases that the deportees from Vienna and all the other cities had been relieved of. The two older girls, then in their late teens, were used for farm work and for cleaning the houses, and the youngest, only eight years old at the time, was permitted to stay with her family on the whim of the SS man in charge of the selection.

Within the next few months, during one of the many small "operations," Mrs. Gruenberg was taken away from her sewing machine and shot. The oldest daughter, Regine, after having been sent outside the farm to do some unspecified work, never returned. Gruenberg and his two remaining daughters heard all about the liquidation of the ghetto in September 1943 as well as about the transports that had left Minsk for Poland. Somehow they still felt safe. As more and more people from the farm disappeared over the next few months and the remnants numbered no more than about 100, Isaak Gruenberg realized that he and his children were doomed unless he acted. Isaak, together with his daughters and several Russian Jews who also could see the end coming, fled into the forest as soon as it was warm enough. Not long afterward, the Soviet army liberated the forest dwellers and the three Gruenbergs lived to tell the miraculous tale of their survival once they returned to Vienna.

Of the very first transport from Vienna that had landed in the Minsk ghetto, Ferdinand and Tusnelda Trausel of Graz, a middle-aged couple, returned home to Austria after the war, the only survivors of that transport. Both had worked outside the ghetto, both had realized that they were doomed, and both had decided to flee. They did so, together with a small group of Russian Jews known to them from working together, and were successful.

Thus, the total survivors of the approximately 9,500 Austrian Jews who were sent to Minsk numbered only nine.

The Death Camps in Poland: 1942

The number of Jews still present in the Reich was dwindling, and especially so in Austria where deportations were conducted quite vigorously, thanks to the presence of Eichmann and his henchmen, the two fiercest of whom were Alois and Anton Brunner.

There were no longer any official schools for the few Jewish children left in Vienna; learning was available only in the two remaining day-care centers. The *Piper Heim* offered three classes and the Jewish Girls' Home offered six. By June 1942, however, all instruction was ordered to come to an end. Although smaller children were still permitted to be at these two centers, they were forbidden to receive lessons or engage in any educational activities. All they had, in addition to some toys, were the books left behind by other students.

Foreign language classes, so popular among adult Jews, were cancelled too since there was to be no more emigration. To be sure, the Jews were still leaving, but the places to which they were going did not require the knowledge of foreign languages. In fact, these places required no knowledge at all. The Jews had ceased to exist as human beings, their knowledge and/or their skills were neither needed nor appreciated; all that was important were their possessions, which were stolen outright, their hair, their gold teeth, and perhaps their ashes to fertilize the fields in Poland.

In the Vienna of early 1942, ever more restrictions were felt among the Jewish population. No longer were they permitted to send mail to the Litzmannstadt ghetto, nor were they allowed to inquire about the deportees, either at the Red Cross offices or at the *Kultusgemeinde*. For a while longer,

they could still send money to their families and friends in Lodz, but not directly to the persons involved; all monies had to be sent to the ghetto's bank. Thus, no matter what had happened to the person in the meantime, the Germans were sure to keep even those meager funds.

As did the rest of Europe, Vienna too experienced a very cold winter with much snow and ice. Since many of Vienna's Aryan males were busy at the various fronts fighting, or, just as likely, working hard in the concentration and extermination camps, the male Jews still in Vienna at the time had to clean the city's streets of snow and ice. As most of them were working at other places during the week, they had to do this cleaning—without remuneration—on Sundays. Among these workers was my uncle Nachman. As luck would have it, he was part of a detail cleaning Thaliastrasse in the sixteenth district, not too far from where he had lived all his life.

After the war, my mother found out from former neighbors who had seen him that he had been in good spirits. He talked about us to my father's schoolmate Willy Tatschek and told him that we had been sent to Riga; he also said that he had been able to send us food while we were at the Sperlschule. This information cleared up the mystery of who had sent us a loaf of bread the day before we were "shipped out" to the East. Despite having so little himself, he still wanted to help his brother and his brother's family!

Even though the male Jews of Vienna were cleaning the city's streets, they were hit with still another restriction: They were no longer permitted to use public transportation on Sundays, making it thus extremely difficult for them to reach those streets. In fact, the use of public transportation by Jews was forbidden altogether by early summer, unless the distance to one's job was greater than 7 kilometers each way.

In June of 1942, the world famous Rothschild Hospital, which belonged to the Jewish community, was summarily confiscated. The patients were transferred to the older hospital at Malzgasse 16, in the second district, and the Jewish administrators were strictly forbidden to transfer any of the modern equipment or instruments.

Although this order was not followed to the letter, its circumvention did not make much of a difference. With deportations going full steam as the months went by, the number of patients dwindled rapidly. That was true of the physicians and nurses as well.

Despite the fact that two-thirds of Austria's Jews had fled that inhospitable country and thousands had already been deported, with most of them being murdered, the authorities claimed that there was still a need for more apartments in Vienna. It was therefore obvious to the various agencies

concerned with the "final solution" of the Jewish problem that the transports to the East had to be stepped up but in such a way that the regions involved would not suffer from "overpopulation."

Thus, in line with the plans made at the Wannsee Conference of January 20, 1942, and despite the death of the man whose name the operation would bear, "*Aktion Reinhard*" became a reality.[20] Spring and summer of 1942 saw the erection of camps containing their own gas chambers, rather than relying on gas vans, which were then still in use in Chelmno, Riga, and Minsk.

These death camps, literally called *Vernichtungslager*, that is, camps of annihilation, were situated near large cities having even then a sizeable Jewish population, both indigenous and foreign. Three of those camps, Belzec, Sobibor, and Treblinka, were used for extermination purposes only. The other four made use of the prisoners as slave laborers both inside the camps and/or in outside industries. Belzec was the first of these camps to be established, then came Sobibor, Treblinka, Majdanek, and finally, the very symbol of evil, Auschwitz. The last two camps, Majdanek and Auschwitz, contained non-Jewish prisoners too, and had been concentration camps before the addition of gas chambers and crematoria.

Extermination facilities were used mainly on Jews, although in Auschwitz, before the grand-scale extermination of Jews began, some invalids and a number of Russian prisoners of war were selected for "special treatment," so that the effects of Cyclon-B could be evaluated. Also at Auschwitz, gypsies were exterminated, just as they had been in Kulmhof (Chelmno), to where they had been sent from the Lodz ghetto. While Kulmhof was definitely a death camp, it was not part of the newly erected *Aktion Reinhard* camps, but as has been demonstrated, had started operations in the part of Poland that was now part of the greater German Reich as early as the winter of 1941. Kulmhof closed its operations in March 1943, but was reopened in the summer of 1944. For several weeks, it served as an auxiliary site to Auschwitz, where most of the inmates of the Lodz ghetto were sent. Several thousand Jews were added to the ongoing burning of corpses once the final liquidation of the large ghetto proceeded. Shortly afterward, all evidence of mass murder was eliminated. According to Polish sources, published in *Przewodnik po Upamietnionych Miejscach walk i meczenstwa: Lata wojny 1939–1945* (Guide to Remembrance of Places, Battles, and Suffering in the War Years 1939–1945), Kulmhof alone claimed 350,000 victims, with most of them from the Lodz ghetto and environs.

The four death camps envisioned by Heydrich were all in the Lublin district of the General Government. Having learned useful methods of liquidation from the early euthanasia program in Germany, as well as some

hands-on experience at Kulmhof, the administrators of these camps, headed by Odilo Globocnik and his deputy Christian Wirth, did not expect any difficulties, even though the scope of their present operation was much larger and more complicated than the euthanasia program had been.

Belzec, located in the province of Zamosc, was the first of these camps to be established and started operating on March 16, 1942. Joseph Goebbels made an entry about this event in his diary on March 27, thinking it noteworthy enough! At that time and for the next five months, Wirth was the commandant. The gas chamber in Belzec, at first nothing but a flimsy wooden shack, was very often in a "holding pattern" because the diesel engine that supplied the carbon monoxide gas was in the habit of breaking down. Sometimes the victims were locked in the gas chamber for several hours while efforts were made to replace or repair the faulty engine. In such cases, as the Jews stood inside, body pressed against body, their cries were heard all over the camp.

A description of this torture was given by Rudolf Reder in the monograph *Belzec*. A Jewish businessman from Lvov, Reder was the only survivor of Belzec. His engineering degree bought him time at the camp, for upon his arrival, he was put in charge of the camp's steam excavator, needed for the ditches. He was the only man there who could handle the machine and one day, when it broke down, he was sent to Lvov, accompanied by two SS men, to buy a replacement for the faulty part. Having grown up in that city and knowing it well, he managed to give his two escorts the slip by entering a house that had a second exit. He hid with gentile friends and after the war wrote his memoirs, describing the makeup of the camp, its administrators, and the scenes where victims had to wait for their death due to technical difficulties.

Reder's report was borne out by SS *Obersturmfuehrer* Kurt Gerstein, who witnessed such a scene. Gerstein, an expert on poison gas in general and Cyclon-B in particular, was so shocked by his experience that he tried to inform the Papal Nuncio in Berlin of what was going on, but was denied entry because he was in uniform. After this fiasco, he approached the Swedish diplomat Baron von Otter who took his report to Stockholm. After the war was over, the Swedish government admitted that it had not done anything about it. Gerstein, who was caught and incarcerated, committed suicide in his cell at Fresnes, France, on July 17, 1945.

Sobibor, the second camp, was established during May 1942 and began operations much like Belzec, relying mainly on diesel engines used to gas the Jews from nearby towns, as well as from far away cities, as for example Vienna. On June 7, in a regular train, a transport of Jews, led by the Austrian

policeman Fischmann, was handed over to the Austrian commandant of Sobibor, Franz Stangl. Stangl had learned his trade at Schloss Hartheim in Austria, where he had been deputy supervisor of the euthanasia program. From there his orders took him to Lublin and he was then promoted to commandant of Sobibor. His deputy commandant was his fellow Austrian Gustav Wagner, who had also worked at Schloss Hartheim.

Stangl's resourcefulness and obvious success brought him a transfer to a bigger camp, Treblinka, in September 1942. In his file there is a letter from Globocnik, describing him as the best commandant in all of Poland.

Wagner stayed on at Sobibor, but functioned as Stangl's deputy at Treblinka whenever necessary. The Jews called him "wolf" behind his back and survivors remember him as a beast in human form who "could not eat a meal without having killed someone first." In contrast to Wagner's cruel and bloodthirsty behavior when receiving transports, Stangl was rather polite, even though the result was the same. Whenever convoys arrived at the camp, he was there to "greet" the victims, dressed in white riding breeches, acting accommodating, answering questions, and seemingly friendly.

After the revolts of Treblinka and Sobibor, in August 1943 and October 1943 respectively, both Stangl and Wagner were transferred to Italy for the express purpose of fighting partisans. Afterward, although both were arrested by the Americans in 1945, there seemed to be nothing to tie them to the monstrous crimes they had committed. All the Americans knew about them was that they had fought against Yugoslav partisans. As a result, Stangl was turned over to the Austrians, who knew much more about him. Wagner had easily escaped from the detention camp and settled in Graz.

Despite the fact that he was to stand trial for his role at Schloss Hartheim and the euthanasia program, Stangl was kept at a so-called "open" jail in Austria. One day, he simply walked out the door and joined his friend Wagner in Graz. Both men combined their resources and with the help of Bishop Hudal in Rome, a native of Austria, managed to obtain Red Cross passports. They made their way first to Syria and then decided to settle in Brazil.

In 1967 Stangl was turned over to the West German Republic and, after a well-documented trial, was sentenced to life in prison. During his incarceration, Stangl was interviewed by the journalist Gitta Sereny. In a book based on these interviews, entitled *Into That Darkness*, Sereny described Stangl's telling her the story of *Oberkapo* (Foreman) Blau, which she later checked during an interview with SS *Unterscharfuehrer* Franz Suchomel. Blau and his wife, both Austrian Jews, arrived at Treblinka with a transport from Kielce, after that ghetto's liquidation. They evidently knew Stangl quite well, for Blau had been a horse and cattle trader in the vicinity of

Stangl's own section of Austria, near Wels. Blau, upon seeing a familiar face on the platform, expressed his delight.

According to the Polish Jew Samuel Willenberg, quoted in Donat's *The Death Camp Treblinka*, Stangl immediately separated Blau and his wife from the other members of the transport. He made Blau the *Oberkapo*, that is, chief of all the other *kapos*, and made her the camp's cook. Willenberg asserted that this was the only time in the history of Treblinka that such a thing occurred. He also maintained that Blau was an informer and had collaborated with the Gestapo already earlier in the Kielce ghetto. Stangl did not describe Blau as an informer, and neither did Suchomel, who told Sereny that Stangl just favored Blau as a fellow Austrian and never made a secret of the fact of having known the Blaus. He added that "old Mrs. Blau" was a great cook.

Stangl recalled an occasion when a very disturbed Blau came to his office to tell him that his eighty-year-old father had just arrived with a transport from Theresienstadt and asked what could be done about him. Stangl, quoted by Sereny, then told him, "Really, Blau, you must understand, it's impossible. A man of eighty . . ." Blau accepted this, but asked for two favors—he wanted Stangl's permission to have his father shot rather than gassed, and he wanted to take him first to the kitchen for a good meal. Stangl granted these requests and told Sereny earnestly that Blau came to him later that day to thank him, with tears in his eyes! As for the Blaus' subsequent fate, Stangl had forgotten what happened to them, but Sereny asked Suchomel and he could give her the following information: First of all, he remembered that Blau asked Stangl to relieve him of being *Oberkapo*; he had evidently developed some trouble with his heart. He asked to be allowed to work in the kitchen and he did so, at least until the uprising. After the uprising, Blau was part of the cleanup detail and then, together with another 100 Jews, he and his wife were brought to Sobibor, including Suchomel and other SS men.

After several weeks Suchomel found out that the whole group was to be gassed on the next day. He went to warn the Blaus, and they took poison. Suchomel, in a philosophical aside, told Sereny that "it was better that way."

There were, to be sure, many other Austrian Jews brought to Treblinka, once all the small ghettos in Poland were liquidated, but none of them had the good fortune to know the commandant personally, and thus went to the gas chambers upon arrival, unknown and unknowing.

Franz Stangl died in 1971, at the age of sixty-three, and never showed the least bit of remorse. In fact, he maintained that he did not hate Jews, but did despise them because "they accepted their fate in such a docile manner."

In one of his last conversations with Gitta Sereny, he emphasized that he had to accept the jobs at Schloss Hartheim, at Sobibor, and finally at Treblinka, to save his family and himself from the wrath of Globocnik and others.

Gustav Wagner, Stangl's deputy, was never apprehended. He lived an opulent lifestyle near São Paulo, Brazil, and consented to be interviewed for the BBC television in 1980. He declared during the interview that "murdering Jews was for him just another job that had to be done." Nevertheless, he sought the services of a psychiatrist that same year and after watching the movie *Holocaust*, committed suicide on October 3, 1980. He was sixty-nine years old.

After Sobibor, the camp to be established next was Treblinka. Started up in June 1942, it was located not too far from Warsaw, which in fact was to supply most of the victims. The methods used at Treblinka were slightly different from those used at Belzec and Sobibor, and although more efficient than the previous ones, the three small gas chambers proved to be inadequate for the task at hand, that is to exterminate these masses of Jews arriving daily at the camp. Thus, according to the records presented at the Nuremberg trials, for the first few transports arriving from the Warsaw ghetto, large ditches were prepared and the Jews were murdered in two ways—some in the gas chambers and some by the same method used by the *Einsatzgruppen* in the East, the "old-fashioned way," by shooting the victims after they had lain down in the ditches.

It was not long, however, before the personnel of the camp, consisting of Ukrainians and Latvians in addition to the few Germans there, learned to pace themselves better. The large courtyard vis-à-vis the railroad station was camouflaged as a street with barracks and a hospital and began to serve as a holding arena until everyone could enter what was called the *Himmel-strasse*, that is, "the road to heaven."

In his award-winning film, *Shoa* (the Hebrew name for Holocaust), Claude Lanzmann used Franz Suchomel as a witness relating the details about the camp. The man had a remarkable memory and even sang the Treblinka Song for Lanzmann. Suchomel also commented that although the Ukrainians were extremely brutal, the Latvians were the worst.

According to Suchomel, additional, "better" gas chambers were added by the end of August 1942, so as to speed up the destruction process. But there were still occasional problems with backlog and there is no doubt that trains meant for these death camps in Poland were occasionally sent to other destinations than the one on the loading list. Furthermore, since many transport invoices in France, Belgium, Holland, Germany, Austria, and

Czechoslovakia are often just marked "*nach dem Osten*" (to the East), instead of indicating the exact place of arrival, the transport leaders, presumably after making phone calls, went farther or perhaps closer than originally planned. This was done quite frequently. Despite there being a definite place of arrival on the manifest, it still happened that the transport would be shunted to another camp, making it difficult for the researcher to arrive at exact numbers for each individual camp. Even at this late date not all transports are fully documented, but one thing is certain: The passengers of those transports are all dead, killed either at the camps in the Polish General Government or perhaps in the environs of Riga and Minsk.

That was the case with the aforementioned Viennese transport which arrived at Sobibor on June 17, 1942. In his report, transport leader Reserve Lieutenant Fischmann, quoted in Christopher Browning's *Ordinary Men*, described the loading of 1,000 Jews at *Aspang Bahnhof* and clearly stated that the transport travelled to Sobibor rather than to Izbica, as had been indicated earlier. He mentioned the cities and towns through which the train had passed and reported that at the Lublin railroad station, fifty-one Jews between the ages fifteen to fifty were removed from the train and taken to a labor camp. At the same time, three cars containing the passengers' luggage and food were left in Lublin as well. Another three cars, also containing luggage and food, were delivered to Trawniki, which he correctly identified as a Jewish camp. After that, the remaining 949 Jews were brought to Sobibor and delivered to First Lieutenant Stangl. Fischmann called Sobibor a "work camp" and closed his report with the notation that there were no untoward incidents on the journey or during stopovers at train stations. This is not surprising. First of all, the Viennese Jews did not foresee what was to happen to them upon arrival. Secondly, they travelled in regular, third class railroad cars and not, as Christopher Browning assumed, in closed cattle cars. They were, moreover, by this time (as opposed to the earlier transports), permitted to get water at prearranged stops. All this was done to prevent panic, and it succeeded only too well.

Despite the detailed report by Fischmann, the transport list as well as the railroad manifesto still indicate that the Jews were sent to Izbica.

Several days after the transport from Vienna had arrived, Stangl received about 5,000 Jews, including some Viennese from the Majdanek camp, owing to the fact that Heinrich Himmler had wanted Majdanek to be cleared of Jews. He changed his mind when it became evident that many of the ghettos in Poland continued to send their able-bodied Jews to Majdanek, and these were supplemented by young men taken from the trains arriving from the Reich and other parts of Europe. It was Globocnik who pointed

all this out to Himmler and thus, Majdanek, which had up until then been a concentration and labor camp, was now equipped with all the trappings of still another death camp, while retaining some of its old character.

Majdanek was outfitted with seven small gas chambers, 5 by 5 meters each and able to hold 200 to 250 people at one time. A much larger crematorium was added to the existing one. People were burned on a daily basis, around the clock, owing not only to the ongoing liquidation of new arrivals selected for instant death, but also to deaths due to sickness, starvation, and punishments. The brutality of the guards, among whom Hermine Braunsteiner of Austria was considered the worst, took its toll especially on the helpless women prisoners who ended up in smoke.

The large field where the selection of new arrivals took place was called the "Rose Garden." Quoted in Ingrid Mueller-Muench's book *Die Frauen von Majdanek* (The Women of Majdanek), the Polish Jewess Rachel Murmann, a survivor who was an important and effective witness at the Majdanek trial held in Duesseldorf, Germany, in 1975, said "one was chosen to live—at least for a while—or for going to heaven right after one's arrival at the camp."

Located next to Field I, the gas chambers looked like ordinary stone buildings, connected to somewhat larger dressing rooms. Unlike the gas chambers at Belzec, Sobibor, and Treblinka, they did not use diesel fuel exclusively through the exhaust contraption, but were also outfitted with small skylights in the ceilings from which Cyclon-B crystals were poured in once groups of 200 to 250 per chamber had been assembled.

Alexander Werth, in *Russia at War, 1941–1945*, described how the Majdanek camp looked one month after the Russians had taken Lublin on July 23, 1944. He wondered what the Jews were thinking about once they were standing in those stone buildings, pressed so close to each other and not being able to move, and what they felt when the "pretty pale blue crystals of Cyclon-B were showered down on them." The men who were busy with the cleanup after each gassing could have told him about the expression of sheer, unmitigated terror on the faces of the doomed, of how the strongest were on top to get that last lungful of air, and of the unnatural positions of the bodies, young and old, some of which had to be separated with crow bars. There was no majesty in their dying.

Right next to the gas chambers were nineteen huts filled with incredible loot taken from the living as well as from the dead. People often hid jewelry in their bodies' orifices, and these were searched after gassing. At that time, gold teeth were removed as well. Prisoners worked in five buildings behind these nineteen huts. After sorting the various items brought into the build-

ings on cars filled at the huts, the loot was transferred to a very large warehouse in Lublin, from where the best items were sent to Germany.

There was also an enclosure where about 200 fierce dogs were kept, and last but not least, there was a huge funeral pyre; it was used to augment the two crematoria located on the other side of the camp, which were often unable to handle all the bodies. In charge of the crematoria was *Obersturm-fuehrer* Erich Mussfeld.

During 1942 and 1943, for unknown reasons, several small transports of Jews, men and women, left Majdanek for Auschwitz and other camps. At the time of their selection for such transports, they were, for the most part, wary, and many tried to avoid leaving. As described in "Lena's Story," included in *The Holocaust Kingdom* by Alexander Donat, people had family members at the camp, or they had attained better jobs and positions, or they had been there long enough to carve out a niche for themselves. Thus, many of them made every effort not to be included in those transports, especially since it was a camp credo and most of the time a true one, that every change during those years was for the worst. In fact, even though the majority of those who finally left perished, there were, however, some survivors. That cannot be said of the Jews who did remain in Majdanek.

During the last two weeks of October 1943, both in the camp itself and at the nearby Krempecki Forest, 300 Polish and Russian prisoners were ordered to dig several huge pits, over 100 meters long, 2 meters wide, and very, very deep. At that time, there were still about 18,000 Jews in Majdanek itself, and over 20,000 in Trawniki and Poniatowo. In addition, there were some remnants in various locations.

About 10,000 Jews were killed at Trawniki and Poniatowo on November 3; the other 10,000 together with small groups, were taken to the Krempecki Forest. Inside Majdanek, under the command of Mussfeld, the Jews were driven to the pits on November 3 and 4, to the accompaniment of popular music, blaring from loudspeakers. They were made to disrobe, lie down, and were then murdered by machine gun fire. And so it went; layer after layer, in an orgy of blood.

The Germans called this atrocity *Aktion Erntefest* (harvest festival). When it was all over, the Polish prisoners of Majdanek, according to Prince Christopher Radziwil, an inmate since 1939, had a party and drank a toast to the fact that the hated Jews were gone. A single paragraph in *Das Nationalsozialistische Lagersystem* (The National Socialist Camp System), edited by Martin Weinmann, under the heading "*Aktion Erntefest*," asserts that these killings were a response to the Jewish resistance attempts in the various death camps that year and cost over 40,000 lives. Mussfeld's

handling of the *Aktion* in Majdanek was rewarded with a position in Auschwitz, where he was put in charge of Crematorium II.

By the time the bodies in Majdanek were disinterred and burned, he was gone. This may account for the fact that the work done by the burning commandos was rather sloppy. According to Werth, it was still possible to find bones, teeth, and mounds of ashes when walking through the area of the massacre. In addition, he reported that the stench was all pervasive. As for the Krempecki Forest, Werth was astonished to discover that the people who had been murdered there were shot while still dressed. There had been no time to exhume and burn the bodies and many were not covered up sufficiently.

His astonishment was due to what he had learned in those few days: He found out that the Germans never wasted anything, and especially not in such a major industry as the "final solution" of the Jewish problem had been. He illustrated that principle of nothing going to waste by describing a huge, barnlike structure containing 850,000 pairs of shoes. He went on to say that by the end of August, half of these shoes were gone. Hundreds of Poles living in the Lublin area had come and taken away bagfuls of shoes.

Werth further described the thousands of suitcases and trunks, piled high, with addresses carefully written on the sides. He wrote about the thousands of women's dresses, of overcoats, of men's suits, and of shelves filled with toys and children's clothes. There were also heaps of junk containing sheet music and piles of loose documents. One such document showed that in the first few months of 1944 alone, eighteen railroad cars, filled with goods from the Lublin warehouse, had been sent to Germany, in response to requests by civilians!

As has been stated, in charge of murder, robbery, and the administration of these four death camps—Belzec, Sobibor, Treblinka, and Majdanek—and reporting directly to *Reichsfuehrer* Heinrich Himmler, was none other than SS *Gruppenfuehrer* Odilo Globocnik, the Austrian with the rather scandalous past. Due to some financial swindle while *Gauleiter* of Vienna during 1938 and part of 1939, Globocnik had forfeited that position, but thanks to Himmler had been made *SS und Polizei Fuehrer* of the Lublin district in November 1939. By the spring of 1942, he was elevated to head the *Aktion Reinhard*. Despite Globocnik's obvious failings, Himmler appreciated him for his fierce anti-Semitism and his brutal methods, as well as for his talent of choosing the right people to assist him. Globocnik's deputy, for example, was Christian Wirth, who had perfected the gassing of the insane and retarded as early as 1939 and 1940 at Grafeneck, Branden-

burg, Hadamar, and Schloss Hartheim. Thus, Himmler had every right to be satisfied.

There is no doubt that the euthanasia program was the forerunner of the gas vans and gas chambers, so important for the success of the "final solution" of the Jewish problem, and while there was strong objection from the church to the euthanasia program, nothing was said about the destruction of the Jews.

On December 15, 1943, several months after *Aktion Reinhard* had come to a close, Globocnik was ordered by Himmler to give him a detailed statement of the operation's profits. According to that statement, which was presented at the Nuremberg trials, Globocnik reported that the total value of the monies, valuables, gold (including melted down teeth), silver, jewelry, and furs, amounted to nearly 180 million Reichsmark net. As was to be expected, a rather large part of what was taken from the Jews ended up in his pockets and those of his assistants, and the real sum must have been even more staggering.

It is generally assumed that the four death camps under Globocnik's control "did away" with approximately two million Jews. Looking at the profits, therefore, it is clear that not only was unprecedented murder being committed without remorse on a scale never attempted before, but the industry of death enriched the murderers in such a way that the act of killing Jews was reinforced by the huge profits to be made. For most of them the operation represented a "getting-rich-quick" scheme, never again to be duplicated. The irony of it was that in the case of Wirth and Globocnik, they did not have much time to enjoy their ill-gotten gains. As happened with many of the upper echelon of the death camps, they, too, were sent to Italy in order to take care of partisans. Stangl saw Wirth being killed during a street fight in Trieste in May 1944. As for Globocnik, he managed to get back to Austria and to Weissenstein, Carinthia, where he was picked up by a British unit. Not willing to face the consequences of his crimes, on May 31, 1945, he swallowed cyanide and died.

Just three years earlier, between April and June 1942, six transports from Vienna had made their way to the General Government, to be held in little towns near the death camps, until their own turn for liquidation would come.

The first transport left on April 9 for Izbica; originally, it had been scheduled to go to Riga on March 23, but the orders were changed when there were some difficulties with the choice of date and location. As has been stated earlier, just then, in the last two weeks of March 1942, thousands of German, Czech, and Austrian Jews were murdered in the forests around Riga. Selections had been held at the Riga ghetto on March 15 and at Camp

Jungfernhof on March 26. The Austrian police who were to guard the March 23 transport and had in fact already been paid to go to Riga, had to give back some of the money received since the distance to Izbica was less than to Riga and, thus, they did not deserve that much.

On the way to Izbica, the train stopped in Lublin. A number of young men were taken off the train and brought to Majdanek. The luggage, too, remained behind in Lublin, and the impoverished Viennese Jews were brought to Izbica, which is located between Chelm and Zamosc, about 50 kilometers north of Belzec, which would eventually be the final destination. In the meantime, the newcomers were added to the local Jews, or, if these had already been murdered, were given their shacks in the little villages where they had lived.

The next transport in this series left on April 27; although the title page of the Gestapo transport list reads Wlodawa, a small town 30 kilometers northeast of Lublin very close to Sobibor, the pages containing the names of the deportees read Izbica. Once again, the same mode was employed. The train stopped in Lublin, some young men were taken off together with the luggage, and the remainder were sent either to Wlodawa or to Izbica. Since it was only for a few days or, at most, for a few weeks, it really did not matter. They ended up either in Belzec or Sobibor.

The next three transports from Vienna all went to Izbica. They had left on May 12, May 15, and June 5. Over 300 men from these transports were added to the Majdanek camp; the others were temporarily placed in the small villages all around the death camps. Father's brother Nachman and his wife Bertha were part of the May 15 transport. Since he was over forty-six years old at the time, it is highly improbable that he was taken off the train in Lublin and selected for work. It can be assumed that the Merlins were added to some little town in the vicinity, and stayed maybe even in Izbica itself. After a while, their lives ended in the gas chambers of either Belzec or Sobibor, whichever one was ready to receive another batch of Jews for what the Germans called *Sonderbehandlung* (special treatment).

In all these cases, even though the trip from Vienna to the General Government was made in regular railroad cars, the last journey from the little towns to the death camps was never in so elegant a fashion, but was made in cattle cars, where the unfortunate victims had barely place to stand, much less to sit down. By the time those trains reached the death camps, many Jews had already died en route.

As has been pointed out earlier, an exception had been made with the sixth and last transport in this series, which left Vienna on June 14, 1942. After short stops at Lublin and Trawniki, it went straight to Sobibor. When

the passengers got off their railroad cars, they did not have to wait long to experience the special treatment. Upon arrival on June 17, their hopes, their dreams, as well as their fears and doubts about the future went up in smoke.

Other Jews from Austria, who had been deported during 1941 to such places as Opole, Kielce, Modliborzyce, and Lagow-Opatow and had settled there or in one of the surrounding little towns where they had found help and friendliness from the indigenous Jews, ended up in either of the four death camps as well. Their stay in Poland had thus been a rather short one.

Whether the Jews had lived in those towns and villages in the Lublin district of Poland for generations, or whether they had been sent there from far away, their fate, with very few exceptions, would be the same. All ended up in the gas chambers. Even during the last hours that remained to them on this earth, they had to suffer the brutality of the monsters who did the actual killing, the so-called *"Hi-Wi's,"* a shortened version of *Hilfsfreiwillige* (volunteer helpers), made up of Latvians, Ukrainians, Lithuanians, and Estonians.

Driven out of the trains, first the men—for reasons of security—and then the women were made to undress and walk through a passage that led to the gas chambers. While their men were murdered, the women's hair was shorn to be used in German submarines as insulation and packing material for the hulls. After that, they too were murdered.

Men, women, and children—so many children—pushed into those gas chambers, never to realize all the good things that they thought would be theirs once the war was over. Ashes to ashes, dust to dust, only because they were Jews . . . no other reason.

As far as the four death camps were concerned, Belzec was the first to stop operating. During the summer of 1943, the buildings were removed, and after exhuming the bodies and burning them, grass had been planted and all looked peaceful and ordinary. The townspeople, however, once the war was over, continued to dig up the earth, hoping to find valuables overlooked by the Germans. Sometimes, indeed, they found a ring or an earring, or perhaps a gold coin—just enough to motivate them to go on looking for more. Eventually, they were made to cease this macabre occupation, the grass was permitted to grow again, and the camp, over a period of years, became a sort of shrine, right at the edge of town. It is estimated that between 200,000 and 250,000 Jews lost their lives at Belzec.

On August 2, 1943, the 800 Jews at Treblinka who had been permitted to live a little longer so as to do the work involved in sorting, repairing, and dispatching the belongings of their murdered brethren, staged a revolt. No longer were they ignorant of their fate as they had been upon arrival, and

since they knew they were doomed in any case, they were unwilling to go to their death quietly. Their plans went awry and only a few of them were able to flee and survive the massacre that followed their revolt. Although they had managed to destroy much of the camp, they had not been able to blow up the sturdy gas chamber. In the next two weeks it was used on the Jews of Bialystock and after that last operation, all evidence of murder was obliterated. Grass and trees were planted and the site looked peaceful and innocent.

Once the war ended, with the tacit approval of the Polish government, many stones, big and small, were brought to the site by Jews coming back to Warsaw and the vicinity. Each stone represented a town, or a village, or a city, from where Jews had been delivered for annihilation. The townspeople of Treblinka remembered the camp very well and also the hundreds and hundreds of trains that came there filled to capacity, and leaving totally empty. In his film *Shoa*, Claude Lanzmann interviewed the townspeople and it is clear that they felt remote then, and still do, from the suffering that went on right next to them. The number of Jews killed at Treblinka is thought to be at least 900,000, but Gitta Sereny, when working on her story about Stangl, interviewed a former member of the Polish underground, who had been sent to Treblinka in order to keep score. According to him, the number was far higher. He arrived at 1,200,000.

On October 14, 1943, there occurred an uprising at Sobibor as well. Very few Jews managed to survive the ensuing massacre, and once the rest had been exterminated, what followed was much the same as in the other two camps. After the bodies were exhumed, burned and the large bones crushed with a special mechanical bone breaker manufactured in Bavaria, all traces of the camp were obliterated. The site was thoroughly cleaned, the Jews who had done the grisly work were killed and burned on the same pyres that they themselves had constructed, and it was hard to tell what grievous sins had been committed there. Approximately 300,000 Jews were killed at Sobibor, but there may have been more.

Of the four death camps, only Majdanek continued to exist, but not so much as a death camp than as a sort of transit camp. Even after the Polish and Russian inmates were evacuated in the early part of 1944, all installations were left standing and were found in July when the Soviet army took Lublin earlier than expected. The indefatigable Alexander Werth sent a detailed report to the BBC in London, but the editors refused to air it. They thought it was nothing but a Russian propaganda stunt and it was not until the discovery in the West of Buchenwald, Dachau, Ohrdruf, and Bergen Belsen among others, that they were convinced about the reality of Maj-

Theresienstadt

It was to be a ghetto for prominent Jews: for Jews who had medals conferred upon them during the Great War, Jews who were living in old-age homes, Jews who had been married to Aryans who had either divorced them or had since died, Jews who were working at the *Kultusgemeinde*, Jews who had connections, Jews who were well-known authors or artists or scientists or aristocrats, Jews whose names were recognized all over the world; in short, a model ghetto meant for the formerly rich and famous. All that was needed was to change the already established ghetto at Theresienstadt into a ghetto for the prominent and that was exactly what Heydrich was going to do. He advanced this plan at the infamous Wannsee Conference on January 20, 1942, at a time when the extermination process was already in full swing. Up to that time, each transport to the East had contained Jews who fit into all these categories, but now there would be a ghetto just for them.

Actually, in practice, even transports that left the Reich for the East after the Wannsee Conference still contained scientists, authors, artists, the aged, as well as former soldiers in the Kaiser's armed forces. Eventually, though, Heydrich's idea would prevail and there arose Theresienstadt, a ghetto for the privileged.

What it became, however, was a vast collection point for transports going to Riga, Izbica, Piaski, Rejowiec, Lublin, Warsaw, Zamosz, Sobibor, Ossowo, Zulia, Trawniki, Minsk (Maly Trostinec), Treblinka, and Auschwitz.

Yet, during 1942, 1943, and 1944 every Jew still in Vienna at that time, hoped and prayed and schemed (with some of them even succeeding) to go to Theresienstadt and not to those other places where people were never heard

from again. They had no idea that a constant stream of transports was leaving the *Prominenten ghetto* (ghetto for the prominent) for just exactly those places!

Theresienstadt, *Terezin* in Czech, had been a fortress built by Emperor Joseph II and named after his mother, the Austrian empress who had hated Jews with such a passion. A small town abutted the fortress and it was that small town that would become the ghetto.

When the first Austrian Jews arrived there in June 1942, they found a teeming ghetto already containing Jews from all over Germany as well as from Czechoslovakia. Later on, there were to be Jews from many countries occupied by Germany, such as Danish Jews, Dutch Jews, Slovakian Jews, Hungarian Jews, and Polish Jews. Finally, just weeks before the end of the war, several death marches ended up in Theresienstadt and long trains came from all over, bearing more than 15,000 half-dead Jews, most of whom could not be saved. They brought spotted typhoid fever and the ghetto had to contend with a quarantine. Excluding these last 15,000 Jews, about 145,000 passed through the Theresienstadt ghetto from the time of its establishment as a regular ghetto in December 1941 to the spring of 1945.

There were three hierarchies in Theresienstadt. On the highest rung of the ladder were the Czechs. After all, this ghetto was in their country and they had been the "builders" of it. On the second rung were the Austrians, with whom the Czechs had once shared imperial Austria. The last large group were the Jews from Germany. Later on, however, the Danish Jews would move up to the top, mainly because they received food packages from home.

The Czech Jews had arrived at Theresienstadt when the town itself was still inhabited by Czechs. It made sense, therefore, to house them, at least temporarily, in some of the old barracks at the fortress. By June 1942, however, the local citizens had been forced to leave and from then on the town became the ghetto, housing the German administration and the guards in a separate section. The fortress itself was used to incarcerate both Jewish and non-Jewish prisoners, who were, for the most part, political or had infringed upon some of the myriad of rules and regulations. Nikolaus Martin, in *Prager Winter* (Winter in Prague) described life in the fortress and the SS men who ruled there. One of the men in charge of prisoners was the Austrian Stefan Rojko. He had been a policeman who transferred to the SS.

Oberscharfuehrer Rojko, aptly named "the butcher of Theresienstadt," still referred to prisoners as "pieces" while on trial in a Graz court in 1963. The judge sentenced him to life in prison.

The "pieces" who were in his charge at the fortress were cramped into the same small cells where during the Great War the Austrians had held spies and assassins. One of those assassins incarcerated there until his death

in 1918 was Gavrilo Princip, who had shot Crown Prince Ferdinand and his wife in Sarajevo, precipitating what became World War I.

Several weeks after the Jews from Prague and Brno had arrived at Fortress Theresienstadt, two thousand of them, in two separate transports, one on January 9, 1942, and the other on January 15, 1942, were shipped to the Riga ghetto, where they formed the Prague group, one of ten groups identified by the name of their city of origin. Among them were several Austrian Jews who had fled to Czechoslovakia in 1938. In the ghetto they met other Austrian and German Jews, who had been deported to Riga directly from their homes. Thus, these newcomers informed the inhabitants of the Riga ghetto about Theresienstadt and the conditions there. What they reported did not sound like such a good deal, at least not at the time. Neither the German and Austrian Jews nor the newly arrived Czech Jews, now together in the Riga ghetto, could have foreseen that this sleepy garrison town they had just left would be known as a model ghetto for "deserving" Jews during the next three years. None of us could have guessed that this so-called model ghetto of Theresienstadt would serve as an antechamber to death with a vast collection of overcrowded houses, rampant diseases, and hunger and desperation, and thus not very different from our own ghetto or other ghettos in the East. As for the intensive cultural life it enjoyed, it was created by its Jewish prisoners and by no one else. The artists gave of themselves and succeeded in bringing life into darkness, more so than in other ghettos owing to their preponderance there.

With the exception of several members of the aristocracy, all other inmates of Theresienstadt were packed together into the old houses that had not been modernized since the time of Emperor Joseph II, or so it seemed. The very, very prominent, in addition to the aforementioned nobility, were housed in a small building at the edge of the ghetto. When they spoke to each other, they never forgot to use their proper titles. One of the building's cleaning women, a Jewess from Hamburg, Kaethe Starke, in her fascinating book *Der Fuehrer Schenkt den Juden eine Stadt* (The Fuehrer Presents the Jews with a City), commented on that charming Viennese idiosyncrasy of holding on to titles, no matter what. Despite titles and somewhat better living conditions, however, these prominent human beings starved just like the rest of the ghetto's populace. Hunger was one of the greatest scourges there and much harder to cope with than the dirt, the vermin, the overcrowding, and even the diseases. Yet, despite these unfavorable conditions, people wanted to remain in the ghetto. It slowly became clear to its inhabitants that they would eventually be part of a transport to the East and even the die-hard optimists were terribly afraid.

In the meantime, though, almost from its inception, the death rate in the ghetto was extremely high and thus, these lovely old people, prominent though they were, with most of them having done so much for Austria and having loved it so well, finally found the only peace there was: death itself.

Some houses in Theresienstadt had names of the cities in the Reich from which the Jews had come, others were numbered as on a grid so that their location could immediately be realized. With small exceptions, sexes lived in separate houses and so did the children. Thus, the streets were crowded at all times as inmates tended to visit each other. Furthermore, people did not cook for themselves, but went to the kitchens with their little pots and pans to get the day's ration; they could warm it up once they got to their rooms, but only if they were lucky enough to have a little stove and if so, if they had wood. Privacy or personal hygiene were virtually unobtainable. Lice and bedbugs made life miserable and, worse, brought diseases. People's tempers snapped, and there were frequent arguments. The model ghetto was hell on earth and yet, it was still better than the East, that dreadful place with its sinister meaning.

Adolf Eichmann visited the Theresienstadt ghetto quite often and once even attended a concert there. During the ghetto's existence the three successive commandants were all Austrians, belonging to the circle of "his" men. The first commandant was *Hauptsturmfuehrer* Dr. Siegfried Seidl, the second commandant was *Hauptsturmfuehrer* Anton Burger, and the third and last commandant was *Hauptsturmfuehrer* Karl Rahm.

Seidl served from spring 1942 until July 3, 1943. He had made several blunders during his tenure, but he was forgiven by Eichmann, who trusted him. One of those blunders concerned Karl Loewenstein, the returnee from Minsk. Seidl had made him head of the Theresienstadt Jewish police and after a while, Loewenstein's well-trained 400 young men were seen as dangerous to the German administration. They were replaced by men over forty-five years old and Loewenstein was kept in jail at the fortress for several weeks.

After leaving Theresienstadt, Seidl served for a short time in Bergen Belsen and afterward, at Eichmann's behest, became very active in Hungary during the deportation of that country's Jews in summer 1944. In fact, by assisting *Sturmbannfuehrer* Hermann Krumey, he was responsible, to a degree, of bringing several thousand Hungarian Jews to Austria after they could no longer be sent to Auschwitz and were needed as a labor force. In fall 1945, Seidl was caught in Austria and was brought to trial there in 1946. He was condemned to death and duly executed.

Anton Burger took over in July 1943, but left Theresienstadt on February 7, 1944, becoming involved with the deportation of Greek Jews. Shortly after that job, much like Seidl, he helped with the deportation of Hungarian Jews, working closely with Eichmann. He managed to escape from Camp Marcus W. Orr, where the Americans had held him ever since he was caught in 1945. Upon leaving, he left his jailers a sarcastic note to the effect that he did not really belong there. Four years later, the Austrian police "found" him in his hometown, Neunkirchen, brought him to the *Landesgericht II* (the country's court) in Vienna, and let him escape once again. Despite the fact that he was in contact with his parents and wife in Neunkirchen, he was never found!

Rahm remained at his post until May 5, 1945, and then fled to Austria. He was arrested in 1946 and extradited to Czechoslovakia where he was brought to trial and sentenced to death by a Special People's Court.

The Jewish elders of Theresienstadt, in succession, were Jakub Edelstein, Dr. Paul Eppstein, and Rabbi Benjamin Murmelstein.

Edelstein, a Czech Jew, did much to create order out of chaos in the early months of the ghetto's existence. Burger did not like him and had him arrested on November 9, 1943. He was held at the *Kommandantur* until December 15, 1943, when he was added to transport DR, which went to Auschwitz. Ludmila Chladkova, in *The Terezin Ghetto*, reported that Edelstein was shot in Auschwitz on June 20, 1944.

The second ghetto elder, Paul Eppstein, also a Czech Jew, was not as able an administrator as his predecessor had been. After a run-in with Rahm, he was arrested on September 27, 1944, and was taken to the Small Fortress where he was shot; his execution, however, was not made public and his wife continued to bring food for him in the mistaken belief that he was still alive. She was told that he would be on a transport for Auschwitz and she boarded what she thought was the same train, still unaware that he had been dead for several weeks. She was gassed upon arrival.

The next ghetto elder was a Jew from Austria. Rabbi Benjamin Murmelstein, an expert on the writings of the renegade Jewish historian Josephus Flavius, served as ghetto elder until the very end. Many people intensely disliked the pugnacious, arrogant man and blamed him for a series of events over which he had no control. It must have been his personality, for he was equally disliked while still an official at the Vienna *Kultusgemeinde* before his deportation. A large, imposing man with a vile temper, Murmelstein, after the war, survived several attempts by higher authorities to punish him for what was called "using his powers to the detriment of fellow Jews." He and his family came back to Vienna in the summer of 1945 and were

eventually able to leave the continent and live in peace, at least from outside sources.

Many of my parents' friends and several elderly relatives were among those approximately 15,000 Jews sent to Theresienstadt from Austria, but not one was alive when the war was over. Among the younger people, however, some acquaintances and a few of the children with whom I had gone to the various schools after the summer of 1938, returned to Vienna either directly from Theresienstadt or from camps to which they had been sent. Some of their adventures deserve special mention, as for example that of Rosi Mausner, which is a story of spunk and luck.

Rosi, born in 1923, had arrived in Theresienstadt together with her mother Josephine Mausner on October 12, 1942. Rosi's father, Jacob Mausner, had left Vienna in 1939 for Italy, but had not been able to bring the two women out of Austria. His son Leo had left for America in early 1939 and was working at an uncle's place of business in New York City. He enlisted in the U.S. army shortly after Pearl Harbor was attacked and was eventually promoted to sergeant. By war's end, his unit was stationed near Cologne. Leo used his furlough to go there and fill out a questionnaire at the Red Cross offices, inquiring about his mother and sister.

At the time he was trying to get this information, Rosi was back in Vienna. She and her mother had remained in Theresienstadt until May 18, 1944, when the two women, together with a large transport of 2,500 people, were sent to Auschwitz. There was no selection upon arrival, for as had been done before, the newcomers from Theresienstadt were put into a so-called "family camp."

It has never really been made clear why the Germans resorted to such a ruse, since most of the people within the three successive family camps were doomed anyway. The first family camp of Jews arriving from Theresienstadt was established on September 6, 1943, and contained over 5,000 men, women, and children. No selection, no prisoners' clothes, no hair cutting, totally different from the way in which the other arrivals were treated. The family camp was described in Rudolf Vrba and Alan Bestic's *I Cannot Forgive*; Vrba indicated that it gave the other prisoners a sense of hope although to the clerks working in the statistics office, that hope was soon dashed. The identity cards of these people from Theresienstadt, who felt so safe, were marked SB 3/6, meaning *Sonderbehandlung* (special treatment) to be given on March 6, 1944, exactly six months later. Indeed, after the selection of a few hundred very strong and healthy prisoners for outside work, the remainder, numbering close to 4,000 Austrian, German,

and Czech Jews were gassed two days after the target date, on March 8, 1944.

Both Vrba and Filip Mueller, a member of the *Sonderkommando* (special task force) and author of *Eyewitness Auschwitz*, were extremely depressed, since both of them had hoped for a general uprising to prevent the massacre.

The second family camp lasted from December 1943 to June 1944, also a period of six months. Once again, the Jews from Theresienstadt represented some kind of normalcy in their enclosure, but the scribes and the members of the *Sonderkommando* working in the crematoria knew from experience that there was no escape. As before, there was one last selection and the remaining people, already decimated by natural deaths, were gassed on June 20.

The third family camp, of which the two Mausner women were a part, lasted only two months. On May 15, 16, and 18, 1944, 7,503 prisoners were sent to Auschwitz, ostensibly to relieve the overcrowded conditions in Theresienstadt, where a commission was to inspect the *Prominenten Ghetto*. After undergoing several rigorous selections in Auschwitz, the remainder were gassed and that last family camp ceased to exist on July 7, 1944. Among those gassed was Josephine Mausner. Rosi, together with a few hundred women, was added to the regular women's barracks and stayed there a few weeks until she was sent to the concentration camp Gross Rosen.

After several days at Gross Rosen, she was made part of a convoy consisting of 1,500 women and was sent to a labor camp in Christianstadt an der Bober (Bobrawa). The women were ordered to rebuild railroad tracks. Other women worked in the nearby munition factory under equally horrible conditions. Many died not only because of the backbreaking labor but also because of cold, hunger, and sickness. Rosi Mausner and her Czech girlfriend Lisa Selig were determined to survive, no matter what. Their chances were not too good.

On February 2, 1945, all the women working in the vicinity were driven out of their barracks and told that they were being evacuated to another camp, supposedly Bergen Belsen. Some of them eventually ended up there, while others came to Flossenburg, among them Gerda Weissmann Klein, who, in *All But My Life* describes the death of all her friends on that same march.

Altogether, only about 200 survived the death march, a phenomenon occurring during the last phase of the war, when the Germans took their Jewish captives from one camp to another and shot all those along the way who could no longer walk. This last torture cost the lives of thousands and thousands, at a time when Germany had already lost the war, but did not let go of its victims.

Rosi was now part of such a march. The women were guarded by regular SS, who did the shooting, and some older men, called *Volkssturm*, representing the last remnant of Hitler's reserves. One such older man, an Austrian, walked next to Rosi and Lisa and told them in no uncertain terms that great trouble was in store for them. After three days on the road, with rest stops in barns along the way, he handed Rosi a map of greater Germany. Rosi and Lisa took the hint and escaped that same night, leaving the barn for a nearby forest with several other Czech girls. They took off the yellow stars on their coats and sewed the resulting holes as well as they could. Waiting until the column had disappeared the next morning, they made their way south.

There were many German civilians on the road, with their household goods heaped high on wagons, all trying to escape the Russian advance. Whenever the girls were asked where they came from or where they were going to, they, too, pretended to flee the Russians after having worked for German firms in the East.

February 14, 1945, found the six young girls outside Dresden. They became witness to the air raid inferno and although they were extremely frightened, they had little sympathy for the inhabitants of the city. Their own losses were just too overwhelming to feel pity for the enemies.

One subsequent night was spent at a German girls' home. When the woman in charge promised them baths and medical attention to be given on the next morning, they fled in great haste, for all of them had their numbers tattooed on their arms and even a cursory examination would have meant death.

Upon reaching Zwickau, the girls separated. The Czech girls tried to get into Czechoslovakia, and Rosi, now by herself, continued south, first passing through Bavaria and then into Austria. Skirting large cities, resting in deserted barns, begging for food, keeping clean by using snow to wash her face and hands, sometimes walking with others, yet always alert, always wary. When asked, her answer was that she had become separated from her group and was going back home. Owing to her unmistakable Viennese accent, she was readily believed.

When she arrived in Linz, Austria, Rosi had a break that she considered a good omen: a truck driver going to the capital offered her a lift and by nightfall she found herself on the outskirts of Vienna, in Huetteldorf, right next to the famous Vienna Woods. It was April 10, her twenty-second birthday and she had been on the move for ten weeks.

The night was dark, lit up by burning buildings; the city was under siege, and she had to find the ninth district, Czerningasse 2, where friends of her

parents and, incidentally, my own parents, lived. The husband, Mr. Landau, was a Jew, his wife was an Aryan, and she had managed to save him and their four children. It was dawn when Rosi reached their house. Uncertain of the reception, she knocked and one of the teenage sons opened the door. When he yelled "*Papa, Mama, die Rosi Mausner ist wieder da*" (Dad, Mom, Rosi Mausner is back again) and she found herself hugged and kissed by everyone, Rosi felt wonderful. Only two days after her arrival, on April 12, Vienna was liberated by Soviet forces; the female members of the family, including Rosi, had to hide from maurauding Russian soldiers looking for women, any women, young or old, it made no difference to them, but that time passed and she was truly free at last.

Owing to the general chaos, she registered with the relocated *Kultusgemeinde* at a much later time and thus, Rosi, in addition to over forty other returnees, was listed as having perished in the East by the otherwise excellent *Totenbuch Theresienstadt: Deportierte aus Oesterreich* (Book of the Dead in Theresienstadt: Deportees from Austria) by a committee, whose members used only the earliest lists of returning Austrian Jews.

In October 1945, Rosi's father, who had been liberated by the end of 1944, having been saved by Italian monks, returned to Vienna and just as we had done and so many others too, went from the railroad station straight to the *Kultusgemeinde*. That very same day, Rosi went there to register. It is almost impossible to describe their joy, when father and daughter met in such a miraculous fashion. After a number of years, first Rosi and then her father joined Leo in the United States. As the years passed, Rosi, unable to cope with questions, had a surgeon remove the number A4047 from her arm, but the scar is still there and so are the scars of her memories.

A similar fate is described by Ruth Klueger in *Weiter Leben: Eine Jugend* (To Continue Living: Youth). Ruth, born in 1931, talked about her life that was very much like Rosi's. She, her mother Alma, and grandmother Katherina were sent from Vienna to Theresienstadt on September 24, 1942. The grandmother died there, in the hospital, and Ruth, then only thirteen, together with her mother were sent to Auschwitz on May 16, 1944. With the help of another prisoner, Ruth managed to get through a selection and both she and her mother, after a short time in Gross Rosen, were made part of the labor camp at Christianstadt. They, too, fled when they had a chance and ended up in Straubing, Germany. Two years later, mother and daughter made their way to the United States. Ruth, just like Rosi, is listed in the *Totenbuch* as having perished. The moving account of her life, both because of her age at the time of the Holocaust and her subsequent erudition, is a welcome addition to survivors' biographies who were children at the time

and had to grow up under very difficult circumstances, in a milieu ruled by terror.

The members of my own family were not as fortunate as Rosi or Ruth had been, nor were they any longer young enough to even try changing their fate. Bubi's mother, Chaja Merlin, for example, then seventy-nine years old, had left Vienna for Theresienstadt on August 28, 1942, together with many others living at the Old Age Home on Seegasse in the ninth district. She stayed at the ghetto for the prominent for just one month. On September 26, 1942, she and her sister-in-law Paula Rintel, my grandfather's older sister, who had come to Theresienstadt on August 23, were taken to Maly Trostinec. If those two old ladies did not die on the way, they found their brutal death at the hands of the ever-obliging *Sonderkommando*.

Only a day or so after the transport had left, Paula's daughter Clara Rintel, aged fifty-five, arrived in Theresienstadt. Clara had hurt her spine in a riding accident several years before Hitler annexed Austria. At the time of her deportation she was an invalid and could perhaps have stayed in Vienna for some time longer. The thought of joining her mother at the "privileged" ghetto caused her to volunteer for the transport which left Vienna on September 25. To her dismay she found out what had happened. Heartbroken and bereft, Clara died in Theresienstadt on October 18, not quite four weeks after her arrival.

That particular transport on September 26 to Maly Trostinec contained many Viennese Jews. The new arrivals had very little time to become accustomed to their surroundings. In retrospect it seems that during the fall of 1942, there was a veritable frenzy of killing these old people, and of that there was no escape. The ghetto for the prominent, seen as salvation to the Jews but in reality an antechamber to death, functioned perfectly.

Transports leaving at a later time and undergoing selections gave at least some people a chance to survive.

Of girls my own age, with whom I had been friendly, only two came back. Hertha Gerstl had been my classmate in the afternoon Hebrew School before 1938, and Vera Korkus was my classmate at the *Piper Heim* in 1941. Both had gone through Auschwitz, both had lost their parents there, and both of them, just like the author Ruth Klueger, looked back upon Theresienstadt as a place where they could be children, where, despite hunger and crowding, they felt at home and where even the hardships could be tolerated. Both hated to speak of what had come afterwards.

Other youngsters known to me, although older, came back too. One of those, for instance, was Ignaz Mucinic, called Nazl, whom we knew from our time at the *Piper Heim*. He was the last person from the "outside" whom

we had seen at the collection point, the Sperlschule. Two days after we had been taken there, Nazl gained entrance and brought us some sandwiches on orders from the home's director, Israel Piper. Piper knew that very little food was given to those who were soon to be deported. It was his duty, as Nazl told us, to do this act of mercy for all the students of the *Piper Heim*, and he was well known to the Jewish "*Ordners.*"

Curiously, when my mother, my sister, and I returned to Vienna on June 1, 1945, we were told by an agent of the *Kultusgemeinde* to take up quarters at what was once the *Piper Heim*. Nazl's was the first familiar face we saw. He had come back just four days earlier, gaunt and obviously ill. Only the smile was the same, as the tall boy ruffled my sister's and my very short hair.

Ignaz and his father Joszi Mucinic had been sent to Theresienstadt on September 25, 1942. (His mother had died when he was a small boy.) Once at the ghetto, his father, a master carpenter, was put to work immediately with Nazl helping him and learning his craft. At night he played with the band, for he was a very good drummer. His knowledge of Czech was of help, for most of the other musicians were from Czechoslovakia.

Despite his usefulness at the ghetto, Joszi Mucinic was sent to Auschwitz on May 16, 1944. Nazl volunteered to go with him. Although Joszi was only fifty-eight at the time, there was something wrong with his lungs, stemming from his service in the infantry during the Great War. After spending several weeks at the family camp, Nazl was selected for work, but his father was gassed together with the others on July 7.

Nazl continued as a carpenter at the camp, fixing barracks or building shelves for the camp's administrators. Sometime during December 1944 he contacted typhoid fever and was kept alive only by the care of some friends he had made. When the evacuation of Auschwitz began on January 17 and 18, he did not heed their advice to leave, but stayed with a few other like-minded men. According to him, he just did not care anymore, nor did he have the strength. As it turned out, his apathy saved his life, for only a few days later, on January 27, the Soviet army liberated Auschwitz. After regaining his health, at least to some extent, he made his way back to Vienna and arrived there on May 27. In January 1947 he left for the United States, where he died an untimely death at the age of thirty-three in 1959. His name, too, is listed erroneously in the *Totenbuch*, as having perished in Auschwitz.

While those three large May transports had left for Auschwitz in 1944, four small transports, containing only ten Jews each arrived in Theresienstadt from Vienna between May 17 and June 21. They were just in time to witness the greatest sham perpetrated on the outside world by the Germans: The special ghetto, Theresienstadt, was going to be paraded in front of an

official Red Cross commission, sanitized and changed beyond recognition. Everything was clean and shiny, the children received new clothes just for the occasion, and with the commission members looking on, they were offered food they had not seen in ages. According to Kaethe Starke in the aforementioned book *Der Fuehrer Schenkt den Juden eine Stadt*, they were given sardine sandwiches and had been coached to refuse them, saying, "Again sardines . . . no thanks!"

The buildings visited by the commission were spotless inside and outside, devoid of decay, and the library had been prepared to look truly impressive. The commission, however, failed to come there, but they did go to see the newly installed *Kaffeehaus* (coffee house), which looked as if it had always been there, organized in truly Viennese fashion, supplied with newspapers, vintage to be sure, and *Ersatz* coffee. In short, the ghetto seemed like a terrific place, beautiful enough to warrant being called a model ghetto.

Questions asked of the Jews by members of the commission had to be answered according to a script and a rehearsal had been held under the direction of the elder Paul Eppstein and attended by the commandant *Hauptsturmfuehrer* Rahm.

The bulk of the very old people, who could not be beautified, had been hidden away; only a few could be seen sitting in the sun at the "*Stadtpark*," listening to a band playing on a small, roofed podium. The repertoire consisted of Viennese operettas composed by Jewish artists; these haunting, sentimental melodies had not been heard in the Reich for several years.

To make the deception complete, there were sham store windows exhibiting clothing items and linens taken away from Jews long since deported to the East and turned to ashes. It was now June 23, 1944, and all the Jews' hopes engendered by the visit of this Red Cross committee were dashed, for the members of the commission saw perhaps only what they wanted to see, and worse, they obviously believed what they saw.

After this farce was over, the Nazi authorities in charge of Theresienstadt commissioned a movie to be called *Der Fuehrer Schenkt den Juden eine Stadt*, from which Starke took her book's title. The direction of the film was in the capable hands of Kurt Gerron, a former actor and director in Berlin. Gerron started filming in August and used some of the prominent inhabitants of the ghetto as extras, as for instance the judge of the ghetto's court, Professor Dr. Heinrich Klang from Vienna. Klang was filmed while choosing a book in the spruced-up library. A similar role was played by Dr. George Stoehr, a former colonel in the Austrian army as well as a physician. Both

men came back to Vienna in the summer of 1945. Klang was then seventy and Stoehr seventy-four. The movie has never been shown anywhere.

For the Jews who had stayed at the ghetto or who arrived there from Vienna during July, August, and September 1944, Theresienstadt was a much nicer place than what it had been before its extraordinary beautification. Thus, what followed was even harder to take: Sooner than anyone had expected, the dreaded transports to the East started up once again. There had been no deportations from Theresienstadt since May, but starting on September 28 and ending exactly one month later, a total of 18,402 Jews, with thousands of Austrian Jews among them, were sent to Auschwitz. The artists who had worked so hard to make the ghetto into a place that transcended its ugliness were part of these transports, and it seemed as if the German authorities wanted to kill off everything that was good and beautiful during this unexpected orgy of murder.

To arrive at an exact number of all Jews sent to Theresienstadt from Austria, it seemed prudent to use the figures given by Zdenek Lederer in *Ghetto Theresienstadt* rather than just relying on the records at the *Kultusgemeinde*.[21]

Thus, during 1942, thirteen transports arrived in Theresienstadt from Vienna. They left on June 20, June 28, July 10, July 14, July 22, July 28, August 13, August 20, August 27, September 10, September 24, October 1, and October 9 and their journey usually lasted only a day or two. These thirteen transports contained 13,922 Jews.

The Theresienstadt transports were interspersed with transports going to Minsk and there is some mystery about one transport that left Vienna on July 17. It is listed as having gone to Auschwitz via Theresienstadt, but neither there nor at Auschwitz is there a notation of its arrival. The orders for the transport's guards do read Auschwitz as point of disembarkation, but, as has been shown, that was not always true. For purposes of accounting, I have included it in the Auschwitz roster, but for all we know, the transport may have gone to Riga, since just about that time, according to rumors in the ghetto, there were lots of suitcases with Viennese addresses in the warehouses of the city, and there was much activity in the forest next to the Salaspils camp.

During 1943, eighteen additional transports from Vienna, Linz, Waidhofen/Ybbs, and Kremsmuenster arrived in Theresienstadt, ranging from just one person to 203. That "big" transport brought the remainder from the Old Age Home and many of the deportees were over eighty years old, with several having reached an age of over ninety. Among the other small transports were Jews who had earlier been left behind because of ailments

and had now recovered, recently widowed Jewish spouses of Aryans, as well as members of the *Kultusgemeinde* personnel. The total number for 1943 was 1,103.

In 1944, 227 additional Jews from Austria, in fourteen separate transports were sent to Theresienstadt, among them Jews by Nazi standards only. Some of them had never even practiced that religion, and it happened sometimes that when Jews of that sort were sent to Theresienstadt or earlier, to other camps, their sons were fighting at the front, never realizing that a parent was slated for destruction while the soldier, in his field-gray uniform, was about to give his life for the *Fuehrer*. These 227 came from Graz, Ried im Innkreis, Traunkirchen, Linz, and Vienna, ranging in groups from one to eighty-four members.

Some more Jews came to Theresienstadt in 1945, among them a transport from Amstetten containing seventy-seven Jews, which arrived on April 15, three days after Vienna had been taken by the Russians. In addition, there were another twenty-two Jews from Salzburg and Vienna and perhaps some more who were added to a very large transport made up of Hungarian Jews that had left Vienna on March 8, 1945. I did not include them in the final count and neither did Moser, but they are registered in the *Totenbuch* as having come from Vienna.

Altogether then, during 1942, 1943, 1944, and 1945, a total of 15,351 Austrian Jews came to Theresienstadt.

According to the records kept at the ghetto, 6,228 died right there, and 7,526 were murdered in the East. Since that last figure includes the fifty Austrian Jews who were listed as having perished, but who did, in fact, return from Auschwitz and other camps, I have reduced that figure to 7,476.

There were several others who were murdered but were not listed anywhere and such is the case with Aaron Menczer. While it was possible to find the ones who did return, there was no way in which to find those who perished and were not listed, unless, as in the case of Menczer, the persons were especially noteworthy.

Subtracting 6,228 and 7,480 from 15,351, we are left with 1,647 Austrian Jews.

In February 1945 a transport of 1,200 Jews was permitted to leave Theresienstadt for Switzerland. One source mentioned that there were 154 Austrian Jews among them, but there is no list available. I have, however, included the 154 among the survivors. In addition, there were 149 men and women who returned from a variety of camps. Then, in May of 1945, those Austrian Jews who had never left Theresienstadt and had the good fortune to be liberated there were counted and registered. They numbered 1,270.

Arriving at a total, therefore, of 1,573, it can be seen that there are 76 unaccounted for. They may have been among those who died during the typhoid epidemic raging through the camp in April, or were among those left off the roster of persons sent to the East.

At any rate, the 1,573 survivors constituted the largest single group of all deportees who came back after the war was over. This figure represented slightly over 10 percent of all the Austrian Jews who were sent to Theresienstadt and survived despite the high death rate there and the transports to the various annihilation centers.

Owing to the age of the survivors, however, and the physical and mental trauma they had suffered, almost half of the returnees died in 1945 and 1946. No matter; they had survived and had experienced freedom once more, even if it was for only a very short time.

The Elimination of the Ghettos in the East

In accordance with resolutions made at the Wannsee Conference on January 20, 1942, and the beliefs of Heydrich's successor, Dr. Ernst Kaltenbrunner, the ghettos in the East, seen as large holding pens by the end of 1942, were no longer considered viable or necessary.

Throughout that year, therefore, inroads on the ghettos' populace were made in the form of selections and subsequent liquidation either in the vicinity of the ghettos' locations or by transfer to any of the death camps. Owing to most of these ghettos' sizes, however, everything was on a much smaller scale than the deportations from Theresienstadt or from the Warsaw ghetto. Smaller ghettos, especially in many Polish towns and villages, were liquidated altogether during 1942, some of them right in the middle of these towns in the market place, or adjacent to those towns, perhaps in nearby forests. For the most part, however, the inhabitants of the ghettos were taken to the railroad station nearby and from there to one of the death camps. Since quite a number of Austrian Jews had been resettled into exactly such small ghettos during 1941, they were among the first to perish in that way.

Kaltenbrunner had been named Heydrich's successor several months after the latter died on June 4, 1942, as a result of wounds inflicted by Czech partisans on May 27. It was Kaltenbrunner who implemented the policy of emptying the ghettos and transferring the younger, healthy Jews to concentration camps. Some of them, despite their usefulness, were added to the aged, the ailing, and the children and taken care of at the Polish death camps.

SS Gruppenfuehrer Dr. Ernst Kaltenbrunner had taken over Heydrich's exalted position, pleasantly surprised by Himmler's decision and with great

zeal. He was especially interested in the killing process by gas, and saw to it that the "final solution" was carried out without fail and mercy. Enjoying the benevolent trust of both Hitler and Himmler, Kaltenbrunner persuaded Himmler shortly after his promotion to do away once and forever with the entire ghetto system, most probably realizing that despite the harsh conditions in the ghettos, there was a sense of some autonomy, no matter how precarious. As long as families could be together, they could nurture each other and find the strength to face each day. By moving them into actual concentration camps, their physical and psychological breakdown was much more rapid and thus hastened the process of their destruction.

Kaltenbrunner, a massive giant of a man, had gone to school in Linz, Austria. One of his best friends there was Adolf Eichmann. Following in the footsteps of his grandfather and father, both of whom were lawyers, Kaltenbrunner studied for his Doctor of Jurisprudence at the University of Graz and, at the age of only twenty-three, opened an office in Linz. His entry into the NSDAP and his subsequent connections and dealings with the Nazis led to his being arrested by the Dollfuss regime. After spending six months in jail, and despite the suspension of his lawyer's license, he continued his illegal activities, working ceaselessly to effect a union of Austria and Germany. Kaltenbrunner's career took off once this union became a reality; it soon became clear that he seemed to have a hand in every policy decision pertaining to criminal activities or what was seen as such. His interests stretched from prisoners of war and their eventual fate, to spies and counterspies, the secret service, and last but not least, to the total destruction of the Jews.

As the war neared its end, in March of 1945, Kaltenbrunner moved his headquarters to Alt-Aussee in Austria's Steiermark. The Americans took him prisoner; he was tried and sentenced to death at Nuremberg, where he was hanged on October 16, 1946, unrepentant to the end.

As for the larger and more prominent ghettos, among the earliest to be liquidated was the ghetto of Cracow, on March 13, 1943. The young and strong of that ghetto were transferred to the nearby newly erected concentration camp Plaszow; a similar policy was followed in other regions as well.

When the Cracow ghetto was liquidated, the children and older people, provided they survived the carnage in the ghetto, were brought to nearby Auschwitz where most of them were gassed upon arrival. In charge of the liquidation was the Austrian *SS Hauptsturmfuehrer* Amon Goeth, heir to an old bookbinding and printing firm in Vienna. He was then made commandant of Plaszow, where his very sight evoked terror. Goeth considered himself an intellectual; in reality, he was a totally corrupt sadist, drunkard,

lecher, thief, and cold-blooded murderer. He had been in charge of the Tarnow ghetto's liquidation as well as that of Cracow and left a carnage behind in both cases. Before that, he had "worked" in Lublin. His mentor there was his fellow Austrian, Odilo Globocnik.

True to his upbringing and cultural background, Amon Goeth loved music, especially Viennese *Heurigen* (new wine) songs, waltzes, and operettas. He often gave parties at his villa in the Plaszow camp, and to entertain his guests, the Rosner brothers, Henry on the violin and Leopold on the accordion, played for them. The Rosners and their siblings were all born in Cracow, but Henry, the oldest, had studied music in Vienna and had lived there for several years. After his marriage to Marianne, a Viennese Jewess, he came back to Cracow, shortly before the *Anschluss*. Goeth not only enjoyed the Rosners' performance, but also their abject terror of him, which was evident whenever they were summoned to his villa.

Eventually Amon Goeth got what he deserved; after being incarcerated by his fellow Nazis for excessive thievery—excessive even to them—he was handed over to the Poles once the war was over and was hanged in Cracow on September 5, 1946. His last words were *"Heil Hitler!"*

There were a number of Viennese Jews in Plaszow, as quite a few of them had earlier been in the ghetto; in 1938 they had fled to Poland, which, in many cases, had been the birthplace of their parents when that part of Poland was still Austria. They had felt very much at home in Cracow, precisely because it resembled the well-remembered districts of Vienna, having been part of the Austrian empire for so long. These Jews had been caught up in the war without any further possibility to escape, although a small number of them managed to make their way to Hungary. Very few ever came back to Vienna, but Henry Rosner, his wife, and their son did. They had survived thanks to the German industrialist Oscar Schindler. After a short stay in Austria, the Rosners made their way to the United States, with Henry playing his violin at a number of fine supper clubs and restaurants until well into his seventies.

There were other gentiles besides Schindler who, having dealt with Jews in the General Government, tried to help as best as they could. Among them were the Austrian industrialists Julius Madritsch, Raimund Titsch, Dr. Adolf Lenhardt, and Maria Herling. All four of them worked both in Cracow and in Tarnow, and all four of them were Viennese. For their help in those bad times, they were recognized as "Righteous Gentiles" with a tree planted for each of them in Jerusalem. In addition, as described in Erika Weinzierl's *Zu Wenig Gerechte* (Not Enough Righteous), the Viennese policeman Oswald Bosko, a former headwaiter, was caught by the Gestapo and executed on

September 18, 1944, for having helped Jews to flee during the liquidation of the Cracow ghetto.

Although the title of Weinzierl's opus indicated that there were not enough righteous people among the Christians, it must not be forgotten that according to the Talmud, he who saves one life, saves the whole world.

The camp at Plaszow was not meant just for the survivors of the Cracow ghetto. Other Jews, culled from the many small towns surrounding Cracow, were brought to Plaszow, and one previously mentioned transport of Polish, German, and Austrian male Jews came from as far away as Minsk; they had passed through Treblinka, Majdanek, Budzyn, and Rzeszow, working along the way for the Heinkelwerke (manufacturers of airplanes), and, after spending some time at Plaszow, were sent to work in the nearby salt mines at Wieliczka.

Plaszow had several satellite camps; there was quite a turnover and much movement between camps. While there was a good amount of killing going on at Plaszow itself, the Jews, who could no longer work and were selected in larger numbers, were sent to nearby Auschwitz, as was one transport of children in the spring of 1944.

Shortly thereafter, in early summer, however, there was a switch: It was now Auschwitz that sent a transport to Plaszow! It consisted of approximately 1,000 Hungarian Jewesses who were added to the depleted workforce of the women's camp. It did not take long until they looked like their Polish counterparts, emaciated and begrimed. By the end of 1944, Plaszow too was liquidated and the survivors were taken on death marches or death trains and brought to German and Austrian concentration and labor camps, where only the strongest would be alive at the end of the war.

Poland's largest ghetto, the Warsaw ghetto, was liquidated in April 1943. Its liquidation marked a special page in the history of the Holocaust thanks to the heroic struggle of its young defenders. The majority of its inmates had been murdered in Treblinka, mostly during the year before the famous uprising. Among the lists of the murdered and the survivors were the names of a few Austrian Jews who had earlier been sent to Warsaw from Theresienstadt.

In August 1943 the ghettos of Sosnowiec, Bedzin, and Byalistock were liquidated, with a desperate and futile uprising ensuing in the latter one. Thus, while the Jews from Sosnowiec and Bedzin were brought to Auschwitz and underwent a selection, no such consideration was given to the Jews of Bialystock; a small group of women was sent to Stutthof and the remainder was brought to Treblinka and gassed upon arrival. As has been related, over 1,200 children were separated from their parents at Treblinka

and brought to Theresienstadt. From there, some time later, they, too, were deemed expendable and gassed at Auschwitz.

In September 1943 the Minsk ghetto was liquidated; the majority of the inmates were killed at Maly Trostinec and those considered fit were sent to Poland. A small group of Jews that remained at the farm of Maly Trostinec for another few months were murdered shortly before the Russians took the city in the summer of 1944.

Also in September, the ghetto of Vilno, Lithuania, was liquidated. Its commandant, the civilian deputy commissar of the Vilno district, was the sadistic Austrian Franz Murer, ably assisted by another Austrian, SD man Bruno Kittel, whom the inmates called "the liquidator." While Murer and Kittel represented everything that was evil, there was another Austrian in Vilno, who represented everything that was good and decent. Army Sergeant Anton Schmid had to pay with his life for helping the Jews. Schmid was appalled by what he observed and, in an attempt to alleviate some of the desperation, he helped the Jews by supplying them with food and medication. He also aided and abetted the escape of some of the would-be partisans among them and saw to it that they reached the forest safely. It was not long before his fellow soldiers found out about it and reported him. He was tried and executed on April 13, 1942. His letter of farewell to his wife and daughter was reproduced in *Zu Wenig Gerechte*. Schmid apologized to his loved ones, but said he could do no less. He was recognized by the Israeli government posthumously and a tree was planted for him on the Street of the Righteous in Jerusalem. His fellow Austrian Franz Murer was exonerated by an Austrian court despite bloodcurdling evidence of cruelty. He had sent the old, the sick, and the children of the Vilno ghetto to the forest at Ponar, where they were slaughtered in the "old-fashioned" way, by bullets. And he had killed Jews wantonly as well, just for the sport of it. Finally, after the last selection, those able to work were brought by train to the Kaiserwald concentration camp in Riga.

They arrived at the camp on September 25, 1943, and had many stories to tell to the Jews they met there. There were Latvian Jews, German Jews, and Czech Jews, and also Austrian Jews who had been brought to Kaiserwald from the nearby Riga ghetto, which was to be liquidated several weeks later, on November 2, 1943.

Already during the summer, several transports from the ghetto had arrived at the camp, first on foot and later in vans. From Kaiserwald they were sent out to work, sometimes even to the same firms or installations where they had toiled while still in the ghetto. Now, however, something new was added: Many of those companies were permitted to make arrange-

ments whereby these workers would not only work there, but live there as well, either in adjacent houses, or old factories, or makeshift barracks. This method served to keep them there and prevented sending them back to the camp each evening, thus wasting valuable time. Soon the majority of inmates lived in those satellite camps and Kaiserwald itself never had more than about 2,000 people in residence. The commandant of the camp, *Obersturmbannführer* Albert Sauer, who had been commandant at Mauthausen in Austria, had learned his trade quite well. He treated the inmates of Kaiserwald with distaste and left the camp's administration in the hands of professional criminals, who were often worse than the SS men in charge.

After the Riga ghetto's liquidation and the advent of another harsh winter, in late November of 1943, there were no more than about 8,500 of the former ghetto inmates left alive, with approximately 2,000 to 2,500 native Latvian Jews and the others a mixture of *Reichsjuden*. It is rather difficult to judge how many of them were Austrians. Before the ghetto's liquidation, no more than 900 Austrian Jews had still been alive and among them were quite a number of older people and children, all of whom had been sent to Auschwitz on November 2, 1943, in a transport containing almost 2,500 Jews. According to Auschwitz registrar Dr. Wolken, 596 were received at the camp. The others either died en route or were gassed upon arrival. Of those 596, only two men survived, both from Germany.

The remnants of Austrian Jews, now stationed at Kaiserwald and its satellite *Kasernierungen* (small outside camps), amounted to perhaps 650, if not less. All four of us, my father, mother, sister, and I, worked at the *Feldbekleidungamt der Luftwaffe* (supply depot of the air force), situated in Riga, with its warehouses right next to the River Daugava. It was always a relief to leave the camp in early morning, when the sky was still dark, for at our place of work we were treated far better than at Kaiserwald. Each evening, when we returned, we did so with apprehension. The situation at camp was extremely stressful and no one knew what to expect. We dreaded Sundays, when we had to move piles of earth or stones or sand from one place to another and then back again. This kind of "game" was played in most of the concentration camps, sapping the strength of the prisoners. At other times some of us were required to work nights at the Anoden *Kommando*, smashing batteries to be recycled. When morning came, we hardly recognized each other, as we were covered with soot. This *Kommando* was part of the Allgemeine Elektrizitaetsgesellschaft (AEG), one of the many companies that profited from slave labor.

We were ill treated by the criminal prisoners, but even the political prisoners, of whom we expected more, were also quite cruel. Altogether, a mixture of both types had come, in March 1943, from Buchenwald to Riga to build the camp, with the help of a small group of Jewish prisoners. During the summer, 400 were sent back to Buchenwald, and when the Riga ghetto was liquidated and the last Jews came to Kaiserwald, only 100 of the Aryan prisoners, who were our overlords, were still there. Ultimately, of these perhaps twenty remained.

From November 1943 to January 1944, we also suffered at the hands of fifty female prisoners brought from Ravensbrueck. For the most part, they wore the black triangle next to their number, identifying them as asocial, that is, as whores. They treated us in a very cruel fashion. Luckily, they were sent back to their camp after they had been caught on New Year's Eve during an orgy in their barrack.

Life in Kaiserwald was hard not only because we were constantly harassed and were always hungry but also because of the deprivations, such as the facts that all our belongings had been taken away and some of us did not even have underwear; family communication was curtailed because men and women lived in separate camps and could speak to each other only through the double fence of barbed wire; and because of the depressing realization that the ghetto was a veritable paradise compared to life as we now knew it. In fact, it seemed that every change of venue throughout these bitter years brought us into worse situations.

Kaiserwald, just as Plaszow had been for southern Poland, became a collection point for the remainder of all the liquidated ghettos in the Baltic states. After the survivors from Vilno came the survivors from Libau, and from Dvinsk, and from Siauliai. Some even came from Kovno, although their ghetto would be functional for another year.

Then, in May 1944, a large contingent of Hungarian Jewesses came from Auschwitz. Five hundred of them were kept at Kaiserwald, and the other 4,500 were sent to the labor camp at Dundaga, in northwest Latvia, where they worked under terrible conditions. Two thousand of them remained in Latvian soil forever; such was their treatment. An excellent description of this camp and the fate of its inmates can be found in Abraham Shpungin's tale "The Terrors of Dundaga" in *The Unfinished Road: Jewish Survivors of Latvia Look Back*.[22]

Thus, by the end of 1943, with the exception of the Litzmannstadt ghetto in the Warthegau and the Kovno ghetto in Lithuania, both of which existed until the summer of 1944, and perhaps some small remnants here and there, Kaltenbrunner's efforts to do away with the ghetto system had

Deportations to Auschwitz and Other Camps: 1943–1944

By October 15, 1942, only 8,100 Jews were living in all of Austria according to a report from the Council of Elders to the Gestapo. (The *Kultusgemeinde* was now called the Council of Elders, or "*Aeltestenrat*," making this last Jewish remnant into a ghetto rather than the community it had been.)

Of the 8,100 registered Jews, 1,200 were *Volljuden*, meaning "Full Jews," which indicated that they had no other trace of blood in them. Many of them were still living in the Old Age Home. The other 6,900 were products of mixed marriages, partners in mixed marriages, or Jews with foreign passports, some of whom had lived in Austria all their lives, but were still considered foreigners.

Eichmann and his men could be proud of themselves, for it had not taken them all that long to make the city almost *judenrein* (cleansed of Jews). Although Eichmann and his men were busy elsewhere now, as for instance in France and Greece, there were a good many minor officials left to finish the job. Even if the so-called U-Boats (i.e., Jews in hiding) were added to the 8,100, the total number of Jews in late fall of 1942 did not even reach 5 percent of the prewar total. Transports to the East had left in several waves and had emptied the city of its Jews rather speedily. In addition to the latest wave, which had been called the Theresienstadt wave, the officials had interspersed the transports with several smaller contingents of Jews to Auschwitz. These Jews had "broken the law" and had therefore been sent to Auschwitz as a punishment.

During November and December 1942 there was a lull. The administrators and clerks at the Council of Elders, reduced to a skeleton crew, worked

in several areas. Some finished up the records, others took inventory in the empty, desolate apartments from where the Jews had been deported, and others saw to the needs of the shrunken community, where people still died, had to be supported with food, or had to be moved, so as to empty still more apartments. When the inventories were completed, duly recorded, and assessed, everything was handed over to the Gestapo and was then given to "deserving" Austrian Nazis.

Did the general population notice that there were hardly any Jews left? There are no reports and little has been written about it, but it does seem likely. The Austrians who profited by getting apartments, furniture, clothing, jewelry, and many other items that had once belonged to Jews, must have been aware of the fact that the rightful owners of all these things had disappeared into a void. How safe they must have felt when there was absolutely no outcry by an aggrieved party about this outright theft! Since there has been little, if any, restitution, these loyal Nazis did not even have to give back what they had stolen, despite their "fall from grace," which in most cases did not happen. Lucky for them, the rightful owners never returned from the East and those few who did were not able to obtain their property either, unless they resorted to drawn-out court proceedings.

By January 1943 deportations started once again. Although the Gestapo lists are useful, the names and numbers of those who left are often not the same as are shown on the records in Vienna, nor do they agree with the records kept at Theresienstadt and Auschwitz. Furthermore, several times during the next two years, transports from Bulgaria, Greece, and Hungary were sent to camps in the East via Vienna and it often happened that Austrian Jews were simply added to these transports as was the case with the aforementioned Hungarian transport to Theresienstadt at the late date of March 20, 1945.

By fall 1943 Auschwitz had superseded all camps in the General Government; the original camp had been enlarged by the addition of hamlets and estates, such as Budy, Rajsko, and best known of all, Birkenau.

Much earlier, in 1940, Rudolf Hoess, on Himmler's orders, had actually built the camp. In his autobiography, he told of the many difficulties that had faced him. He also mentioned that his colleagues, with whom he had served in several concentration camps on German soil, were only too glad to see him "banished" to Auschwitz, owing to the fact that he was a hard taskmaster and a workaholic.

Until early 1942, the largest group of prisoners in Auschwitz were Poles, who, according to Hoess, realized that they would have to stay in camp until the war was over. The question of who would survive to see that end was

on everyone's mind, since the conditions within the camp were not seen as optimal. There was, first of all, insufficient food, insufficient clothing, and the hard work of building roads and barracks. The sanitary state in those early years was such that many of the Poles died of diseases brought about by vermin. Hoess wrote that the prisoners could have escaped but did not do so only because they knew that their families would suffer reprisals.

The next largest contingent of prisoners just then were Russians, who had been brought to Auschwitz from a prisoner of war camp at Lamsdorf, Upper Silesia. Most of them were in very bad physical condition, owing to the situation at Lamsdorf. They were, however, needed to build an extension to Auschwitz to accommodate the expected influx of Jews. That extension was Birkenau.

Of the 10,000 Russian prisoners who had arrived in Auschwitz in October 1941, only about 1,500 were still alive in February 1942, when the construction of Birkenau started in earnest; by the summer of 1942, however, no more than 450 of them had survived the hard labor and the terrible conditions.

The next large group described by Hoess was the gypsies. They lived in what was called a family camp and their barracks, according to a report published in 1956 by Lucie Adelsberger, entitled *Auschwitz: Ein Tatsachenbericht* (Auschwitz: A Factual Report), were desperately overcrowded. She wrote that there were 16,000 gypsies in Auschwitz by 1943. Approximately 4,000 had died of "natural" causes during 1942.

Starting in late fall of 1942, the most numerous group in the camp were the Jews. This remained the case until the very end of Auschwitz in January 1945. Between fall 1942 and fall 1943, on Himmler's orders, the four most effective gas chambers and crematoria of any camp were built; the work was directed by the Austrian *Hauptsturmfuehrer* Walter Dejaco. Years later, that same Walter Dejaco built some houses and even a church or two in his hometown Reutte, Austria. For that work and effort he was highly praised by Bishop Rusk of Innsbruck in 1963. Nothing was said about his excellent work in Auschwitz.

During the period of building and expansion, Himmler came to Auschwitz twice. Rudolf Vrba in *I Cannot Forgive* described Himmler's first visit in the summer of 1942 when things were still rather primitive, and the other visit, in 1943, when mass murder was streamlined and efficient, and the operation could be compared to a conveyor belt.

There have been discussions and arguments about the number of Jews who were gassed or died of "natural" causes in that place of evil. Much of the controversy was due to the inscription on the stone tablets at Birkenau, erected by the Polish government, which proclaimed that four million

victims of fascism had been murdered in the Auschwitz complex. It was thought that of these over three million had been Jews. Since that figure seemed indeed to be on the high side, Holocaust deniers had a field day and historians of all denominations tried to whittle down the figures, often with preposterous results.

Relying on the best sources, therefore, I found that Filip Mueller, the only surviving member of the *Sonderkommando* who worked inside the death machinery, Rudolf Vrba, the registrar at the quarantine camps, and Rudolf Hoess, the commandant of Auschwitz, came to the same conclusion: All three of them, working independently so to speak, arrived at a total of two million murdered Jews, with another half a million victims consisting of gypsies, Russians, Poles, and a sprinkling of other groups. As for those so-called scholars who doubt the capacity of the crematoria, for example, let it not be forgotten that there were enormous mass graves adjacent to the camp from which bodies were exhumed and turned into ashes.

Auschwitz/Oswieczem. Symbol of Evil. *Anus Mundi*. A small town, west of Cracow, once upon a time almost entirely peopled by Jews. A perfect site for a perfect factory of death. Attached to it is a place called Birkenau . . . glen of birches . . . Brzezinka.

Starting in 1943, it was in Birkenau, where the rails ended, where the selections occurred, and it was mainly in Birkenau where Jews from all over the world, including Austria, were brought by the thousands, to be turned into ashes. Most of the time the new arrivals, still innocent, as it were, did not realize the purpose of the selection conducted by actual physicians such as the infamous Dr. Josef Mengele. More experienced "campers," however, tried to look young and healthy, all in an effort to prolong life. Precious life, despite the inhuman conditions, despite everything.

To live, to hope, to go to work, to be useful, to persevere, to triumph over all that was evil, to be allowed to go on with one's existence, not to be noticed by a guard, a *kapo*, an SS man, to blend in, to be invisible, to survive, not to go into the dreaded gas chamber, not to go up in smoke. It is impossible for sane people to imagine the constant terror and dread, forcing the weakened bodies to perform, keeping step with one's neighbor when marching in or out of the camp, thinking of food, talking about the finest dishes imaginable, and then eating foul, smelly potatoes swimming in an undefinable liquid as if it were indeed nectar and ambrosia. Inadequate clothing, feet rubbed raw from the wooden clogs, little time or inclination to keep clean, waking up while darkness was still enveloping the camp, lit only by the giant five chimneys where perhaps just then a father, a mother, a brother, a sister, a husband, a child was burning. And still, one wished for life. Incredible.

Those Austrian Jews who arrived at Auschwitz and lived to tell about the experience could do so mainly because they were sent out to other camps, with the majority of them leaving in the fall of 1944. At that time, the "family camps," which consisted of Jews who had come from Theresienstadt, had been totally liquidated, with the older people, the sick, and the children being sent to the gas chambers, and the young and strong found worthy to live on as slave laborers.

Before that, back in Vienna, on March 3 and on March 31, 1943, two transports were marked "*nach dem Osten*" (to the East) by Moser, and "*nach Auschwitz*" (to Auschwitz) by the Gestapo. According to the Auschwitz registrar quoted by Danuta Czech in *Hefte von Auschwitz* (Auschwitz Folders), only the first one, which left Vienna on March 3, arrived at Auschwitz. It contained seventy-five Jews. The second transport, although marked *nach Auschwitz*, and containing eighty-five Jews, of whom a few were from Germany, went a different route. According to witnesses, it arrived at Treblinka, either following or as part of a larger transport of Bulgarian Jews. These witnesses worked at Treblinka and survived the subsequent uprising. They are Samuel Rajzmann, Yankl Wiernik, Stanislaw Kon, and Samek Warszawski. All four were interrogated in Warsaw after the war, all four commented on the Austrian commandant Stangl's reaction to seeing Jews arriving directly from his native country, and all four were quoted in *Dokumenty i Materialy* (Documents and Sources).

Their story covers the events that started on March 22, 1943, when over 3,000 Bulgarian Jews had been forced to leave their own country from the Danube port of Lom Palanka. They arrived on several barges at the pier near the *Reichsbruecke*, one of Vienna's longest bridges, on March 26 and were then transferred to trains at the nearby Danube railroad station. From there, they were sent to Treblinka. Within the next few weeks, there were additional transports that passed through Vienna on the way to Treblinka. They came from Zagreb and Skoplje in Yugoslavia, and also from Saloniki in Greece. The stopover in Vienna involved a changing of the guards and most often, the addition of some local Jews, who had for one reason or another missed an earlier transport or had been found out for some infraction and had therefore been marked for deportation to the East. Frequently, despite the general attempt of keeping records as thoroughly as possible, the names of these Jews were not necessarily transmitted to the Council of Elders.

In addition, during 1943, there were several small, very special transports leaving Vienna, containing foreign Jews who, up until then, had been "safe" in comparison to those Jews who were Austrian citizens.

The official document, which changed their safe status, was dated September 23, 1943, but even as early as March of that year the administrators working on Jewish affairs in Vienna foresaw the possibility of taking "legal" steps to get rid of these foreign Jews. Among other, more obscure places, they held passports of Italy, Romania, Turkey, Hungary, and Russia.

For the remaining part of 1943, there were two more transports to Auschwitz. One left on October 7 and contained twenty-one people. The manifest of the other one, which left on December 1, did not indicate who or how many Jews were part of it. The official paper stated that one person died en route and the registrar at Auschwitz wrote that thirteen men and eleven women were given numbers after the usual selection; if there were any others, they must have been gassed. Neither Moser nor Danuta Czech offered additional information.

Altogether, during 1943, approximately 130 Austrian Jews were deported to Auschwitz, 85 Jews to Treblinka, and 200 to a variety of concentration camps, as described earlier. There were several who had gone to Auschwitz in 1942 already, and there were some who left later, but it is hard to read the documents; all are marked "secret," and only the smudged duplicates were found at the various districts' police stations in Vienna after the war. The originals had been burned shortly before the city's liberation.

Military and political events during 1943, such as the enormous losses at Stalingrad, the highly charged situation in Italy, and the ever increasing air raids over the German lands, did not cause the slightest letup in the destruction process of the Jewish people. Furthermore, although there was dire need for workers, especially in industries concerned with the war effort, many transports did not even undergo selections; instead, all deportees, even the young and strong, were driven into the assorted gas chambers, both in the Polish death camps and at Auschwitz. As for the former ghetto inmates who were now part of the concentration camp system, having successfully weathered a series of selections, they still had another year and a half to endure and their chances for survival did not look promising. The way they were treated, the backbreaking labor, the insufficient food, the cold, the vermin, the diseases, and worst of all, the ever new selections with the specter of the gas chambers always on their minds, their survival looked unlikely. Yet, as long as there was life in them, there was hope.

During 1944, albeit on a very small scale, the deportations in Vienna continued. On February 1, five Jews, all Argentinian citizens, were sent to Bergen Belsen. On February 24, forty-one Jewish men were sent to Auschwitz. Only four of them were selected for work and given numbers; the other thirty-seven were gassed upon arrival.

On April 26, nineteen Jews were sent to Auschwitz. Of them, five were permitted to enter the camp and given numbers; the others were gassed. On June 27 and 28, two further transports left Vienna for Auschwitz. The first one contained seventeen women, of whom eight received numbers; the other nine were sent to the gas chambers. The second transport contained thirty-eight men, of whom only six received numbers; the other thirty-two were gassed.

On August 22, three Jewish women left Vienna for Auschwitz and all three are listed as having arrived there and been given numbers. On September 1, another twenty-nine Jewish women were sent to Auschwitz and it took them six days to get there, due to air raids. Four of them were selected for work; the other twenty-five were gassed.

After that transport, the registrar at Auschwitz did not enter any other transports as having come from Austria, although the Council of Elders in Vienna registered some more people as having left as late as October. By that time, conditions both in Austria as well as in Auschwitz were chaotic and record keeping was very much neglected. Officially, 152 Jews had left Austria for Auschwitz.

The year 1944 had been a very busy one for Auschwitz. Selections continued to be as fierce as ever, even though it was illogical to kill potential workers at a time when manpower was needed so badly. From a vantage point of fifty years later, it seems clear that logic had nothing to do with it. The Germans simply wanted to kill as many Jews as possible before the final curtain. By 1944 most of them knew that the war was lost and very few believed in the promised miracle weapon. The killing of Jews, however, was a number one priority.

Starting in May 1944, among the masses of Hungarian Jews that arrived in Auschwitz, there were quite a number of Austrian Jews who had found refuge in Hungary during 1938 and 1939. From May through August, the remnants of the large Litzmannstadt ghetto came, and all throughout the year, the transports from Theresienstadt came, culminating in the autumn transports.

Described eloquently by Filip Mueller in *Eyewitness Auschwitz*, in October 1944 the *Sonderkommando* blew up one of the four gas chambers and its adjacent crematorium in the hope of starting a general campwide uprising, thus stopping the killing process. Unfortunately, all the men involved in this heroic endeavor were butchered, and the hoped for uprising did not occur. The death of these men, however, was not in vain. It may have contributed to a lessening of the murderous activities, for while murder

was still being committed, it slowed down to a trickle and eventually, by December 1944, it came to a halt.

The last transport from Theresienstadt to Auschwitz left on October 28, 1944; upon arrival, after a cursory selection, most of the newcomers were marched to the remaining gas chambers, making it the last large group for "special treatment," or *Sonderbehandlung*. From then on, the camp itself supplied its own victims save for a few incoming transports here and there, all very small as far as Auschwitz was concerned. As for Theresienstadt, whoever was left and had not been part of the autumn transports could now start to hope.

In a diabolical twist of fate, during summer and fall of 1944, just as the last Austrian Jews were deported, at least 18,000 Hungarian Jews arrived in Austria! According to Rudolf (Reszoe) Kastner in *Der Kastnerbericht ueber Eichmanns Menschenhandel in Ungarn* (The Kastner Report on Eichmann's Slavetrade in Hungary), bringing Hungarian Jews to Austria was due to his intervention with Eichmann on behalf of them. Kastner's role may well have benefitted his fellow Jews, but he remains a murky figure.

In charge of these Hungarian Jews was Eichmann's assistant, Austrian *Sturmbannfuehrer* Hermann Krumey; his deputy was *Hauptsturmfuehrer* Dr. Siegfried Seidl, former commandant of Theresienstadt. The new arrivals were used as much-needed laborers in factories as well as on farms. Even so, a good number were sent on to Theresienstadt, to Mauthausen, and to camps such as Gusen and Ebensee, among others.

In January 1945 Eichmann sent another 10,000 Hungarian Jews on a death march in the direction of Austria, ostensibly because more workers were needed there. The true reason most probably was that due to the swift advance of Soviet forces into Poland, it was no longer possible to send the Hungarian Jews to Auschwitz; a death march such as the one Eichmann envisioned would take care of them, as indeed it did. Thousands died by the roadside and those few who survived were put to work in the understaffed armament industry or other installations. They were treated cruelly, and even Gerald Reitlinger, who has a tendency to underestimate the number of victims, wrote in *The Final Solution* that of these last 10,000, no more than 3,000 survived the inhuman conditions of their last journey on foot.[23]

Of the 28,000 Hungarian Jews sent to Austria in those last, desperate months, no more than approximately 15,000 survived. While these odds were not the best, they were still better than at Auschwitz. Even after that camp was abandoned on January 18, 1945, with columns leaving it on trains, on vans, and on foot, there was no end to the dying.

It has been demonstrated that from Austria proper not too many transports were sent directly to Auschwitz during 1942, 1943, and 1944. Most of them were quite small and the total for these three years comes to 1,268; according to Moser, however, at least another 200 Jews are not recorded anywhere and probably left Vienna singly or perhaps two people at a time. Of the approximately 1,468, 109 survived.

On the other hand, thousands of other Austrian Jews ended up in the gas chambers of Auschwitz, but they had first suffered the hardships of other camps, as for example Theresienstadt, where they had believed themselves to be safe. Like everything else during those years, it had all been a lie.

Other Austrian Jews whose last stop was Auschwitz came there from France, Belgium, Holland, Italy, Czechoslovakia, Hungary, Poland, and from wherever Hitler's hordes had caught up with them. They also came from the ghettos to which they had been deported earlier. Those few who survived and came back to Vienna after the war were broken in body and in spirit but tried to go on living. Many of them succumbed within a short time, even though they were comparatively young.

The statistics for returnees are a measure of the tragedy that befell the Jewish people in general and one-third of Austrian Jews in particular. Unfortunately, many of the victims remained unrecorded and thus unmourned.

An Accounting of Survivors
Who Fled from Austria

On November 10, 1941, the *Kultusgemeinde* published the Loewenherz Report, a compilation of the countries to which two-thirds of Austria's Jews had fled. It asserted that approximately 115,000 had been admitted into safe countries and/or continents. As for countries on the European continent, which, on account of being taken over by Germany, turned out to be unsafe, the report is not always reliable. Neither the Baltic states, Norway, Greece, Romania, Luxembourg, nor Czechoslovakia are mentioned, even though Austrian Jews most certainly fled to these countries just as they did to all the others that were listed. These were Italy, Poland, Yugoslavia, Hungary, and Holland, in addition to France and Belgium, which were discussed earlier in this book.

Using the Loewenherz data, of the 4,460 Jews who fled to Italy, it can be assumed that perhaps over half of them were able to travel farther, mainly illegally to Palestine. Others, as for instance my aunt and uncle, Esther and Bernhard LeWinter, went to the United States. Some may have reached other safe places, but those who remained were sent to a variety of camps. Moser estimated that 500 perished. Only twenty-four Jews who had originally fled to Italy returned to Vienna after the war; eight had been in Auschwitz and satellite camps, two in Buchenwald, thirteen in the Italian camp Ferramonte, and one man, Jacob Mausner, had lived in Civitella de Tronte where he had been hidden for over a year by kind monks.

Loewenherz listed 2,260 Austrian Jews as having fled to Poland. Of them, eleven came back, having survived such camps as Auschwitz, Gross Rosen, Lublin, and Czenstochowa, among others. Moser's figure of 1,850

having perished seems to be on the low side. This is no doubt due to a problem of accounting for the Polish Jews who had nowhere to go, and therefore, once the war was over, registered in Vienna during the summer of 1945; several remained there and settled in Vienna for good. It was extremely difficult to ascertain how many of them had originally lived in Austria; that could only be said with certainty about the above mentioned eleven. One was Toni Mantel, who left Vienna in 1938 for Lemberg (Lvov) and later survived the Warsaw ghetto. Another was Heinz Schenker-Gottesmann, liberated at the Gross Rosen camp. There were further Elias Wygodski, who survived Auschwitz, as did Karl Altbach. Others were Helene and Joseph Spiegel, Helen and Rudolf Hirsch, Alfred Paulus and Rudolf Stadler, all of whom were liberated at the labor camp of Czenstochowa. The eleventh, Alfred Leicht, survived Plaszow. The other survivors listed on "*Befreiungsort-K.L. in Polen*" (Place of Liberation-Concentration Camp in Poland) at the *Dokumentationsarchiv des Oesterreichischen Widerstandes* (Archive of Documents of the Austrian Resistance) were presumably Polish Jews.

For Yugoslavia, the Loewenherz report listed 1,644 Jews as having gone there, and of them, eleven returned. Owing to the fact that many others went across the border illegally, the official figure was too low. According to Moser, at least 1,660 perished. As for the eleven who had survived, one man had been sent to Buchenwald, two had been in camps in Yugoslavia, and the other eight had lived among the Serbs.

Loewenherz listed 915 Jews as having fled to Hungary; this figure, however, was certainly incorrect. Jonny Moser, who was himself in Hungary together with his family, believed that over 3,000 Austrian Jews perished right there and at places to which they had been sent from Hungary, such as eastern Poland and, of course, Auschwitz. Of those countless and obviously unrecorded Austrian Jews who arrived in Hungary between 1938 and 1941, with a few as late as 1942, sixty-five came back to Vienna. Of them, nineteen had survived Auschwitz, there was one each for Buchenwald, Bergen Belsen, and Sachsenhausen, and two for Mauthausen. The remainder, for the most part, had been interned in Hungarian camps.

In *Dimension des Voelkermordes* (Dimension of Genocide), trying to set the record straight, Moser, in addition to making the quoted corrections, also listed the countries left out by Loewenherz, generally arriving at logical and believable conclusions. Moser wrote, for example, that approximately 600 Austrian Jews perished in the Baltic states. As there is a scarcity of records, it will never be known how many had gone there, but those I interviewed did not dispute these figures. Among the Austrian Jews who

had fled to Latvia in 1938 was Bernie Clarke, formerly Bernhardt Klughaupt. He was able to leave and make his way to the United States via Japan, and he told me that he had been part of a large group of young Austrian Jews, most of whom had remained behind to stay with their parents. With only a few exceptions, they had all been murdered. These "exceptions" had been deported to Siberia by the Russians. That was the case with Leontine (Lilly) Halpern, then only twenty, who, together with her new husband, the Latvian Jew Jakob Rishik, and her parents survived the war years in the Siberian gulag and later made her way to the United States. The eminent historian, Herbert Rosenkranz, was also among those who, with his family, fled to Latvia and was sent to Siberia, thus escaping certain death by the invading Nazis. He returned to Vienna and later settled in Israel.

Not so lucky was the Viennese lyricist and composer Victor Hahn. In 1938 he had fled to Libau (Liepaja), a city in the Kurland section of Latvia, where he became the conductor of the Libau Opera House. According to Aaron Vestermann's "Survival in a Libau Bunker," a vignette in *Muted Voices*,[24] the aged Hahn, whom Vestermann calls Walter Hahn, and his family were among the first Jews to be murdered by a Latvian mob egged on by the German invaders. Since Austrian Jews fled to Estonia and Lithuania as well as to Latvia, Moser's estimate on the Baltic states is most probably correct.

The Loewenherz report listed 1,151 Jews as having fled to Holland between 1938 and 1940. Of these, nine came back after the war. Moser estimated that 750 perished. It seems likely that the others made their way to Belgium and France and were sent to Auschwitz from there. The chance for survival in Holland was almost nil, thanks to the efficiency of *Reichskommissar* Artur Seyss-Inquart and his deputy Hans Albin Rauter, both Austrians. They knew how to deal with Jews.

Of Austrian Jews who perished in Czechoslovakia, Moser's estimate of 2,710 victims for Bohemia, Moravia, and Slovakia seems much too low. Considering the information about Litzmannstadt and Minsk, to which transports had gone from Czechoslovakia that included Austrian Jews, the numbers come to about 2,500 just for that group. In addition, there were those who had fled to Prague and had been caught and sent to Theresienstadt, ending up in Auschwitz, as evidenced by the seven survivors who returned.

As has been pointed out earlier, discrepancies of that sort are the result of the *Kultusgemeinde*'s closing in the early days after the *Anschluss* at exactly the time when thousands of Austrian Jews went across the border

to Czechoslovakia. It was a chaotic situation and these Austrian Jews cannot be traced, as most of the documentation was destroyed. Weighing all the evidence, there is reason to believe that at least 3,500 Austrian Jews perished in Czechoslovakia, and even that is a conservative estimate.

The seven Austrian Jews who had found refuge in Czechoslovakia and returned to Vienna after the war had gone through several camps. Three of them had last been in Auschwitz, one had been found at Bergen Belsen, one had been at the Kielce ghetto, one had ended up in Ravensbrueck,and one of them had been part of the Nisko experiment. Although he was of Czech origin, he lived in Vienna until 1938 and then fled to his native country; he then lived in Bruenn and was sent to Nisko from there. After crossing the border into Soviet territory, he was sent to a gulag in Karaganda; upon release, he decided to go back to Austria, settling in the sixteenth district, in Ottakring, where he stayed until his early demise.

For Romania, Moser listed 1,320 as having perished; the figure seems reasonable. In her book *Five Chimneys*, Olga Lengyel wrote about the many Viennese refugees who had come to settle in Cluj, her hometown; all of them, as did she, ended up in Auschwitz. In addition, there were reports by Romanian Jews about Austrian Jews who had temporarily lived in Bukarest and Czernowitz, as well as in other towns along the border with the Ukraine during the war, having arrived there during 1938. Of the Jews who had fled to Romania, only one man, Israel Granierer, came back in 1946; he had spent some time during the war in a Polish labor camp.

While there were not too many Jews who had fled to Greece, a number of small groups, consisting mainly of families, lived in Athens and on some of the Greek isles. Moser estimated that fifty were killed. Only one woman, Margarethe Katz, came back to Vienna via Auschwitz. It will never be possible to arrive at an exact figure. That is true also for Mauthausen, Ravensbrueck, Bergen Belsen, and once again, Buchenwald. During 1943 and 1944 small transports containing Jews who had either been picked up for some offense, or who had, up to then, been safe as foreigners, were sent to either one of these camps. Most of them were not recorded anywhere. Based on survivors' accounts, a conservative estimate for Mauthausen is the number 200, with 14 returnees; for Bergen Belsen 100, with 5 returnees; for Ravensbrueck also 100, with 10 returnees; for Flossenburg 50, with 2 returnees; and for Sachsenhausen 50, of whom none returned. The three small transports to Buchenwald contained approximately fifty Jews, of whom eighteen survived. They were added to the earlier list of Jews who had been there for six years.

Still another group of Jews who made their way back to Austria came from the Isle of Mauritius. They had tried to enter Palestine illegally, had been caught by the British, and had been interned on that African island for the duration of the war. Conditions on the island were awful. The fate of the internees is described in the fictionalized account by Maureen Earl, *Boat of Stone*. Of the forty-seven Jews who returned to Austria, several left for Israel and the United States only a short time later, seven died soon after their return, and twenty-eight stayed in Vienna.

In the previously cited *Die Judenverfolgung in Oesterreich, 1938–1945*, Jonny Moser asserts that during 1943, 1944, and 1945, 1,721 Jews were deported to the camps mentioned earlier. Subtracting this figure from the 8,100 registered Jews accounted for in October 1942, we arrive at 6,379. In Vienna and Lower Austria, however, by the end of 1944, according to official records, there were only 5,917 Jews left, and that number was still smaller when the war in that part of the country ended. The missing 462 Jewish victims were among those unrecorded additions to transports, a number of natural deaths, and two last-minute tragedies. One occurred several days before the Russians entered, during an air raid, when a bomb hit Seitenstettengasse, the site of Vienna's last remaining synagogue and the attached offices of what was now the Council of Elders and had formerly been known as the *Kultusgemeinde*. Almost everyone sustained wounds, and thirteen Jews lost their lives.

The second tragedy occurred on April 11 during the siege of Vienna. It was the day before the SS hordes fled to the upper regions of Austria, yet they took time to execute nine young Jews hiding in a basement. The nine had been denounced by the superintendent.

Approximately 5,600 "Jews" had survived the war in Austria. Of them, 5,000 were Jews only by dint of Germany's racial laws and soon reverted back to their former denominations. Of the 600 actual Jews, 150 were technical workers for the firm of Wittke and Grimm, 35 were clerks and officials of the *Kultusgemeinde*, 35 were veterans of World War I who had somehow been overlooked, over 100 were foreign Jews who had never been picked up for deportation, and perhaps 60 were in different jails. There were, furthermore, 150 to 200 so-called U-Boats. In *From Prejudice to Persecution: A History of Austrian Anti-Semitism*, Bruce Pauley wrote that there were 700 U-Boats. While this inflated number may have been correct for 1940, it was not true in 1945.

The *Kultusgemeinde* made its new home in the first district, at Schottenring 25, and stayed there until its old offices and the beautiful synagogue were fully restored. Its small staff was augmented and every official tried

his or her best to make the homecoming of returning survivors as easy as possible.

Jonny Moser and Herbert Rosenkranz arrived at a figure of between 65,000 and 66,000 victims (i.e., one-third of all "racial" Jews present in Austria in March 1938). My own findings more or less agree with this figure, since it was based on the same data available to both of these historians. We all used the archives of the *Kultusgemeinde*, of the *Dokumentations archiv* in Vienna, of Yad Vashem; we also used the available Russian, Polish, Czech, German, and Hungarian records deposited at lesser documentation centers; and we consulted American, British, and French files.

My presentation of events, however, is quite different. First of all, I was in Vienna until February 1942 and thus an eyewitness to the hardships suffered by the remaining Jewish community. Both Rosenkranz and Moser had long since left. There were, in addition, my own observations of being deported to the East, living in a doomed, moribund ghetto, existing in several concentration camps, and surviving a death march. Due to that incisive experience, my relations with survivors are different, and so is my awareness of what the official records say and what they do not say. Last but not least, I used an anecdotal method to bring the Holocaust into a more personal focus.

With two-thirds of Austria's Jewish community having found refuge in safe countries, and one-third having perished, only a handful of "racial" Jews were left in Vienna on that April 12, 1945. Clearly, the authorities had tried until the very end to make the country *judenrein*, but they never actually achieved this goal, even though the effervescent, enlightened, and creative Jewish presence in Austria was for all purposes lost and would never again give Vienna that special, cosmopolitan flavor.

The Homecoming

It was a desolate city to which my mother, my sister, and I returned on June 1, 1945. We had been away only three-and-a-half years, but it seemed much longer. Despite the fact that so few of us came back to the city of our birth, there was no joy in those who saw us once again. We were not greeted with open arms, as some incorrigible optimists, myself included, had hoped for. The reception we had dreamed about in those long, cruel years that had robbed us of our youth, sapped our strength, and taken away our loved ones, was not forthcoming. There were no kind words; instead, there was the typical exclamation, something like "you people always come back," and with that we had to be satisfied.

When we tried to reclaim what had been ours, all we got were insults. The same people who had been in power when we left still had their positions in the various agencies where we tried to find redress for our losses. It seemed that everyone, except the survivors, suffered from a convenient kind of amnesia and quite often we were told of all the suffering the local population had experienced because of the air raids and then, after being defeated, by the marauding Russian troops. Safrian and Witek, in *Und Keiner War Dabei* (And No One Was There), point out that the Austrians, once the war was over, saw themselves as innocent victims and felt very sorry for themselves. Those who robbed the Jews and harmed them in a variety of ways during 1938 and later, pretended to have been the most righteous all along and were absolutely unwilling to part with their ill-gotten assets. They exhibited only hatred, Safrian and Witek maintain, an ice-cold hatred for the returnees, which once again was called anti-Semitism.

We thought it would get better once more of our people returned. But there were only very few who came back and in the meantime, all of us, almost without exception, lived from hand to mouth, getting help mainly from the soup kitchen of the *Kultusgemeinde*, occasional packages from the American Joint Distribution Committee, from the *Agudath Yisroel*, and once, at Passover of 1946, oranges and wine from Palestine, just in time for the holiday. To make our lives easier, my clever mother reverted back to her talents developed during the Hitler years, travelled to Hungary and brought home badly needed food, some of which she sold on the Black Market. While this activity was illegal and fraught with dangers, to someone like her it was child's play compared to how daring she had been while we were incarcerated.

Other returnees, not as daring, were in bad shape. While many of the survivors had never been ill during their incarceration, they suddenly experienced a great number of physical problems. The reaction had set in and the Jewish hospital on Malzgasse was very busy. Among the people who had returned from Riga, four died within the first few months after liberation. Wilhelmine Hochermann (52) did not even get to Vienna but died on the way, Ruth Kuttenplan (18) died only two weeks after she returned in July 1945, Fritzi Bottwin (45) and Elizabeth Winternitz (46) both developed cancer of the uterus and died in early 1946. Just now, when they could have started a new life, these comparatively young people died, and we were affected and hurt by the unfairness of it all.

We seemed to live in a state of limbo and what I remember best about these days is the waiting . . . everyone hoped this one or that one would come back. Arthur Hochermann, who had fled to France and had survived Auschwitz, came back and was overjoyed when told his wife was on the way. Then, when it became clear that she had died at just about the time when he had entered Vienna, he broke down. He died a short time afterward.

Our daily pilgrimage to the *Kultusgemeinde* on Schottenring 25 became a ritual. We wanted to find out who had returned. Most of us, however, waited in vain although from time to time, there were miracles, and we treated them as such.

Despite the unwillingness of Austrians to face their past, some arrests were made and trials against our former tormentors took place, ending at times in well-deserved death sentences, as that of Anton Brunner, who had sent us to the East. Brunner's death did not make up for his brutal treatment of the thousands who were to be murdered, but during his trial it became clear how Austrian officials had dominated the destruction process, not only in their own country, but in all of Europe under the sign of the swastika.

We followed the Nuremberg Trials on radio and we became ever more cynical; it seemed that all of the defendants had only "followed orders," no one had really known what had been done, and no one had participated in genocide. The men on trial, when shown films of bloodbaths in the forests, in the ghettos, in the camps, and in some market places of small towns, behaved as if they were seeing all that carnage for the first time. To add insult to injury, they were unrepentant.

After having registered at the *Kultusgemeinde*, Jewish concentration camp survivors found out that "Aryan" political concentration camp survivors could and did register at City Hall. At first there seemed to be no difference, but after a while it became obvious that the non-Jewish returnees were able to get apartments, clothing, and even food directly from the city of Vienna and in far greater amounts than their Jewish counterparts. Our sustenance came from the *Kultusgemeinde*, which in turn received their main support from agencies abroad. Thus, while we did have the aforementioned soup kitchen and packages, as well as some clothing, the *Kultusgemeinde* had no power to give us either our previous or another apartment. When the Jews, considered to be "racially persecuted," therefore wanted to join the newly created *K.Z. Verband* (concentration camp organization) with its ties to the government, the political prisoners refused to accept them into their ranks, and there were many instances of rather vituperative fights. It is perhaps because of these occurrences, that many Jews, born and bred in Austria, realized that there was no future for them in that country and emigrated, leaving the field to the political concentration camp survivors, who may have been anti-Nazi, but were also anti-Semites.

Not surprisingly, when Austria finally paid a pittance to the few survivors still left at some time in the 1970s, it was the political exprisoners and not the Jews who received the restitution of 880 *Oesterreichische Schilling* for each month of incarceration not only earlier, but also with less trouble, such as bringing witnesses, documents, and other proofs of our ordeal. The authorities did not want to bother looking at the readily available Gestapo transport lists! We still did not count. Neither were we given restitution for the time between the *Anschluss* and our deportation, nor did it matter that we certainly did not lead normal lives.

Despite the daily worries, the happiness of being free was ever present. Of course it was overshadowed by our losses, but there were get-togethers and especially the young tried to make up for all the formal education they had missed. Foreign language classes started up again, special courses were offered to prepare for "*Matura*" without which better jobs would not be available, and mundane courses such as typing, stenography, and others

were also given and well received. Moreover, the Zionist movement, hopeful and desperate at the same time, started to attract the returnees.

After the end of the war in Europe, the leaders of the victorious nations, President Harry S Truman, Marshal Joseph Stalin, and Prime Minister Winston Churchill, met at Potsdam near Berlin. While preceding conferences had outlined only tentative plans for the post-war period, the main task at Potsdam was to establish occupation zones, assess quotas of reparation, set up administrative offices for the enemy territory, and arrange for peace treaties. These points were embodied in the Potsdam Agreement.

Once more, Austria, even though no longer united with Germany, would share the latter's fate: The country was divided into four zones, and Vienna, while situated within the Russian sector, was divided into four zones as well, each to be administered by one of the Allies, including France, even though it was not always clear to us in what way France had been a winner. The Jewish members of these military forces came to several organized functions of the *Kultusgemeinde*, especially to the well-attended Chanukah Ball 1945, supervised and directed by none other than my former teacher, Dr. Gertrude Neumann, who had survived the war in Hungary together with her daughter Lisa. Her husband, Arpad Neumann, did not survive. Only four years earlier, it had been a totally different world for all of us. Among my teachers, only Dr. Neumann and Paul Stagel had survived. As for the students of the *Piper Heim*, my sister, Vera Korkus, Ignatz Mucinic, and I were all who were left. There were several who had been with us at the *Palaestina Amt* and had come back from the camps, but most of them were older, with the exception of Vera Kisch, who was fifteen when the war ended.

At that first Chanukah Ball of our new lives, most of the guests were survivors, and all of us were delighted to have Jewish soldiers in our midst. After some of us had entertained the crowd, the candles were lit and the *Maos Zur* was sung. There was not one dry eye among us, even though we should have been very happy, for our survival was indeed a great miracle too.

For the next few years, Vienna and other cities in Austria served as collection points for Polish and Hungarian Jews on their way to either Palestine or the United States. Despite fears expressed by xenophobic politicians, only very few of these foreign Jews remained and settled there. Of the native Jews, the same could be said. The majority left, the older people who had survived Theresienstadt died rapidly, and only a small group remained who made Vienna their home once more.

While members of the government were ostensibly friendly to Jewish concentration camp survivors, with some of them having spent time in camps themselves, the reality was quite different. The British historian Robert Knight

unearthed records at the Vienna State Archives dated 1945 to 1952 that show a very ugly picture. Perusing those records, it becomes frighteningly clear how differently the members of Parliament expressed themselves when they were among themselves compared with what they said in public.

State Chancellor Karl Renner, the later president of Austria, for instance, found it impossible for the country "to be responsible for whatever was owned by those Jews who had been no more than small tradesmen and peddlers," and Austrian Chancellor Leopold Figl, in a discussion about restitution, said, "all those Jews would like to get rich quickly," and then energetically denied, when confronted by Austrian Jews living in the United States and England, that anyone in his government was anti-Semitic. In this obvious untruth Figl was seconded by the Viennese Mayor Theodor Koerner, who called the Austrians "too cosmopolitan to be prejudiced against Jews."

Perhaps Koerner should have been enlightened by those of us who had survived the camps and had been deathly afraid especially of Austrian personnel there! Whenever we heard the well-remembered dialect, we did our best to become invisible. To this day, many of us ask, of course in vain, "Why did they hate us with such a passion?" The very songs they hummed and loved were composed by Jews, much of the literature they appreciated was written by Jews, everything that pointed out that they were special because they were Austrians had its origin in some Jewish brain, and still, they disliked us intensely and did their best to eliminate us from this earth.

Robert Knight published the protocols he found in 1988, in Germany, under the title *Ich bin Dafuer, die Sache in die Laenge zu Ziehen*, the infamous sentence that refers to restitution for the Jews and which can be translated into "I would suggest to let the matter take a rather long time." It was spoken by *Unterstaatssekretaer* (Under Secretary of State) Georg Helmer at a meeting on November 9, 1948. While some of the other ministers present felt that in order to aid the few Jews in Vienna, most of them poor, the *Kultusgemeinde* should at least be given a loan by the government, so as to ease those surviving Jews' precarious situation, the majority felt as Helmer did. He claimed that even the English and the Americans no longer cared for the Jews, either in Austria or elsewhere, after having seen how cruel Jews had been during the 1948 liberation war in Palestine! Helmer went on to say the Austrian government should just tell the Jews "we'll see what can be done," and let it go at that.

That same evening, however, November 9, 1948, at a ceremony commemorating the ten years which had passed since *Kristallnacht*, Chancellor Figl reassured those present that he hoped for a new growth of a Jewish community in Vienna, despite all the atrocities that had occurred there. He

did not tell the Jews present that evening, that he, together with the other members of his government, had decided not to accept any more claims of restitution for the time being!

Owing to the unwillingness of the Austrian authorities to do right by the few survivors, it took twenty years for my mother to get restitution for our business and for the apartment. As for my sister's and my own claims as far as loss of schooling was concerned, we were summarily denied. They did, however, give us a few hundred Schilling for having to wear the yellow star from September 1941 until our deportation in February 1942. In addition, my mother received a small amount for the loss of her husband, but we, even though we were so young when the war ended, were not considered orphans under Austrian law with so much time having passed. This same scenario was played out with all other Viennese with whom we kept in touch, no matter whether they had managed to flee to a safe country or had been, like us, deported and had survived. Again, the question to which none of us found an answer, came up: Why did the Austrians hate us so bitterly?

The contributions made by Jews to the country's cultural *niveau*, to medicine, to science, to literature, to the law, to the theater, to journalism, to the arts, and especially to music, left even the small, truncated Austria after World War I in the limelight. Despite being much like a head without a body, Vienna was still considered a glittering, cosmopolitan city, which retained its fascination long after it had ceased to be the capital of an empire. Jews could be found in every field, contributing to the city's glory. Therefore, "why the hatred?" must one day be answered. In the meantime, the hurt runs deep and Austria, for all practical purposes, while not completely *judenrein*, is on the way to becoming a country without Jews.

In fact, today's Austrians prefer not to think back to the flourishing, vibrant Jewish community that existed before 1938, which had enriched their country and which, posthumously, is still doing so. Few of the younger people care to know or acknowledge that most of the plays and operettas, indeed most of the music offered as entertainment, now perhaps more than ever, was created by those same Jews who were either forced out of the country, or worse, were deported and slaughtered. On the other hand, a segment of Austrians puts on exhibits dedicated to all those Jews, dead of course, and, if lucky, of old age. In 1945, however, when some of them were still alive, little or no attempt was made to get them back from where they had sought safety.

In the spring of 1992, the Vienna Museum of History organized an exhibition entitled *"Sag beim Abschied . . ."*[25] These three words are the start of a song where a leave-taking lover is admonished to just say good-bye and then let it go at that. The exhibition concentrated on Jews who had been

forced out of Austria in 1938; it had as its main theme the contributions they had made in the areas of operettas, Viennese popular music, opera, stage, film, cabaret, and also literature.

The catalogue describing the exhibition was written by Robert Dachs, who indicated that it was the Jews to whom Austria in general and Vienna in particular owed the distinction of being the center of music. Dachs further wrote that after 1945, not one of the artists then in Vienna, with the exception of City Council member Victor Matejka and the actor Willy Forst, tried to convince the exiles to return.

The list of composers, librettists, singers, writers, and other artists is quite extensive. One of the songs mentioned is the *Fiakerlied*, written by the Jew Gustav Pick. It ends with the plaintive statement by the carriage driver, the "Fiaker," that he is a "real child" of Vienna. When looking at all the names listed by Dachs, it becomes clear that although most of them were from the crown lands, they were real Viennese "children" in their hearts and managed to convey it through their art. Dachs compared the Jewish absence at this time to an open wound that cannot heal and bemoans the fact that today's youth has no idea what they had missed and what they will never know.

Peter Malina's essay "Nach dem Krieg" (After the War) in *Oesterreicher und der Zweite Weltkrieg* (Austrians and the Second World War), tries to offer some explanations for the Austrians' insufferable behavior exhibited toward those of us who had dared to survive, both in camps and in safe countries. His main argument is that there was the fear we would ask for what had been taken from us to the detriment of those who now lived in our houses, wore our jewels, and held our former positions. Economics aside, he believes that they did not want to be reminded of having been "real Germans" during those heady years. Now, having returned to being "good old Austrians," they knew absolutely nothing about the murder of so many Jewish citizens. At any rate, Malina went on to say, there was no regret during the Hitler years, not is there any regret at this time.

Brigitte Bailer, in her new book on restitution for Austrian Jews *Wieder-gutmachung Kein Thema* (Restitution is not on the Agenda), found that the main reason for the unwillingness of the Austrian government to extend a helping hand to the Jewish victims, was the belief that Austria was Hitler's victim and should therefore not be held responsible. In fact, facing criticism by foreign governments, Austria found a way to circumvent admitting its guilt. For every law passed that helped their Jewish victims, a similar law was passed benefitting their former tormentors. Bailer wrote that such laws were often formulated at the same session of Austria's National Council members.

The records of SS officers who served between 1933 and 1945 are kept at the archives of Ludwigsburg, Germany. A copy of these records is held by the Anti-Defamation League in New York City, containing 42,000 names in eight volumes. Eight thousand of those listed were citizens of countries outside greater Germany, such as Latvia, Lithuania, Czechoslovakia, the Ukraine, the Netherlands, Italy, Poland, Spain, and even France, Great Britain, and the United States.

Of the remaining 34,000 "German" SS officers, over 5,000 were from Austria, or, as it was then called, the Ostmark. Although the Ostmark, with its six million inhabitants, represented only 8 percent of greater Germany, it supplied more than 14 percent of SS officers, with many of them being members of the party and the *Sicherheits Dienst*. Among those officers were aristocrats, lawyers, physicians, and doctors of philosophy.

In addition to the officers, there were thousands of Austrians serving in the lower ranks of the SS. According to Simon Wiesenthal, in *The Murderers Among Us*, one-third of *all* personnel having to do with the "final solution" of the Jewish problem were Austrian.[26]

While there is no real explanation for this phenomenon, it may be that the Austrians wanted to prove what good Germans they were. On the other hand, maybe they enjoyed their power over life and death vis-à-vis Jews. All we know is that not too many of them were ever taken to task for their murderous activities.

In the following pages, I have made an effort to list every registered survivor of the various camps, who, after the war was over, returned to Vienna. I have also included several who did not do so, but had, after spending time in hospitals located near their places of liberation, thought it best to go somewhere else. I have also included those who survived but died on the way to Vienna. Wherever possible, provided it was so indicated on the deportation lists, I have listed the year of their birth.

The bibliography pertains mainly to the contents of this book. Using the fate of the members of my family and friends as examples of what happened to the Jews of Austria made the tragedy come alive in a way that mere statistics never could. It is a foregone conclusion that the death of even one person through violence makes a witness feel outraged and violated as well. When the figures, however, speak about thousands or even millions, the awful events become meaningless and do not convey the tragedy properly. We do not want to see the victims as statistics, but as people. Thus, when imagining an exiled woman such as my aunt Antoinette meeting her fate in the gas chambers of Auschwitz, we should remember her witty letters, her

love for poetry, and the pride she exhibited when looking at her two beautiful children. Likewise, when thinking of my father's cousin Bubi, as he was pushed down the stone quarry in Mauthausen breaking his neck in the process, he should be remembered also as a good son, a man who loved life, an individual who did not have one enemy in the world. Or, when thinking of young Bernhard, my cousin, seeing him being murdered in Yugoslavia on his way to the Holy Land, he should be remembered as playing soccer on the Schmelz, a meadow in the fifteenth district of Vienna, hoping to make the big time. Then, the statistics turn into real people, not just numbers.

Finally, there is the memory of my father. Like so many of his generation, he was a Viennese extraordinaire, suffused with a love for his country that seems ludicrous from a vantage point of half a century. During the Great War, he was willing to give his life for this country and then, three decades later, his life was indeed forfeited in Buchenwald, only this time he was considered the enemy of a state that included his beloved Austria.

Never again would he saddle his horse Fuchsel or teach his daughters the waltz, never again would he take us to the Prater when the chestnut trees there were in bloom, never again would he walk with us on the beautiful Schoenbrunner Allee, never again would he take my mother to see *The Zigeunerbaron* or *Countess Maritza* or a new film, never again would we all go to the Krapfenwaldl and swim surrounded by the Wienerwald, and never again would we hear him sing "Gluecklich ist, wer vergisst, was nicht mehr zu aendern ist!"[27] Never again.

Appendix

DACHAU AND BUCHENWALD

Sent between April 1938 and September 1939	7,958	Men
Released between February and August 1939	(approx.) 5,000	
	2,958	
Sent between 1942 and 1945	(approx.) 50	
	3,008	
Returned	71	
Perished	2,937	

List of Survivors:

Jakob Alastraky	Victor Erber
Moritz Alastraky	Otto Fischer 1897
Jakob Apfel 1920	Ernst Fischl 1901
Dr. Gerhard Arnstein 1906	Armin Freudmann 1915
Benzion Bacher	Rudolf Friedenthal 1921
Robert Bauer	Hermann Geppert 1913
Friedrich Beck 1910	Victor God 1902
Erich Bock 1909	Hermann Gottlieb 1920
Viktor Brust 1887	Karl Gruen 1904
Erich Dawird	Paul Gruenberg 1923
Leopold Deutsch	Otto Herschmann 1907
Heinrich Diamond	Gustav Hirschkron
Moses Einhorn 1905	Hermann Hirschler

Alfred Hrabek 1921
Alfred Klapper 1905
Fritz Kleinmann 1923
Gustav Kleinmann 1891
Samuel Knoll 1922
Karl Kocheles 1887
Julius Kodicek 1915
Viktor Kohn 1917
Erich Kohut 1918
Ernst Kolben 1926
Fritz Kollmann 1908
Berthold Kornitzer 1908
Fritz Kornitzer 1906
Otto Kornthal 1917
Fritz Krakauer 1896
Dr. Gustav Kreisler 1886
Oskar Kurz 1906
Lazar Leitner 1917
Akim Lewit 1893
Hans Lichtenstein 1901
David Lopper 1921
Adolf Luster 1922
Alfred Lustig 1907

Jakob Margulies 1900
Ludwig Max Matzner 1904
Hugo Monschein 1903
Isak Neumann 1893
Samuel Petschaft 1921
Hans Plohn 1908
Bela Pordes 1895
Heinrich Preis 1923
Fritz Rosenblatt 1917
Ing. Fritz Roubicek 1913
Paul Schapira 1894
Hermann Schiffer 1886
Josef Schiller 1914
Adolf Smilowitz 1923
Paul Spitzer 1908
Leo Stechler 1899
Peter Sturm 1909
Markus Wassermann 1907
Hermann Weber 1897
Kurt Weinber 1909
Ludwig Weinber 1911
Fritz Weiss 1914

NISKO, POLAND

Transport of October 20, 1939	912	Men
Transport of October 27, 1939	672	
	1,584	
Returned to Vienna on April 16, 1940 and subsequently deported	198	
	1,386	
Returned from Karaganda	71	
Perished	1,315	

List of Survivors:

Jakob Bem 1897
Salomon Berkowitz 1902
Josef Biller 1888
Hersch Birkenfeld 1897

Mordko Birkenfeld 1894
Hans Braunwald 1891
Leopold Brill 1880
Schick Diamant 1889

Richard Fink 1915
Adolf Fischer 1895
Karl Fischer 1903
Oskar Flaschner 1896
Egon Frankenstein 1899
Heinrich (Chaim) Fries 1885
Herbert Fuerth 1903
Hans Gold 1899
Moritz Gruenfeld 1896
Armin Guenser 1895
Josef Hahn 1899
Hugo Hirschl 1897
Richard Hittner 1899
Friedrich Hoffmann 1906
Richard Hoffmann 1898
Felix Huttrer 1903
Otto Jellinek 1907
Hugo Karpfen 1900
Leo Kihn 1903
Friedrich Koch 1903
David Koenigsberg 1888
Erwin Kornfeld 1898
Jakob Krakauer 1892
Samuel Krassotozky 1889
Ladislaus Kummer 1920
Friedrich Kuerzer 1913
Heinrich Laser 1898
Samuel Lebzelter 1906
Wilhelm Littner 1896
Leopold Loeffler 1895
Philipp Meller 1893
Leopold Meutner 1905

Siegfried Pick 1905
Rudolf Pollak 1914
Johann Pordes 1890
Rafael (Chaim) Preis 1909
Hermann Pulgram 1901
Oskar Ullitzer 1893
Ignaz Reisfeld 1893
Siegfried Reismann 1897
Gerome (Jerazo) Rosenfeld 1901
Siegfried Rosenzweig 1903
Leopold Rudoll 1913
Leo Salmann 1899
Solomon Schaffer 1904
Robert Schlemmel 1904
Victor Schlesinger 1898
Walter Schlesinger 1900
Ernst Schwimmer 1900
Heinrich Silber 1901
Ernst Simon 1916
Viktor Sommerfeld 1899
Leopold Sonnenfeld 1892
Markus Spira 1897
Alfred Spitzer 1899
Arthur Stricker 1899
Josef Vogel 1901
Leopold Vogel 1902
Karl Weiner 1912
Max Weinfeld 1899
Otto Weiss 1920
Rudolf Wessely 1888
Paul Zilsel 1897

OPOLE VIA PULAWY, POLAND

Transport of February 15, 1941	1,005	People
Transport of February 26, 1941	1,002	
	2,007	
Returned	15	
Perished	1,992	

List of Survivors:

Nelly Adler 1896
Walter Appel 1905
Robert Paul DeMajo 1905
Siegmund Deutsch 1896
Anika Engel 1890
Rudolf Engel 1889
Edith Frischmann 1923
Anna Henner 1879

Fritz Kueri 1903
Selma Ludwan 1905
Alexandra Schaerf 1896
Regie Tuter 1923
Hersch Wenkart 1900
Klara Wenkart 1907
Emilie Wolf 1906

KIELCE, POLAND

Transport of February 19, 1941	1,003	People
Returned	9	
Perished	994	

List of Survivors:

Alice Berger 1895
Bertha Fries 1898
Kaethe Fries 1921
Ignatz Oesterreicher 1879
Hugo Riegelhaupt 1904

Alice Rusz 1922
Irma Weiner 1886
Siegfried Weiner 1887
Berta Weiss 1898

MODLIBORZYCE, POLAND

Transport of March 5, 1941	1,000	People
Returned	4	
Perished	996	

List of Survivors:

Elsa Holzer 1928
Helene Koenig 1890
Dr. Paul Messinger 1914
Salo Weinbaum 1926

LAGOW-OPATOW, POLAND

Transport of March 12, 1941	1,001	People
Returned	4	
Perished	997	

List of Survivors:

Max Beer 1880
Katharina Goetzl 1895
Julia Sinai 1919
Berta Weissberg 1903

LODZ (LITZMANNSTADT), POLAND

Transport of October 15, 1941	1,005	People
Transport of October 19, 1941	1,003	
Transport of October 23, 1941	991	
Transport of October 28, 1941	998	
Transport of November 2, 1941	998	
	4,995	
Returned	18	
Perished	4,977	

List of Survivors:

Wilhelm Abeles 1886
Rosa Breitenfeld 1903
Joachim Dicker 1892
Paula Elges 1901
Siegfried Federidt 1920
Walter Feiden 1928
Hermann Feigelbaum 1894
Cyrill Feilich 1926
Grete Feldberg 1920

Julius (Juda) Feldhorn 1892
Hella Fixel 1921
Anna Glueck 1897
Leopold Hauser 1898
Sofie Rosenkranz 1901
Joseph Saphier 1893
Daniel Steiner 1906
Hilde Ungar 1911
Max Weiss 1919

KOVNO, LITHUANIA

Transport of November 23, 1942	995	People
Perished	995	

RIGA, LATVIA

Transport of December 3, 1941	1,042	People
Transport of January 11, 1942	1,000	
Transport of January 26, 1942	1,196	

Transport of February 6, 1942	<u>997</u>	People
	4,235	
Returned	<u>103</u>	
Perished	4,132	

List of Survivors:

Edith Bettler 1922

Fritz Bettler 1924

Johanna Bloch 1894

Anna Boehmerwald 1898

Hans Boehmerwald 1927

Fritzi Bottwin 1900

Selma Breitner 1907

Fritz Deutsch 1925

Lazar Drimer 1885

Melanie Eckstein 1892

Rosa Eisler 1924

Franziska Engel 1896

Karl Engel 1894

Robert Fischer 1926

Irene Frischmann 1899

Gustav Gelles 1912

Egon Glaser 1905

Erwin Glaser 1922

Rosalie R.Goldapper 1915

Martha Goldfischer 1924

Paula Goldstein 1924

Leah Granierer 1901

Leo Granierer 1927

Minna Gruber 1907

Renee Hacker 1907

Lea Haim 1896

Sally Hauser 1926

Charlotte Hirschhorn 1898

Gertrude Hirschhorn 1928

Rita Hirschhorn 1930

Wilhelmine Hochermann 1893

Erich Jellinek 1924

Siegfried Katz 1899

Kurt Keinersdorf 1926

Malvine Keinersdorf 1896

Hertha Kisch 1899

Vera Kisch 1929

Margarethe Koerner 1890

Fritzi Kohn 1923

Margarethe Kohn 1902

Alexander Kornfeld 1893

Grete Kreitler 1920

Hertha Kuerth 1922

Ruth Kuttenplan 1927

Anna Lampel 1923

Albert Lang 1907

Magdalena Lewy 1909

Gerda Mahler 1920

Regina Malz 1908

Gusta Mann 1897

Mathilde Maurueber 1896

Erich Mautner 1920

Trude Moik 1908

Liane (Baby) Mueller 1924

Rudolf Neumann 1922

Helene Nistler

Trude Oser 1911

Lilly Picker 1895

Dolly Pinkassowitsch 1928

Erich Pinkassowitsch 1923

Erich Pisk 1924

Otto Posament 1911

Lydia Reichmann 1909

Elfriede Rerucha 1930

Hildegard Rerucha 1908

Klara Rosenberg 1900

Felicia Rosenkranz 1924
Gusti Roth 1899
Anna Rothfeld 1893
Inge Rothfeld 1925
Julius Rubin 1928
Paula Sandler 1901
Kurt Sauerquell 1927
Edith Schneller 1927
Mathilde Schneller 1906
Alice Schorr 1906
Herbert Schwarz 1925
Regina Schwarz 1899
Else Sekules 1906
Erwin Sekules 1901
Lea Singer 1898
Ernest Sonnenschein 1926
Harry von Sonnenthal 1906
Nina von Sonnenthal 1917
Ernestine Spitzer 1899

Kurt Steinbach 1922
Eduard Steinitz 1920
Elizabeth Suschny 1907
Otto Toper 1905
Frieda Trost 1907
Oskar Tycho 1926
Kurt Urbach 1911
Elena Weinheber 1910
Elizabeth Weiss 1888
Hertha Weiss 1927
Otto Weissenstein 1896
Lia Weisskopf (Julie)
Hilda Wiener-Rotmueller 1901
Margit Wieselmann 1915
Elizabeth Winternitz 1899
Ruth Wischnitzer 1922
Edith Zinner 1930
Ottilie Zinner 1897

MINSK, BELORUSSIA

Transport of November 28, 1941	999	People
Transport of May 6, 1942	994	
Transport of May 20, 1942	986	
Transport of May 27, 1942	991	
Transport of June 2, 1942	999	
Transport of June 9, 1942	1,006	
Transport of August 17, 1942	1,003	
Transport of August 31, 1942	967	
Transport of September 14, 1942	992	
Transport of October 5, 1942	549	
	9,486	
Returned	9	
Perished	9,477	

List of Survivors:

Edith Gruenberg 1923
Isaak Gruenberg 1891

Lotte Gruenberg 1934
Julie Hochbaum 1903

Marie Mack 1907
Johann Noskes 1921
Hans Schuller 1923

Ferdinand Trausel 1895
Tusnelda Trausel 1894

DEATHCAMPS IN POLAND

Transport of April 9, 1942 to Izbica	1,002	People
Transport of April 27, 1942 to Wlodawa	999	
Transport of May 12, 1942 to Izbica	1,001	
Transport of May 15, 1942 to Izbica	1,006	
Transport of June 5, 1942 to Izbica	1,001	
Transport of June 14, 1942 to Sobibor	1,000	
Transport of March 31, 1943 to Treblinka	85	
Perished	6,094	

THERESIENSTADT, CZECHOSLOVAKIA

13 Transports between June 21 and October 10, 1942	13,922	People
18 Transports between January 6 and December 15, 1943	1,103	
14 Transports between January 11 and November 23, 1944	227	
4 Transports between February 2 and April 15, 1945	99	
	15,351	
Transport to Switzerland, February 5, 1945, among them		154 Austrian Jews
Alive in Theresienstadt on May 5, 1945	1,270	
Returned from Auschwitz and other camps to where they had been sent from Theresienstadt	149	
Perished	13,778	

List of 149 Survivors:*

Ilse Adler 1930
Lily Adler 1925
Adele Aufrichtig 1922
Walter Baier 1912
Heinrich Berger 1924**
Henriette Bisseliches 1919

Emil Breier 1896
Kurt Breitbart 1925**
Susanne Brender 1929**
Herta Buchwald 1921
Robert Buchwald 1900**
Wolf Dennenberg 1892**

*Those returned from various camps to where they had been sent from Theresienstadt.
**Denotes inclusion in *Totenbuch Theresienstadt*.

Eugen Deutsch 1903**
Erwin Diamant 1925
Annemarie Eichberg 1916
Fritz Eichberg
Emil Ernst 1897
Irene Faerber
Melanie Feldsberg
Rudolf Flussmann 1900**
Dr. Victor Frankl 1905
Blanka Fried 1883
Trude Friedlaender 1922
Franziska Frommer 1900
Dr. Jakob Frucht 1897**
Gisela Gelbard 1909
Herta Gerstl 1928
Emil Glass 1898
Olga Glixam 1901
Grete Goldberg 1921
Jaroslav Goldschmid 1898**
Suse Goldschwird 1923
Moritz Goldstein 1921
Emil Gottesmann 1903
Georg Gottesmann 1927
Gitta Gottesmann 1900**
Thea Gottesmann 1928**
Franziska Grab 1899
Marie Gross 1922
Alice Guttmann 1898
Eveline Guttmann 1924
Elsa Gyoery 1895**
Dr. Franziska Haas 1909
Ignaz Haas 1894
Ernst Hacker 1929
Dr. Franz Hahn 1913
Dr. Oswald Hardeck 1910
Kurt Hertzka 1926
Bernard Hindelsz 1892
Eva Hirsch 1927
Therese Hochwald 1906
Berthold Hoffmann 1927
Anny Holzer

Erika Jakon 1928
Hermine Jakon 1898
Jacques Jakon 1920
Josefine Jakon 1917
Therese Jakon 1923
Edith Jedlinsky 1924**
Hilda Jedlinsky 1897**
Albert Jungmann 1925
Edith Jupiter 1923
Otto Kalwo
Zev Kamiel 1901**
Eva Kardemann 1921**
Hans Kessler 1912
Rita Kirmayer 1926
Kaethe Klamper 1904
Stella Klepper 1911
Alma Klueger 1900
Ruth Klueger 1931
Renee Konstant 1927**
Lilly Kopper 1923
Vera Korkus 1928
Israel Koss 1901
Kurt Ladner 1926
Elizabeth Lamberg 1925**
Gertrude Landau 1924
David Lehrer 1901
Johanna Leitner 1910**
Harry Linser 1928**
Anita Loewy 1921**
Leo Luster 1927**
Berthold Mandel 1927**
Fanny Mandel 1908**
Elly Matyas 1925
Rosa Mausner 1923**
Max Max 1892**
Adolf Merkur 1922
Nelly Miczek 1898**
Ignaz Mucinic 1926**
Bernhard Mueller 1925**
Ingeborg Nadbath 1924**
Wilhelm Pekel 1909

Else Rachmiel 1905
Regine Rawitz 1915
Wilhelm Rechnitz 1927**
Hugo Reinfeld 1919**
Hermann Riegler 1924**
Lizzy Rosenzweig 1921**
Margaretha Roth 1908
Thea Rumstein 1928
Egon Schacherl 1908**
Hermann Schaffer 1917**
Frieda Scheindl 1911**
Max Scheindl 1900**
Eva Schick 1927
Lilly Schlimper 1923
Hedwig Schneller 1908
Fanny Scholl 1900
Gertrude Schramek 1922
Herbert Schrott 1926
Erika Schuster 1929
Edith Schwarz 1923
Walter Schwarz 1923
Ernest Seinfeld 1924
Robert Singer 1928**
Rosa Singer 1912
Gusta Slopkowitzer 1902**
Ernst Sonntag 1897**
Ilse Spielberg 1923**
Kurt Spitz 1920

Paul Stagel 1912
Leo Stein 1898
Dr. Otto Stein 1912
Gertrude Steiner 1908
Leopold Stern 1892
Frieda Stern 1906
Rita Sternschuss 1922
Ernst Sterzer 1925
Friedrich Sterzer 1929
Eva Steuer 1921**
Gerty Taussig 1928
Wolfgang Teichthal 1930
Alice Tiegel 1920
Herta Trebitsch 1916
Hermine Vogel 1901
Lilly Vogel 1929
Reinhard Vogel 1901
Berthold Wagner 1916
Raul Wasservogel 1894**
Heinz Wegner 1922
Fanny Weiss 1919**
Oskar Weiss 1898
Julie Wessely 1911
Karoline Widder 1902
Hinde Witrofski 1905**
Walter Wolfgang 1923
Ernst Wulken 1922**

List of Survivors Who Came Back to Vienna from Theresienstadt:*

Laura Avelis 1875
Sarina Aberbach 1882
Hilda Abramoff 1894
Lea Adam 1884
Janka Adler 1901
Julie Adler 1881

Julius Adler 1894
Karl Adler 1873
Karoline Adler 1871
Louise Adler 1872
Richard Adler 1899
Rosa Adler 1902

*Denotes death between May 5 and July 10, 1945.

Simon Adler 1896

Karoline Affenkraut 1868

Karoline Albala 1898

Wilhelm Alt-Rhoden 1892

Elisabeth Altmann 1868

Johanna Altmann 1894

Max Altmann 1875

Rosa Altmann 1876

Dr. Sigmund Altmann 1876

Herta Altschul 1897

Josefine Amon 1883

Wilhelm Amon 1873

Emilie Andreach 1892

Emilie Angelmar 1886

Irene Angerer 1886

Rosa Apfelbaum 1899

Judis Auerbach 1942

Sara Auerbach 1888

David Auersbach 1902

Ernst Aufricht 1890

Stefan Auspitz 1869

Charlotte Bachmann 1872

Helene Bachmann-Arnstein 1877

Sofie Bader 1905

Katharina Balner 1900

Julie Banaschek 1876

Simon Band 1874

Adolf Barasch 1870

Eugenie Barasch 1901

Olga Baroch 1867

Ludwig Barsz 1879

Rosa Barusch 1874

Ludwig Basch 1862

Nelly Baschant 1897

Alma Bass 1880

David Bass 1876

Flora Bass 1867

Nelly Bass 1892

Albert Bauer 1871

Anna Bauer 1868

Leopold Bauer 1868

Marie Bauer 1871

Hans Beck 1924

Rosa Beck 1895

Rudolf Beck 1877

Zdenka Beer 1897

Emil Bellak 1885

Moritz Benedikt 1876

Hermine Benesch 1873

Elise Berczeller 1871

Anna Berger 1907

Auguste Berger 1873

Benjamin Berger 1875

Ferdinand Berger 1885

Josef Berger 1933

Julian Berger 1886

Laura Berger 1866

Therese Berger 1887

Louise Berger-Liebstoeckl 1902

Anna Bergmann 1897

Elfriede Bergmann 1937

Erna Bergmann 1901

Franz Bergstein 1876

Ida Berkowitz 1866

Antonie Bermann 1875

Moses Bermann 1867

Alexander Bernat 1912

Rifka Bernfeld 1875

Fanny Bernhardt 1870

Josefine Bernstein 1903

Max Bernstein 1894

Rosa Bienenfeld 1868

Wolf Bikles 1878

Julie Birkelmayer 1870

Klara Bittner 1872

Leib Blaettel 1870

Adolf Blau 1875

Adolf Blau 1894

Elsa Blau 1899

Emilie Blau 1886

Gisela Blau 1872

Herbert Blau 1931

Rudolf Blau 1882
Rosa Blauer-Kugler 1871
Dr. Arthur Bleier 1874
Karl Bleier 1894
Ottilie Bleier 1879
Berta Bloch 1883
Richard Bloch 1870
Aron Blum 1875
Dr. Emil Blum 1873
Helene Blum 1933
Leonore Blum 1907
Jenny Blumengarten 1868
Therese Bock 1878
Samuel Bock 1875
Therese Boeck 1878
Jetty Bogen-Fuchs 1924
Karoline Bololanik 1918
Rosa Bololanik 1884
Berta Boskowitz 1871
Hermine Braeuer 1886
Ludwig Braeuer 1870
Netti Brand 1871
Therese Brandl 1875
Else Braun 1874
Hilde Braun 1897
Marianne Braun 1889
Fanny Braunwald 1876
Bernhard Braver 1891
Anschel Breier 1939
Ilse Breier 1937
Kurt Breier 1933
Ludwig Breier 1908
Regine Breier 1908
Thomas Breitfeld 1939
Berta Breuer 1863
Ida Brichta 1875
Erich Brueck 1879
Julie Bruell 1894
Rudolf Bruell 1887
Johanna Brunner 1864
Gustav Brunwald 1887

Paula Brunwald 1899
Wilhelmine Brunwald 1856
Gertrude Buchbinder 1910
Hedwig Buchbinder 1883
Peter Buchbinder 1933
Anna Mathilde Buchsbaum 1871
Emanuel Stefan Buchsbaum 1889
Arpad Buechler 1900
Pehsie Lea Burg 1875
Rosa Burstein 1876
Rella Bustin 1886
Gabriele Caro 1868
Vilma Cermak 1876
Franz Cernoch 1901
Georg Cernoch 1938
Lina Cernoch 1906
Helene Chalupka 1883
Charlotte Charisch 1867
Charlotte Chmiel 1868
Rosa Czas 1866
Franz Czinner 1870
Julie Dauber 1889
Dr. Lucian Dauber 1881
Johann Davidovicz 1897
Aloisia Deutsch 1897
Hermann Deutsch 1874
Julie Deutsch 1874
Lene Deutsch 1860
Oskar Deutsch 1885
Regine Deutsch 1868
Thekla Deutsch 1872
Wilhelmine Deutsch 1910
Rosi Dey 1892
Julie Doerfler 1873
Siegfried Doerfler 1868
Dr. Julius Donat 1873
Charlotte Doubek 1925
Flora Drill 1874
Sigmund Dukes 1871
Antonie Duldner 1872
Maria Dzugan-Neumann 1875

Karoline Ebenspanger 1867

Johanna Ebner 1872

Rita Edelhofer 1890

Elisabeth Ehrenfest 1890

Emil Ehrenstein 1868

Ida Ehrenstein 1873

Henry Ehrlich 1900

Karoline Ehrlich 1890

Klara Ehrlich 1875

Leiser Ehrlich 1878

Margarethe Ehrlich 1902*

Esther Eibuschitz 1878

Fritz Eichberg 1875

Chaja Einziger 1903

Regine Einziger 1877

Wolf Eisenberg 1876

Gertrude Eisenstein 1926

Helene Eisenstein 1921

Wigdor Hersch Eisenthal 1882

Dr. Michael Eisler 1877

Magdalena Eisner 1878

Eugenie Elbaum 1899

Mozek Elbaum 1899

Julie Elmer 1886

Leopold Eltbogen 1892

Friederike Engel 1882

Ludwig Engel 1869

Ernestine Erban 1871

Emilie Erben 1896

Marie Erben 1877

Elisabeth Erber 1868

Sara Hinde Erber 1871

Anna Ermes 1882

Sophie Ernst 1898

Paula Eskenasy 1874

Therese Fanta 1868

Josef Fanti 1868

Else Fasal 1877

Oskar Fasal 1874

Leo Fassel 1895

Sophie Feher 1867

Marie Feilendorf 1873

Dora Fein 1872

Sigmund Feitel 1876

Johanna Felber 1861

Max Feldmar 1895

Rachel Feldmar 1895

Ernst Feldberg 1894

Zerline Feldberg 1899

Dr. Isidor Fell 1870

Albert Fellner 1898

Carola Fellner 1901

Jakob Fellner 1874

Margarethe Fessler 1870

Hermine Feyer 1876

Wilhelm Fiala 1891

Johanna Figel 1876

Martha Fink 1885

Friedrich Fischer 1883

Gisela Fischer 1900

Mano Fischer 1893

Samuel Fischer 1866

Dr. Wilhelm Adolf Fischer 1869

Sophie Fischl 1862

Ida Fischl-Rattinger 1895

Clotilde Fleckles 1876

Helene Flesch 1895

Toni Flussmann 1864

Emilie Forstner 1877

Benzion Fraenkel 1877

Charlotte Fraenkel 1896

Paula Fraenkel 1874

Rosa Fraenkel 1867*

Elsa Frank 1895

Georg Frankel 1935

Regine Frankenstein 1865

Kitty Frankfurter 1918

Stella Frankfurter 1892

Jeanne Frankl 1906

Wilhelm Frankl 1889

Sofie Franzl 1883

Friederike Freund 1900

Hellmut Freund 1937

Ignaz Freund 1866

Josef Freund 1936

Klara Freund 1875

Flora Fried 1871

Franziska Fried 1881

Helene Fried 1887

Kaethe Fried 1866

Lucie Fried 1921

Albert Friedmann 1873

Hermine Friedmann 1873

Malwine Friedmann 1878

Sara Frimel 1890

Gertrude Fritz 1897

Auguste Froehlich 1879

Marianne Froehlich 1905

Max Froehlich 1868

Erich Frost 1886

Leopold Anton Frost 1894

Edith Fuchs 1876

Flora Fuchs 1883*

Gustav Fuchs 1882

Josef Fuchs 1874

Maximilian Fuchs 1874

Dr. Sigmund Fuchs 1877

Therese Fuchs 1867

Valerie Fuchs 1877

Benno Fuerst 1874

Hermine Fuerth 1872

Jaroslav Fuerth 1871

Kaethe Fuhrmann 1902

Sigmund Fuhrmann 1896

Eleonore Gaenger 1863

Hedwig Gara 1873

Dr. Heinrich Gans 1874

Olga Gans 1886

Gmendel Garfinkel 1864

Ottilie Gebhardt 1874

Ludwig Geiringer 1871

Josephine Gelbard 1903

Rudolf Gelbard 1930

Seinder Gelbard 1904

Ernestine Geroe 1906

Elisabeth Gerzabek 1883

Caroline Gibien 1867

Rose Giesskann 1876

Theodor Giesskann 1873

Scheindel Gipfel 1876

Antonie Glaser 1873

Franziska Glasner 1862

Helene Glattau 1868

Gertrude Gleiss 1913

Aurun Glogower 1941

Lea Glogower 1907

Sylvia Glogower 1931

Sidonie God 1906

Helene Goetzel 1875

Paul Gold 1892

Regine Gold 1904

Jakob Goldbaum 1896

Elsa Goldberg 1898

Harry Goldberg 1931

Jetty Goldberg 1874

Simon Goldberger 1871

Hermine Goldblatt 1871

Hedwig Goldmann 1905

Lisa Goldmann 1933

Katharine Goldmann-Gold 1867

Leo Goldschmid 1934

Sara Goldschmid 1900

Hani Goldschmidt 1857

Franziska Goldschmied 1873

Martha Goldschmied 1899

Fanni Goldstein 1865

Marianne Goldwerth 1898

Markus Goldwerth 1898

Elisabeth Gollerstepper 1877

Chaje Gottesfeld 1868

Moses Gottesfeld 1867

Caecilie Gottesmann 1872

David Gottesmann 1870

Jetti Gottesmann 1873

Camille Gottlieb 1884

Rose Gottlieb 1868

Hermine Graf 1873

Wilhelm Gram 1914

Erna Granek 1894

Zipa Grebler 1873

Ottilie Groebel 1884

Hermine Groeger 1871

Tony Gronewetter 1867

Abraham Gronich 1890

Hennie Gronich 1887

Albine Gross 1872

Marie Grosser 1907

Leopold Grosz 1869

Nina Grosz 1872

Gisela Gruber 1873

Judith Gruenbaum 1889

Bertha Gruenberg 1899

Bertha Gruenberg 1874

Karl Gruenberger 1866

Sofie Gruener 1881*

Sylvia Gruener 1939

Magda Gruenspann 1895

Emmerich Gruenwald 1896

Julius Gruenwald 1872

Minna Gruenwald 1876

Selma Gruenwald 1901

Gisela Gruenzweig 1876

Rosa Grulich 1883

Helene Guschelbauer 1878

Edith Gutes-Meth 1906

Hilde Gutfreund 1905

Kurt Gutfreund 1938

Abraham Gutherz 1871

Josefine Haas-Feuereisen 1878

Maria Haber 1877

Peter Haber 1879

Karl Hacker 1873

Helene von Haenisch 1872

Victor Hubert von Haenisch 1865

Gisele Hafner 1905

Amalie Hahn 1876

Emilie Hahn 1868

Friederike Hahn 1872

Herbert Hahn 1931

Irene Hahn 1884

Leopold Hahn 1884

Rita Hahn 1931

Walter Hahn 1929

Gisela Hahn-Wurzel 1902

Hermine Haiduk 1881

Regine Hajek-Stern 1876

Regina Halberthal 1870

Franz Johann Halbkram 1879

Josef Halpern 1873*

Emilie Hamber 1867

Jenny Hamber 1875

Ciwja Hamer 1867

Emilie Hamper 1867

Clara von Hartel 1873

Friederike Hartmann 1878

Johanna Hartmann 1867

Stefanie Hartkopp 1886

Fanny Hauptmann 1876

Kaethe Hauser 1872

Helene Hausner 1868

Ottilie Hayek 1900

Margit Marie Heger 1870

Sophie Heinrich 1876

Karoline Heinz 1860

Sabine Heitel 1901

Fanni Helfert 1881

Chana Heller 1876

Ferdinand Heller 1901

Johanna Heller 1869*

Marianne Heller 1874

Rosalie Heller 1877

Hermine Hellreich 1896

Manes Hellreich 1879

Emma Helm 1886

Anna Hendel 1874*

Dr. Sigmund Herbatschek 1872

Fanny Herlitzka 1875
Franziska Hermann 1915
Fritz Herman 1923
Hugo Herman 1872
Otto Herschan 1879
Herta Hersenander 1927
Bertha Hersfeld 1871
Elsa Herzfeld 1908
Helene Herzfeld 1877
Else Herzka 1923
Hanne Herzka 1943
Ernst Herzl 1879
Charlotte Herzog 1857
Dr. Ludwig Hift 1899
Elias Hirom 1889
Sidonie Hirsch 1868
Adelheid Hirschl 1876
Malvine Hirschl 1875
Ilonka Hirschler 1901
Monika Hirschler 1931
Renee Hirschler 1932
Sara Hirsch-Witte 1867
Hermine Hnilitschek 1874
Therese Hochreiter 1867
Dr. Max Hoenier 1877
Marie Hoenig 1875
Anna Hoenigsberg 1864
Ilona Hoess 1905
Sonja Hoess 1941
Norbert Hoffenberg 1885
Hermine Hoffmann 1869
Olga Hoffmann 1875
Pinkas Hoffmann 1876
Josefine Hofirek 1873
Kamilla Holzer 1902
Marie Holzer 1875
Elisabeth Holzinger 1893
Ida Horinek 1868
Heinrich Horn 1904
Lazer Horowitz 1872
Natalie Horowitz 1875

Emma Houska 1926
Hermine Houska 1880
Anna Huber 1876
Mathilde Huss 1864
Othmar Huss 1892
Sabina Hutterer 1867
Gisela Huybensz 1899
Scheindel Itzigsohn 1863
Bertha Jacobi 1872
Emilie Jahoda 1870
Gustav Jakobowitz 1898
Rosa Jamroz 1883
Betti Jellinek 1881
Olga Jiricek 1873
Caecilie Jokel 1863
Erna Jonas 1873
Regine De Jong 1872
Josefine Joseffowitz 1876
Erna Jung 1912
Laura Jungwirth 1885
Nelly Jussau 1930
Anna Kachler 1873
Helene Kadelburg 1875
Prof. Israel Kaestenbaum 1886
Chane Kahane 1888
Rosa Kahane 1923
Scheindel Kahane 1890
Henriette Kaldori 1866
Hermine Kalwo 1876
Gisela Kappelmacher 1878
Samuel Kardemann 1862
Rosalie Karnowsky 1874
Stefanie Karoly 1881
Walter Karpeles 1926
Berta Karpfen 1891
Emil Karpfen 1891
Regina Karten 1868
Marguerite Kary 1886
Jetty Katz 1867
Marjem Katz 1875
Mordko Katz 1873

Otto Katz 1903
Adolf Kauder 1879
Dr. Ernst Keller 1871
Hugo Keller 1876
Andor Kemeny 1874
Jeanette Kempler 1862*
Josefine Kerbel 1875
Friederike Kertesz 1878
Franz Kessler 1886
Karoline Kessler 1861
Elisabeth Khuner 1876
Dr. Ernst Khuner 1870
Henie Kindler 1881
Wilhelm Kindler 1885
Alice Klaar 1892
Dr. Paul Klaar 1887
Dr. Heinrich Klang 1875
Caecilie Klarfeld 1874
Gisela Klauber 1875
Elisabeth Klein 1877
Helen Klein 1897
Hilde Klein 1908
Kurt Klein 1931
Margarete Klein 1882
Therese Klein 1887
Malka Kletter 1892
Paul Kletter 1896
Mini Kligler 1875
Jakob Klipper 1878
Olga Klipper 1876
Jetty Knoepfelmacher 1873
Julie Knoepfer 1868
Emma Knoepfmacher 1885
Kurt Knoepfmacher 1920
Gisela Koch 1875
Gustav Koch 1894
Hermine Koch 1868
Hilda Koch 1906
Rosa Koch 1867
Alfred Kocian 1927
Paula Kocian 1894

Rosalie Koehler 1889
Helene Koenig 1890
Irma Koenig 1874
Josef Koenig 1874
Julie Koenig 1875
Theresa Koenig 1869
Therese Koenig 1883
Gisela Koerpel 1873
Elizabeth Kohlruss 1888
Clara Kohn 1864
Daniela Kohn 1888
Debora Kohn 1874
Emilie Kohn 1868
Erna Kohn 1909
Franziska Kohn 1910
Jakob Kohn 1882
Julie Kohn 1873
Karoline Kohn 1866
Katharina Kohn 1874
Leopold Kohn 1869
Otto Kohn 1907
Rosa Kohn 1865
Ruth Kohn 1923
Seraphine Kohn 1877
Therese Kohn 1872
Elly Kohn-Spitzer 1919
Alexander Kokisch 1875
Hedwig Kokisch 1874
Leontine Kolbert 1902
Anna Kolisch 1866
Arthur Kolisch 1885
Flora Kolisch 1889
Siegfried Kolisch 1891
Johanna Koller 1923
Markus Kollmann 1872
Rosalie Kollmann 1875
Dr. Gustav Kolny 1878
Maria Konrad 1897
Friederike Koppel 1891
Friedrich Koppel 1875
Julie Koppl 1891

Blanka Kormis 1896

Walter Kormis 1925

Lini Korn 1866

Josef Kornfeld 1887

Pauline Kornfeld 1867

Berta Kornitzer 1873

Zirl Krach 1877

Paula Kral 1906

Adele Kraus 1883

Leopold Kraus 1865

Martha Kraus 1917

Moritz Kraus 1881

Lotte Krieger 1867

Walter Kris 1932

Berta Kriss 1890

Susanne Kriss 1919

Norbert Kronberger 1877

Rosa Kronberger 1875

Gisela Kroupa 1877

Gisela Kuhn 1878

Leopold Kuhn 1871

Dorothea Kurt 1927

Marie Kwapniewski 1867

Cila Lacarovici 1894

Simon Lacarovici 1891

Paula Lachmanski 1878

Regine Lackenbacher 1878

Elizabeth Lahner 1931

Henriette Laizner 1877

Hermine Lamberg 1864

Franziska Landau 1895

Franziska Landau 1875

Dr. Rudolf Landau 1874

Hermann Lang 1867

Erna Langberg 1915

Johanna Langer 1887

Hana Lapter 1860

Franz Lateiner 1869

Anna Latzer 1879

Julius Latzer 1882

Hilda Lauer 1893

Mathilde Laumann 1876

Adele Lederer 1892

Eugen Lederer 1889

Therese Lehmann 1863*

Rosa Leiblinger 1867

Sofie Lenk 1877

Berta Lenobel 1905

Ignatz Lenobel 1890

Norbert Lenzer 1873

Isak Lerner 1873

Leopoldine Lessinger 1897

Klara Tatiana Leuthner 1874

Chaim Lewniowski 1877

Cylli Lewniowski 1872

Gabriele Liappi 1898

Alfred Lichtenstein 1884

Charlotte Lichtig 1868

Ilona Liebermann 1888

Marjem Liebling 1883

Markus Liebling 1884

Olga Liebstoeckl 1877

Alice Lissner 1902

Judith Lobmann 1941

Lola Lobmann 1907

Osias Lobmann 1895

Anna Loebl 1895

Amalie Loebls 1863

Maria Etelka Loescher 1897

Margarete Loew 1894

Vera Loew 1901

Ernestine Loewi 1866

Hermann Loewinger 1875

Friedrich Loewy 1906

Grete Loewy 1920

Josefine Loewy 1878

Klara Loewy 1923

Malvine Loewy 1887

Moritz Loewy 1918

Oskar Loewy 1894

Jakob Loewy 1912

Josef Lottner 1885

Riva Lottnere 1897
Golda Luster 1892
Josefa Lustgarten 1865
Eleonore Lustig 1899
Flora Lustig 1888
Theodora Lustig 1924
Friedrich Mahler 1878
Else Maisels 1868
Margarethe Malek 1899
Karoline Maly 1874
Regina Mandl 1877
Rebekka Mannheimer 1871
Johanna Mansky 1892
Elsa Manswirth 1912
Leonore Manzoni 1905
Henriette Manzoni-Menkes 1867
Richard Ludwig Marcus 1895
Rosa Marcus 1895
Gerda Margulies 1874
Lilly Margulies 1908
Herta Maurer 1912
Leopoldine Maurer 1911
Munisch Mautner 1894
Camilla Mayer 1873
Gerda Mayer 1918
Gerdamaria Mayer 1938
Lotte Mayer 1869
Leonore May-May 1869
Sofie Mebus 1892
Karoline Meiner 1887
Eugenie Meinhard 1874
Alfred Meissner 1878
Ida Meissner 1876
Marie Menninger 1880
Ignaz Messinger 1874
Paul Meth 1877
Wilhelmine Michel 1865
Maria Mikoletzky 1882
Amalie Mimeles 1871
Mathilde Mitterlechner 1881
Hermann Moranz 1876

Karoline Morawitz 1876
Jakob Morgenstern 1860
Rosa Morgenstern 1875
Eugenie Moser 1869
Josefine Mucha 1889
Albert Mueller 1870
Helene Mueller 1894
Ludwig Mueller 1876*
Olga Mueller 1878
Dr. Benjamin Murmelstein 1905
Margarethe Murmelstein 1904
Wolf Murmelstein 1936
Rosa Nachmias 1891
Friederike Nagler 1899
Emil Nettel 1878
Hermine Neubauer 1865
Maria Neubrunn 1892
Alfred Neufeld 1920
Johanna Neufeld 1869
Josefine Neufeld 1927
Pauline Neufeld 1892
Salo Neufeld 1885
Berta Neugebauer 1871
Adele Nemez 1889
Dr. Heinrich Neuhaus 1891
Herbert Neuhaus 1923
Wanda Neuhaus 1892
Aloisia Neumann 1887
Chajim Neumann 1866
Hans Neumann 1936
Hencie Neumann 1892
Jenny Neumann 1875
Klara Neumann 1892
Luise Neumann 1873
Markus Neumann 1889
Michael Neumann 1874
Minna Neumann 1885
Rosa Neumann 1874
Sara Neumann 1874
Siegfried Neumann 1872
Agnes Neuner 1867

Margarete Nicklas 1877

Berta Nussbaum 1868

Gustav Obergriever 1885

Oskar Oczeret 1896

Rosa Oczeret 1911

Marianne Offer 1886

Mathilde Offer 1919

Henriette Opad 1893

Dr. Amalie Oppenheim 1878

Regine Oppenheim 1868

Josef Orancz 1885

Berthold Ordner 1889

Olga Ordner 1887

Franz Orenstein 1883

Berta Orienter 1872

Marguerite Orienter 1908

Feiwel Ornstein 1866

Josefine Otto 1876

Klara Padawer 1863

Johanna Parloy 1904

Hilda Parnes 1899

Eleonore Parolla 1869

Ernestine Patak 1871

Marie Pauk 1863

Lea Pekel 1876

Berta Penizek 1914

Anna Perker 1874

Josefine Petersilka 1875

Valerie Peyerl 1886

Rosa Pfeffer 1878

Hilda Pfeiffer 1881

Dr. Robert Pfeiffer 1885

Valerie Pfeiffer 1879

Berta Pick 1876

Emma Pick 1900

Irma Pick 1877

Leopold Pick 1874

Dr. Maximilian Pick 1875

Chajim Pipper 1874

Ida Pisk 1887

Friedrich Pistol 1871

Julie Pitra 1914

Sofie Platschek 1866

Julius Pless 1866

Ludwig Pless 1885

Regine Pless 1871

Sabine Pless 1886

Irma Plohn 1858

Ilona Pohl 1872

Chaje Pohorilles 1885

Josef Pohorilles 1872

Moritz Pokorny 1867

Ida Polatschek 1872

Rosalie Poleiner 1869

Hugo Politzer 1876

Angelo Pollak 1931

Arnold Pollak 1877

Elisabeth Pollak 1936

Ester Pollak 1867

Flora Pollak 1875

Harald Pollak 1936

Helga Pollak 1929

Hertha Pollak 1905

Irma Pollak 1907

Johanna Pollak 1905

Marianne Pollak 1879

Marie Pollak 1905

Resi Pompan 1866

Abraham Popper 1889

Adolf Popper 1874

Berta Popper 1893

Gisela Popper 1879

Gustav Porges 1892

Jeanette Porges 1900

Leontine Porges 1872

Julie Pragan 1884

Max Pragan 1874

Ida Praska 1899

Paula Presinger 1884

Johanna Priester 1874

Robert Prochnik 1915

Rosa Prowisor 1913

Rosa Radda 1873

Martha Raditz 1874

Julius Ranzenhofer 1873

Anna Maria Rappaport 1888

Kamilla Rattinger 1893

Margit Raubitschek 1889

Malvine Reichel 1874

Auguste Reil 1881

Regine Reininger 1875

Rifka Reininger 1903

Rosa Reisch 1872

Josefine Reismann 1903

Adele Reiss 1869

Franziska Reiss 1874

Isidor Reiss 1885

Regine Reiss 1874

Berta Reisz 1868

Elise Reisz 1916

Adele Revesz 1900

Emma Richter 1873

Philippine Richter 1875

Kamilla Richter 1867

Sofie Ricker 1877

Erna Riegler 1925

Walter Riegler 1923

Rachel Riesch 1864

Helene Rind 1905

Sybille Ringel 1910

Aron Rissover 1874

Nadja Rissover 1876

Elly Ritscher-Brod 1912

Margit Ritter 1903

Malvine Robert 1883

Rudolf Robert 1881

Sigismund Rochmis 1873

Leontine Rold 1874

Norbert Rosegg 1868

· Kitti Rosen 1930

Amalie Rosenbaum 1891

Brigitte Rosenbaum 1933

Frieda Rosenblatt 1865

Golde Rosenstock 1874

Fanny Rosenthal 1870

Heinrich Rosenzweig 1871

Therese Rosenzweig 1877

Martha Roth 1872

Berta Rothberg 1897

Hermine Rotter 1864

Edith Rubenkes 1920

Eski Rubin 1890

Karl Rubinstein 1865

Rosa Rubinstein 1879

Berisch Rudel 1869

Emma Rudoll 1874

Viktor Rudolph 1872

Malvine Ruml 1874

Berta Rybaczewsky 1871

Frieda Sachs 1887

Sara Salner 1869

Cornelia Salzer 1881

Gisela Salzer 1884

Simon Salzer 1881

Emma Salvotti 1890

Sophie Sandler 1870

Karl Sattler 1871

Gisela Sauerquell 1903

Prof. Dr. Alfred Saxl 1877

Camilla Saxl 1884

Friedrich Saxl 1874

Hedwig Saxl 1898

Ida Saxl 1868

Josefine Sborowitz 1866

Alois Schafer 1878

Charlotte Schafer 1868

Leonore Schafer 1909

Margarete Schafranek 1896

Max Schafranek 1894

Klara Schaller 1880

Dr. David Schapira 1879

Tina Schapira 1899

Margarete Schechter 1906

Karl Scheer 1876

Leonore Scheer 1882

Helene Scheidl 1886

Dr. Lieber Scheiner 1888

Regina Scheiner 1894

Jenny Scheyer-Tiring 1877

Hermine Schick 1866

David Schild 1871

Debora Schiller 1867

Stefanie Schiller 1902

Berta Schindler 1874

Grete Schindler 1886

Fanny Schlaefrig 1886

Friedrich Schlaefrig 1875

Brane Schmerer 1874

Jakob Schmerer 1872

Caecilie Schmid 1869

Berta Schmidberger 1938

Friederike Schmidberger 1904

Johann Schmidberger 1935

Malvine Schnabel 1893

Malka Schneid 1896

Leonore Schneider 1870

Sigmund Schneider 1871

Sofie Schneider 1887

Berta Schnur 1877

Karl Schnur 1876

Rosa Schoeberl 1872

Sofie Schoen 1868

Hildegard Schoergenhummer 1907

Grete Schorr 1922

Marianne Schossberger 1903

Berta Schotten 1875

Heinrich Schotten 1871

Berta Schrage 1877

Salomon Schrage 1877

Feige Schramek 1874

Louis Schramek 1871

Else Schreiber 1880

Jakob Schreiber 1888

Sabine Schreiber 1933

Sabine Schreiber 1901

Antonie Schreiber-Braver 1901

Mina Schulhof 1871

Henriette Schustermann 1904

Kamilla Schwach 1932

Anna Schwarcz 1919

Sari Schwarcz 1924

Anny Schwarz 1936

Berta Schwarz 1927

Erwin Schwarz 1923

Georg Schwarz 1938

Grete Schwarz 1930

Heinrich Schwarz 1893

Hilde Schwarz 1925

Irma Schwarz 1874

Johanna Schwarz 1894

Julius Schwarz 1871

Kurt Schwarz 1937

Laura Schwarz 1877

Lilly Schwarz 1904

Maria Schwarz 1934

Mathan Schwarz 1874

Rosa Schwarz 1884

Wilhelm Schwarz 1931

Hugo Schwed 1878

Mathilde Schwed 1885

Chaskel Segel 1898

Ester Segel 1887

Schulim Segel 1922

Gisela Seibold 8191

Anny Seidl 1921

Henriette Seidl 1883

Dan Seidler 1940

Davbid Seidler 1868

Grete Seidler 1902

Theodor Seidler 1895

Anna Seinfeld 1868

Johanna Selzer 1868

Caecilie Siebenschein 1866

Ida Siebenschein 1877

Marie Siegelbaum 1875

Fortunie Siersch 1892

Edith Sigmund 1860
Ester Silber 1877
Johanna Silberknopf 1867
Adele Singer 1880
Josefine Singer 1902
Judith Singer 1940
Klara Singer 1905
Louise Singer 1872
Maximilian Singer 1877
Martha Sloup 1911
Ignatz Sobotka 1872
Rudolfine Sobotka 1876
Rosa Soffer 1867
Anna Sommer 1887
Emil Sommer 1869
Dr. Emil Sonnenfeld 1873
Katharina Sonnenreich 1863
Feile Sonnenschein 1939
Berta Spaniermann 1876
Alice Spatz 1922
Bernhard Specht 1876
Risa Specht 1875
Rosa Spennadel 1873
Malke Sperber 1874
Jona Jakob Spiegel 1941
Olga Spiegler 1876
Hugo Spieler 1885
Jenny Spieler 1885
Israel Spielmann 1871
Louis Spielmann 1882
Lilly Spielman-Boehmer 1904
Alois Spira 1880
Rosa Spira 1886
Berta Spitz-Stellich 1874
Charlotte Spitz 1876
Adolf Spitzer 1870
Adrienne Spitzer 1875
Egon Spitzer 1915
Dr. Ernst Georg Spitzer 1877
Gisela Spitzer 1882
Gisela Spitzer 1873

Helene Spitzer 1869
Herbert Spitzer 1931
Leo Spitzer 1903
Marie Spitzer 1909
Siegfried Spitzer 1880
Valerie Spitzer 1938
Pauline Sprechmann 1911
Moritz Spronz 1887
Sari Spronz 1885
Emilie Stadler 1868
Robert Staerk 1870
Salomon Stanger 1889
Marie Stasser 1868
Julius Stecher 1870
Eugenie Steiger 1865
Emilie Stein 1866
Jetti Stein 1873
Robert Stein 1868
Camilla Steinbrueck 1873
Elfriede Steiner 1924
Johann Steiner 1877
Katharina Steiner 1869
Paul Steiner 1895
Rosa Steiner 1892
Emma Steinhardt 1868
Berta Stengel 1870
Mathilde Stermann 1882
Berta Stern 1875
Ernst Stern 1875
Marie Stern 1876
Maximilian Stern 1900
Mina Stern 1904
Therese Steppat 1879
Josef Stiassnie 1928
Rudolf Stiassnie 1885
Ida Stier 1897*
Ernst Stimmer 1906
Dr. Georg Stoehr 1871
Caecilie Stoessel 1878
Hedwig Stoessel 1896
Rachel Storch 1878

Caecilie Coelestine Storper 1905
Leopoldine Storper 1926
Adele Strach 1872
Regine Strakosch 1871
Felix Stransky 1871
Isabella Strassmann-Alexander 1904
Erich Strauss 1932
Leopold Strauss 1871
Leopoldine Strauss 1877
Lilly Strauss 1919
Flora Streicher 1872
Elisabeth Strohs 1878
Edith Stueckgold 1905
Stephanie Stumpf 1880
Bernhard Stux 1874
Kaethe Stux 1925
Paul Stux 1890
Stefanie Stux 1892
Gertrude Stwertka 1920
Regine Subak 1878
Erna Sucher 1912
Henny Sucher 1878
Srul Paul Sucher 1909
Louise Suschitzky 1872
Berthold Suschitzky 1871
Ida Suess 1924
Rosa Suess 1895
Salomon Suess 1894
Deszoe Sussmann 1895
Heinz Sussmann 1930
Lizzi Sussmann 1926
Samuel Sussmann 1902
Ludwig Szendroe 1874
Kaethe Szufel 1902
Flora Szymkowiak 1882
Antonie Tachau 1867
Norbert Taskier 1883
Mignon Taussig 1897
Paula Taussig 1874
Henriette Tausk 1864
Baruch Tenzer 1874

Gisela Tenzer 1887
Lina Thaussig 1878
Friedrich Thieben 1876
Berta Thiel 1876
Antonie Thomas 1889
Ernestine Tichy 1896
Kurt Tintner 1894
Frimel Tischler 1896
Hersch Tischler 1896
Grete Toch 1890
Dr. Siegfried Toch 1884
Eleonore Tomberg 1899
Margarete Trawersa 1883
Selma Treibel 1878
Hilde Treibel-Gelbard 1904
Johanna Tretschik 1874
Debora Tritt 1862
Fanny Tritt 1909
Jakob Tropp 1877
Sure Tropp 1879
Sigmund Tuerk 1879
Regine Tutsch 1868
Ernestine Tyroler 1911
Fanny Tyroler 1889
Milan Tyroler 1885
Frida Ueberall 1892
Therese Uihely 1875
Melanie Ulrich 1868
Friederike Ulrik 1864
Therese Umansky 1876
Dr. Jetty Ungar 1893
Margot Ungar 1923
Berta Urz 1879
Hermine Vecsei 1868
Frida Verstaendig 1929
Franz Vogel 1898
Gertrude Vogel 1923
Rudolf Vogel 1864
Berta Vogl 1894
Toni Vogl 1865
Susanna Vorstein 1908

Hilda Wacha 1912
Rosa Wachtel 1925
Dorothea Wager 1895*
Berta Wagner 1878
Eugen Wagner 1875
Leontine Wagner 1890
Leopold Wagner 1877
Marie Waller 1868
Frida Walter 1878
Rosa Wanek 1869
Elsa Wasservogel 1899
Gerti Wasservogel 1932
Mathilde Wechsler 1868
David Weigl 1881
Kurt Weigl 1926
Therese Weigl 1895
Emma Weil 1899
Ernestine Weil 1856
Hanna Weil 1897
Dr. Kornelius Weil 1886
Kurt Weil 1937
Hermine Weinbaum 1866
Fanny Weiner 1881
Isak Weiner 1880
Rosa Weiner 1873
Sidonie Weiner-Kohn 1915
Luise Weinhengst 1873
Witte Weinreb 1870
Anna Weinstein 1865
Anna Weinstock 1879
Lotte Weinstock 1916
Oskar Weinstock 1878
Guste Weiser 1868
Anton Weiss 1907
Dr. Arthur Weiss 1875
Elsa Weiss 1875
Heinrich Weiss 1898
Josefine Weiss 1875
Julius Weiss 1886
Lina Weiss 1872*
Margarete Weiss 1893

Marie Weiss 1872
Mathilde Weiss 1881
Max Weiss 1874
Dr. Olga Weiss 1885
Rudolf Weiss 1922
Sali Weiss 1866
Sigmund Weiss 1881
Sofie Weiss 1924
Dr. Theodor Weiss 1870
Therese Weiss 1894
Johanna Weissmann 1865
Ida Weisz 1897
Franziska Weller 1896
Berta Welsch 1870
Chaim Welsch 1871
Helene Welsch 1878
Ella Wenger 1869
Martha Wenger 1902
Caecilie Wengraf 1877
Camilla Wengraf 1870
Eleonore Wenzel 1891
Ernestine Wertheimer 1875
Grete Wertheimer 1909
Elizabeth Wessely 1899
Ester Wessely 1861
Pauline Wessely 1871
Zerline Wessely 1898
Regine Wiener 1878
Gisela Wiese 1873
Dr. Hermann Wiesenberg 1873
Rosa Wiesenberg 1870
Malvine Wilhelm 1873
Malvine Wilhelm 1912
Schlome Wilgott 1875
Dr. Konrad Wilheim 1889
Elsa Winkler 1874
Herman Winkler 1867
Dr. Hugo Winkler 1878
Jakob Winkler 1880
Leopold Winkler 1855
Hermine Winter 1864

Jakob Winter 1875*
Sofie Winter 1867
Hermine Winternitz 1867
Maria Wohlmuth 1867
Arnold Wolf 1872
Franziska Wolf 1902
Gerhard Wolf 1937
Gertrude Wolf 1922
Rosalie Wolf 1876
Stella Wolf 1878
Caecilie Wottitz 1863
Emanuel Wurm 1893
Chane Zahler 1940
Elfriede Zahler 1936

Irma Zboril 1886
Auguste Zdekauer 1876
Ernestine Zeichner 1897
Selig Zeichner 1893
Pepina Zelenka 1870
Klara Zelinsky 1897
Moses Zimmer 1889
Erna Zimmermann 1871
Camilla Zrust 1875
Ida Zucker 1873
Paula Zuckerbaecker 1894
Margit Zupnik 1937
Sali Zupnik 1912
Olga Zweig 1885

AUSCHWITZ

July 17, 1942	995	People
1943	121	
1944	152	
Unrecorded (approximately)	200	
	1,468	
Returned*	109	
Perished	1,359	

List of Survivors:

Heinrich Beer
Theodor Brod 1873
Regina Chum 1923
Ilse Chybik 1931
Karl Chybik 1896
Hermine Deiches 1922
Max Erben
Marianne Feuerstein
Hermine Fiala 1899
Jakob Finkelstein 1896
Feige Fleming 1910
Friedrich Flussmann 1902
Ernest Fuchs 1912
Emil Gemeiner 1911

Adolf Gerstl 1926
Isidor Gingold 1899
Kurt Hacker 1920
Egon Hamburger 1923
Georg Heller 1909
Hans Heller 1904
Karl Heller 1910
Josef Herzler 1893
Otto Himmler 1877
Siegmund Hirsch 1877
Karl Hochwald 1903
Walter Immergut 1912
Ernst Jancu 1905
Rudolf Jellinek 1905

*Some survivors may have been in other camps earlier.

Rudolf Jellinek 1929
Leopold Kain 1909
Isak Kanner 1920
Elise Kertesz 1910
Gerda Kertesz 1908
Fritz Klinger 1913
Jenny Koenigsberg 1923
Mathilde Kohn 1924
Robert Kohn 1918
Franz Kollin 1902
Ruth Korkus 1923
Gertrud Kraus
Margarethe Krecny 1911
Dr. Gustav Kreisler 1886
Wilhelm Krell 1902
Max Lanes 1907
Otto Lazner 1893
Kurt Lendl 1924
Fritz Loewy 1897
Anna Mandl 1898
Franz Mandl 1911
Jakob Margulies 1900
Friedrich Mindlich 1924
Martha Moltkau 1891
Ernestine Musil 1921
Erich Nadler 1916
Wilhelm Nuernberg 1920
Josef Obseka 1916
Stella Paneth 1899
Else Pater 1905
Hermann Pflazner 1901
Natalie Poll 1926
Erwin Pollitzer 1918
Margarethe Putz 1902
Lotte Riegelhaupt 1920
Paul Roman 1908
Erna Rosenbach 1907
Trude Rosenzweig 1920
Erika Rudolf 1921
Victor Rueff 1899
Jakob Rumstein 1922

Alfons Sass 1895
Siegfried Schechter 1925
Fini Scheindl 1930
Ernst Schenker 1912
Otto Schick 1921
Lory Schiffnagel 1921
Johanna Schuhmacher 1913
Alexander Schwarz 1878
Dezoe Schwarz 1897
Ernst Schwehla 1925
Alice Silberstein 1899
Arthur Singer 1897
Leonore Skokan 1914
Katharina Spiegel 1912
Malwine Spitaler 1914
Paul Spitz 1909
Joseph Spitzer 1904
Martha Steiner 1925
Leopold Stern 1892
Anna Sussmann 1909
Heinrich Sussmann 1904
Ernst Toch 1912
Leopold Tocker 1897
Max Ullmann 1888
Erna Vogelfaenger 1927
Adolf Volk 1923
Alfred Wachsberg 1913
Regine Wallinger 1923
Hermann Weber 1897
Rudolf Weiner 1905
David Weintraub 1911
Ernst Weiss 1908
Ignatz Weiss 1882
Johanna Weiss 1917
Ernst Wexberg 1915
Hildegard Wilczek 1911
August Wilhelm 1905
Heinrich Wohlmuth 1921
Dr. Otto Wolken 1903
Irene Zausner 1907

MAUTHAUSEN

Approximate total of small transports between 1940–1944   200   People

Returned   14

Perished   186

List of Survivors:

Kalman Gertler 1909	Fritz Muenster 1891
Leopold Hirsch 1898	Ernst Schiller 1912
Rosa Jellinek 1909	Arthur Schneier 1930
Wilhelm Klinger 1893	Richard Wachsler 1902
Hans Kurzweil 1908	Ignaz Wachtel 1924
Aba Lewit 1923	Rosa Zelenka 1909
Mathilde Lewit 1924	Bertha Ziegler 1926

BERGEN BELSEN

Approximate total of small transports from
    Vienna during 1943, 1944   100   People

Returned   5

Perished   95

List of Survivors:

Gertrude Adler

Alfred Hirschhorn 1903

Gertrude Janeba 1910

Barbara Kohn 1899

Gertrude Kornitzer 1910

RAVENSBRUECK

Approximate total of small transports from
    Vienna during 1942, 1943, 1944   100   Women

Returned   10

Perished   90

List of Survivors:

Hedwig Chebat	Elizabeth Koelnberger 1926
Sara Gabay 1905	Judith Rusch 1921
Sultana Gabay 1919	Maria Scheu 1907
Eva Gutfreund 1926	Anna Srp 1917
Edith Heinrich 1913	Edith Wexberg 1919

FLOSSENBURG

Approximate total of small transports from
   Vienna during 1939, 1940, 1941, 1942, 1943, 1944   50   People

Returned	2
Perished	48

List of Survivors:

Siegmund Goldwasser 1920
Moritz Schweigler 1899

SACHSENHAUSEN

Vienna between 1939 and 1944	50	People
Perished	50	

TOTALS

Number of Survivors and Victims by Place

Place	Survivors	Victims
Dachau and Buchenwald	71	2,937
Nisko	71	1,315
Opole via Pulawy	15	1,992
Kielce	9	994
Modliborzyce	4	996
Lagow-Opatow	4	997
Lodz (Litzmannstadt)	18	4,977
Kovno	—	995
Riga	103	4,132
Minsk	9	9,477
Deathcamps in Poland via Izbica and Wlodowa (Belzec, Sobibor, Treblinka)	—	6,094
Theresienstadt	1,573	13,778
Auschwitz	109	1,359
Mauthausen	14	186
Bergen Belsen	5	95
Ravensbrueck	10	90
Flossenburg	2	48

Sachsenhausen	—	50
Insane Asylums		400
	2,017	50,912

Approximate Number of Austrian Jews Who Were Caught in Neighboring Countries to Where They Had Fled

Baltic States	600
Belgium and Luxemburg	800
France	3,200
Greece	50
Italy	500
Yugoslavia	1,700
Holland	700
Poland	2,000
Czechoslovakia	3,500
Romania	1,000
Hungary	3,000
	17,050

Notes

1. The University's Hall of Fame is described in Bernard Postal and Samuel H. Abramson, *The Traveler's Guide to Jewish Landmarks of Europe*, New York, Fleet Press Corporation, 1971, p. 12.

2. The 1475 trial for the murder of the boy Simon of Trient, when Tyrolean Jews were accused of killing the boy and then using his blood for baking matzo, the unleavened bread Jews eat at Passover.

3. Walter Grab, *Der Deutsche Weg der Judenemanzipation 1789–1933*, Munich, Piper 1991, p. 15.

4. Called "*Stadt Tempel*," it was designed in Biedermeier style by the architect Joseph Kornhaeusel and symbolized a compromise between the orthodox and the modern, reform-minded Jews.

5. Friedrich Heer, *Oesterreich: Damals, Gestern, Heute*, Vienna, Oesterreichischer Bundesverlag, 1962, p. 14.

6. Grab, *Der Deutsche Weg der Judenemanzipation 1789–1933*, p. 27.

7. "Table of Jewish Population in Vienna, 1787–1910," assembled in Marsha Rozenblit's *The Jews of Vienna, 1867–1914* Albany, State University of New York Press, 1983, pp. 17, 18.

8. A fictional account of a provincial Vienna without its Jews, written as a satire in 1922 and later made into a film.

9. I interviewed Max Temel at his home in Florida in February 1992. The charming old gentleman told me how the Nazis, once they came to power, harassed his aged parents. He was able to get them out of Austria in the fall of 1938.

10. Guenter Lewy, *The Catholic Church and Nazi Germany*, New York, McGraw Hill, 1964, pp. 212–15. Lewy also writes that the Vatican was not very

happy about Innitzer's "servile attitude" and that he was summoned to Rome, where he signed a declaration that the church per se did not approve of acts incompatible with the laws of God. By then, however, it was too late. The Nazis in Austria made good use of the bishop's indiscretion.

11. *Die Erste Woche* describes the excesses against Jews committed in Vienna in that first week after the *Anschluss*, between March 11–19, 1938.

12. In my talks with Siegmund and Martin Wolfzahn over a period of several years, I realized that they wanted to be heroes like their father, who had fallen on the field of honor in the Great War.

13. Wenn der Tag erwacht,
Eh-die Sonne lacht,
Die Kolonnen zieh'n,
Zu des Tages Mueh'n,
Hinein in den grauenden Morgen.
Und der Wald ist schwarz
Und der Himmel ist rot
Und wir tragen im Brotsack
Ein Stueckchen Brot
Und im Herzen, im Herzen die Sorgen.

Oh, Buchenwald, ich kann dich night vergessen
Weil du mein Schicksal bist.
Wer dich verlaesst, der kann es erst ermessen
Wie wundervoll die Freiheit ist.
Oh, Buchenwald, wir jammern nicht und klagen
Und was auch uns're Zukunft sei,
Wir wollen trotzdem "ja" zum Leben sagen
Denn einmal kommt der Tag, da sind wir frei!

[As the day starts, long before the sun rises,
the columns leave for the day's hard work
marching into the greying morning.
And the forest is black, and the sky is red,
and we carry a small piece of bread in our satchels,
and in our hearts we carry worries.

Oh, Buchenwald, I cannot forget you, because you are my fate.
Those who leave you can first realize how wonderful freedom is.
Oh, Buchenwald, we do not cry nor do we complain
Whatever the future may hold.
We shall say "yes" to life despite everything,
for the day will come when we are free.]

14. Called in July 1938 at the initiative of President Roosevelt, the conference met at Evian, Switzerland, to seek a coordinated international solution to the

refugee problem. Other than lengthy memoranda and the formation of the ineffectual IGCR (Inter-Governmental Committee on Refugees), it proved to be a fruitless endeavor.

15. *A Tale of Two Cities*, first published in Great Britain in 1859, re-issued by Octopus Books, Ltd., London, 1981.

16. Based on the description given to me in several interviews with Abraham Goldmann and Moses Tellmann, and compared with Frank Brandenburg's interview (Ib Melchior and Frank Brandenburg, *Quest: Searching for Germany's Past*, Novato, California, Presidio, 1990, pp. 82, 214–23, 240, 319), the official must have been Professor Hermann Giesler himself. He was one of Hitler's favorite architect-engineers and was made the head of *Organization Todt* in Russia-North after Dr. Fritz Todt had died in a plane crash in 1942. Giesler had taken on the responsibility of constructing military roads, to be accomplished by slave labor. He was sentenced to life in 1948, but was released four years later and died of old age a free man in the 1980s.

17. As a youngster, Alfred Slawik ran around with a group of like-minded thugs in the seventeenth and sixteenth districts of Vienna (Hernals and Ottakring), and was known as a juvenile delinquent, called "Schlurf." It was he who presided over the destruction of my grandparents' restaurant on November 10, 1938, and he was later known as one of Eichmann's men, described in detail by Hans Safrian in *Die Eichmann Maenner*, Vienna, Europaverlag, 1993. Alfred clearly recognized my father, but decided to be civil to him.

18. Heinz Wiesner (former name Wisotzki) was tried in Duesseldorf in 1981 and again in 1984. Up until then he had lived a good life, but was arrested when he applied for an increase in his pension, based on his wartime job!

19. Karl Loewenstein, *Minsk: Im Lager der Deutschen Juden*, Bonn, Bundeszentrale fuer Heimatdienst, 1961, p. 28. In this description of the Minsk ghetto, Loewenstein reports that Ilse's escape had terrible consequences for her co-workers at the Minsk skyscraper and for the people with whom she lived in the ghetto, as well as for some distant family members of hers. All of them were executed two weeks after her escape, when it became clear that she would not be caught.

20. *Akton Reinhard* was named for Reinhard Heydrich, head of the Security Police and the Security Service (*Sicherheits Dienst*), and one of the leading figures in the destruction of the Jewish people.

21. *Karteikarten* were separate cards made up for each individual listed as having been deported, based on the actual transport lists. Returnees are marked with a red sign. Unfortunately, the lists were incomplete since Jews were added at the last minute and not recorded. At the Theresienstadt ghetto, however, the exact number of arrivals was duly registered.

22. Gertrude Schneider, *The Unfinished Road: Jewish Survivors of Latvia Look Back*, New York: Praeger, 1991, consists of a collection of vignettes written by survivors, researched and edited by me. *The Unfinished Road* is the third book in a trilogy.

23. Gerald Reitlinger, *The Final Solution*, New York, Thomas Yoseloff, 1968, p. 485. Reitlinger calls the conditions under which those Hungarian Jews labored "atrocious neglect."

24. Gertrude Schneider, *Muted Voices: Jewish Survivors of Latvia Remember*, New York, Philosophical Library, 1987, second book in a trilogy and nominated for the Jewish Book Award of 1988.

25. Sag beim Abschied
     Leise Servus
     Nicht Lebwohl
     Und nicht Adieu
     Solche Worte
     Tun nur weh.
     Doch das kleine
     Woertchen Servus
     Ist ein lieber, letzter Gruss
     Wenn man Abschied nehmen muss.
     S'gibt jahraus, jahrein,
     An neuen Wein
     Und Neue Liebelei'n.
     Sag beim Abschied
     Leise Servus
     Denn gibts auch kein Wiederseh'n
     Einmal war es doch schoen.

     [When you part, say "Servus,"
     Not farewell and not Adieu
     Words like that only hurt.
     But the little word "Servus"
     is a dear, last greeting
     if you have to part from one another.
     Every year, there's a new wine
     and there are new loves.
     When you part, say "Servus,"
     for even if you never see each other again
     Once upon a time it was beautiful.]

Sag beim Abschied music by Johann Strauss, arranged by Peter Kreuder for the film *Burgtheater* in 1935. Lyrics by J. F. Lengsfelder, a Jew, who asked his friend Harry Hilm to say it was he who wrote the words, since the UFA would not accept lyrics written by a Jew in 1935. (With special thanks to the Austrian Cultural Institute in New York for their help and courtesy.)

26. Simon Wiesenthal, The Murderers Among Us, New York: McGraw Hill, 1967, p. 188. Wiesenthal felt that the Germans assigned Austrians to command as well as to lesser positions in the camps located in all the former crown lands,

owing to the fact that they may have understood the mentality of the populace better than real Germans. This explanation may be as good as any other one.

27. "Happy is he who forgets what cannot be changed." From the first act of *Die Fledermaus*, an operetta by Johann Strauss. The song was my father's favorite. In some ways, he lived by its motto.

Glossary

SS RANKS WITH ARMY EQUIVALENTS

Brigadefuehrer	Major General
Gruppenfuehrer	Lieutenant General
Hauptscharfuehrer	Master Sergeant
Hauptsturmfuehrer	Captain
Oberfuehrer	Brigadier General
Obergruppenfuehrer	General
Oberscharfuehrer	Sergeant First Class
Oberstgruppenfuehrer	no equivalent
Obersturmbannfuehrer	Lieutenant Colonel
Obersturmfuehrer	First Lieutenant
Reichsfuehrer SS	General of the Army, Commander-in-Chief
Rottenfuehrer	Corporal
Scharfuehrer	Staff Sergeant
SS Mann	Private
SS Sturm Mann	Private First Class
Standartenfuehrer	Colonel
Sturmbannfuehrer	Major
Sturmscharfuehrer	Sergeant Major
Unterscharfuehrer	Sergeant
Untersturmfuehrer	Second Lieutenant

PLACES FREQUENTLY MENTIONED

Kultusgemeinde   full name: Israelitische Kultusgemeinde Wien, responsi-
                     ble for all record keeping of its Jewish members, from
                     birth to grave.

Palaestina Amt   Palestine Bureau, Palamt (abbreviation). Its main purpose
                     was to facilitate emigation to Palestine, it also adminis-
                     tered farms in Austria where young people prepared
                     themselves for life in Palestine. It also served as a school
                     for Hebrew and Jewish history; officially until late sum-
                     mer 1941, unofficially until early spring 1942.

Piper Heim   Named for its director, Israel Piper, it started out as a
                     day-care center for after-school activities in the twentieth
                     district. Early 1940 it moved to the second district, where
                     it also served as an auxiliary school in addition to func-
                     tioning as a day care center.

TERMS FREQUENTLY MENTIONED

Aufseherin   female SS guard in charge of women in concentration
                     camps

Einsatzgruppe   Special Task Force. Created by Heydrich, there were 4
                     such groups, A, B, C, and D.

Einsatzkommando   Each Einsatzgruppe had several Einsatzkommandos,
                     which dealt with localities.

Gauleiter   Section Leader, Chief

Gestapo   *Ge*heime *Sta*ats *Po*lizei, Secret State Police

Hoeherer SS und   Higher SS and Police Leader
  Polizei Fuehrer

Kapo   Foreman. Mainly a foreman of a work detail in the camps
                     and in some ghettos.

NSDAP   National Sozialistische Deutsche Arbeiter Partei (Na-
                     tional Socialist German Workers' Party)

Ordner   Officials of the Kultusgemeinde in Vienna, who were
                     used mainly to inform Jews about their forthcoming de-
                     portation; they were also working at the schools serving
                     as collection points.

Sicherheitsdienst, SD Security Service. One component was the Gestapo, an-
                       other the Secret Police.

Sonderkommando	1. auxiliary special groups attached to Einsatzkommandos for killing Jews
	2. within the crematoria, a special task force of Jews working to burn the corpses they removed from the gas chambers
U-Boat	1. Untersee Boot / submarine vessel
	2. Jewish person in hiding within a city, usually hidden by friends
Wehrmacht	Armed Forces, now called the Bundeswehr

Bibliography

Abzug, Robert H. *Inside the Vicious Heart*. New York: Oxford University Press, 1985.

Adelsberger, Lucie. *Auschwitz: Ein Tatsachenbericht*. Berlin: Deutsche Verlagsanstalt, 1956.

Adler, Jacques. *The Jews of Paris and the Final Solution: Communal Responses and Internal Conflicts, 1940–1944*. New York: Oxford University Press, 1987.

Anderl, Gabriele and Walter Manoschek. *Gescheiterte Flucht: Der Juedische "Kladovo Transport" auf dem Weg nach Palaestina, 1939–1942*. Vienna: Verlag fuer Gesellschaftskritik, 1993.

Andics, Hellmut. *Die Juden in Wien*. Munich and Lucerne: Verlag C. J. Bucher, 1988.

Arad, Yitzhak, ed. *The Pictorial History of the Holocaust*. New York: Macmillan Publishing Company, 1990.

Aueracker, Heinrich. *Ein Volk—Ein Reich—Ein Fuehrer*. Munich: Deutsche Staatsdruckerei, 1938.

Bailer, Brigitte. *Wiedergutmachung Kein Thema: Oesterreich und die Opfer des Nationalsozialismus*. Vienna: Loecker Verlag, 1993.

Beller, Steven. *Vienna and the Jews 1867–1938: A Cultural History*. New York: Cambridge University Press, 1989.

Benz, Wolfgang, ed. *Dimension des Voelkermords: Die Zahl der Juedischen Opfer des Nationalsozialismus*. Munich: R. Oldenbourg Verlag, 1991.

Bettauer, Hugo. *Die Stadt Ohne Juden: Ein Roman von Uebermorgen*. Vienna: Gloriette Verlag, 1922.

Bettelheim, Bruno. "Individual and Mass Behavior in Extreme Situations." *Journal of Abnormal and Social Psychology* 38, 1943: 417–52.

Botz, Gerhard. *Nationalsozialismus in Wien*. Buchloe: Verlag Obermayer, 1988.

Browning, Christopher R. *Ordinary Men*. New York: HarperCollins, 1992.

Chladkova, Ludmila. *The Terezin Ghetto*. Prague: Publishing House Naše Vojsko, 1991.

Clare, George. *Last Waltz in Vienna*. New York, Chicago, San Francisco: Holt, Rinehart & Winston, 1980.

Cowles, Virginia. *The Rothschilds: A Family of Fortune*. New York: Alfred A. Knopf, 1973.

Crankshaw, Edward. *Gestapo*. New York: Pyramid Books, 1957.

Czech, Danuta. *Hefte von Auschwitz*. Poland: Wydawnictwo Panstwowego Muzeum w Oswiecemu, 1959–1964.

"Der Gelbe Stern in Oesterreich: Katalog und Einfuehrung zu einer Dokumentation." *Studia Judaica Austriaca* 5, Eisenstadt: Roetzer, 1977.

Dickens, Charles. *A Tale of Two Cities* (first published in Great Britain, 1859). London: Octopus Books, Ltd., 1981.

Dobroszycki, Lucjan. "Wiener Juden im Ghetto Lodz." *Die Gemeinde*. Vienna, 1965.

Dokumenty i Materialy. 3 vols. Warsaw, Lodz, and Krakow: The Central Jewish Historical Commission, 1946.

Donat, Alexander. *The Holocaust Kingdom*. New York, Chicago, San Francisco: Holt, Rinehart & Winston, 1963.

Donat, Alexander, ed. *The Death Camp Treblinka: A Documentary*. New York: Holocaust Library, 1979.

Earl, Maureen. *Boat of Stone*. New York: Permanent Press, 1993.

Eisenberg, Azriel. *Witness to the Holocaust*. New York: The Pilgrim Press, 1981.

Elon, Amos. "Report from Vienna." *New Yorker* 67, no. 12 (May 13, 1991): 92–102.

Fein, Erich and Karl Flanner. *Rot-Weiss-Rot in Buchenwald*. Vienna, Zurich: Europaverlag, 1987.

Fleming, Gerald. *Hitler und die Endloesung*. Wiesbaden, Munich: Limes Verlag, 1982.

Forsythe, Frederick. *The Odessa File*. New York: Viking, 1972.

Fraenkel, Josef, ed. *The Jews of Austria: Essays on Their Life, History, and Destruction*. London: Valentine, Mitchell, 1967.

Gai, David. "Liebe im Ghetto." *Neue Zeit* (Maerz 1989). Frankfurt am Main.

Gerassimow, Jossif. *The Escape*. Belorussia: People's Publishing House, 1991.

Gesellschaft fuer Christlich-Juedische Zusammenarbeit. *Die dem Gewissen Gehorchten*. Cologne: Druckerei Wienand, 1969.

Gilbert, Martin. *Atlas of the Holocaust*. London: Rainbird Publishing Group, 1982.

Gottschalk, Gerda. *Der Letzte Weg*. Constance: Suedverlag, 1991.

Grab, Walter. *Der Deutsche Weg der Judenemanzipation 1789–1933*. Munich: Piper, 1991.

Haas. Gerda. *These I Do Remember*. Freeport, Maine: Cumberland, 1982.

Heer, Friedrich. *Gottes Erste Liebe: 2,000 Jahre Judentum und Christentum: Genesis des oesterreichischen Katholiken Adolf Hitler*. Munich: Bechtle, 1967.

Heer, Friedrich. *Oesterreich: Damals, Gestern, Heute*. Vienna: Oesterreichischer Bundesverlag, 1962.

Heimler, Eugene. *Concentration Camp (Night of the Mist)*. New York: Pyramid, 1961.

Hilberg, Raul. *The Destruction of European Jews*. Chicago: Quadrangle, 1967.

Hilberg, Raul. *Perpetrators, Victims, Bystanders: The Jewish Catastrophe 1933–1945*. New York: HarperCollins, 1992.

Hilsenrad, Helen. *Brown Was the Danube*. New York, London: Thomas Yoseloff, 1966.

Hoess, Rudolf. *Commandant of Auschwitz*. Translated from the German by Constantine FitzGibbon. New York: Popular Library, 1959.

Hoffmann, Heinrich. *Wie die Ostmark ihre Befreiung Erlebte*. Berlin: Staatsdruckerei, 1940.

Israelitische Kultusgemeinde Wien. *Trotz Allem . . . Aron Menczer 1917–1943*. Vienna, Cologne, Weimar: Boehlau Verlag, 1993.

Kaczkowski, Adam. *Auschwitz-Birkenau*. Krakow: Drukarnia Narodowa, 1970.

Karny, Miroslav. "Das Schicksal der Theresienstaedter Osttransporte im Sommer und Herbst 1942." *Judaica Bohemiae* 14, no. 2. Prague: Statni Zidovske Museum, 1988.

Kastner, Reszoe. *Der Kastnerbericht ueber Eichmanns Menschenhandel in Ungarn*. Munich: Kindler Verlag, 1961.

Katz, Josef. *One Who Came Back: The Diary of a Jewish Survivor*. Translated from the German by Hilda Reach. New York: Herzl Press, 1973.

Katznelson, Yitzhak. *Vittel Diary*. Translated from the Hebrew by Dr. Myer Cohen. Israel: Hakibbutz Hameuchad Publishing House, 1972.

Klarsfeld, Serge. *Memorial to the Jews Deported from France 1942–1944*. New York: Beate Klarsfeld Foundation, 1983.

Klee, Ernst and Willi Dressen, eds. *Gott Mit Uns: Der Deutsche Vernichtungskrieg im Osten*. Frankfurt am Main: S. Fischer, 1989.

Klee, Ernst, Willi Dressen, and Volker Riess. *Those Were the Days: The Holocaust as Seen by the Perpetrators and Bystanders*. Translated from the German by Deborah Burnstone. London: Hamish Hamilton, 1991.

Klein, Gerda Weissmann. *All But My Life*. New York: Hill and Wang, 1957.

Klueger, Ruth. *Weiter Leben: Eine Jugend*. Goettingen: Wallstein Verlag, 1992.

Knight, Robert. *Ich bin Dafuer, die Sache in die Laenge zu Ziehen*. Frankfurt: Athenaeum Verlag, 1988.

Kogon, Eugen. *The Theory and Practice of Hell*. Translated from the German by Heinz Norden. New York: Berkley, 1980.

Kohl, Paul. *Ich wunderemich dass ich noch lebe: Sowietische Augenzeugen berichten*. Guetersloh: Guetersloher Verlagshaus Gerd Mohn, 1990.

Kuehn, Guenter and Wolfgang Weber. *Staerker Als Die Woelfe*. Berlin: Militaerverlag der Deutschen Demokratischen Republik, 1976.

Lanzmann, Claude. *Shoa: An Oral History of the Holocaust*. (The Complete Text of the Film.) New York: Pantheon, 1985.

Lederer, Zdenek. *Ghetto Theresienstadt*. London: Edward Goldstone and Son, Ltd., 1953.

Lengyel, Olga. *Five Chimneys: The Story of Auschwitz*. New York: Howard Fertig, Inc., 1983.

Levi, Primo. *Survival in Auschwitz*. Translated from the Italian by Stuart Woolf. New York: Collier, 1961.

Lewy, Guenter. *The Catholic Church and Nazi Germany*. New York: McGraw Hill, 1964.

Liebmann, Hanne. "A Deportation to the West before Wannsee: A Page of History Rarely Told." *Together* 8, no. 1 (December 1993): 3–5.

Liga der Freunde des Judentums, eds. *Oesterreichisch-Juedisches Kulturleben*. Band I, Band II. Vienna: Literas-Universitaetsverlag, 1988.

Loewenstein, Karl. *Minsk: Im Lager der Deutschen Juden*. Bonn: Bundeszentrale fuer Heimatdienst, 1961.

Loewy, Hanno and Gerhard Schoenberner. *Unser Einziger Weg ist Arbeit: Das Ghetto in Lodz 1940–1944*. Vienna: Loecker Verlag, 1990.

Luckner, Gertrude and Else Rosenfeld, eds. *Lebenszeichen aus Piaski: Briefe Deportierter aus dem Distrikt Lublin 1940–1943*. Munich: Biederstein Verlag, 1968.

Malina, Peter. "Nach dem Krieg." *Oesterreicher und der Zweite Weltkrieg*. Vienna: Oesterreichischer Bundesverlag, 1989.

March, Tony, ed. Darkness Over Europe: First Person Accounts of Life in Europe during the War Years 1939–1945. Chicago, New York, San Francisco: Rand McNally and Co., 1969.

Marsalek, Hans. *Mauthausen*. Vienna: Offsetdruck Max Ungar, 1970.

Marszalek, Jozef. *Majdanek: The Concentration Camp in Lublin*. Warsaw: Interpress, 1986.

Martin, Nikolaus. *Prager Winter: Ein Ganz Normales Leben*. Munich, Vienna: Carl Hauser Verlag, 1991.

May, Arthur J. *The Passing of the Hapsburg Monarchy 1914–1918*. Vol. I and II. Philadelphia: University of Pennsylvania Press, 1968.

Melchior, Ib and Frank Brandenburg. *Quest: Searching for Germany's Past*. Novato, CA: Presidio, 1990.

Meysels, Theodor F. *Die Erste Woche*. Jerusalem: Olim Verlag, 1944.

Moser, Jonny. *Die Judenverfolgung in Oesterreich 1938–1945*. Vienna: Europa Verlag, 1966.

Moser, Jonny. "Oesterreich." *Dimension des Voelkermordes: Die Zahl der Juedischen Opfer des Nationalsozialismus.* Munich: R. Oldenbourg Verlag, 1991.

Mueller, Filip. *Eyewitness Auschwitz: Three Years in the Gas Chamber.* Translated from the German by Susanne Flatauer. New York: Stein and Day, 1979.

Mueller-Muench, Ingrid. *Die Frauen von Majdanek.* Hamburg: Rowolt Taschenbuch Verlag, 1982.

Mussmanno, Michael A. *The Eichmann Kommandos.* New York: MacFadden, 1962.

Neugebauer, Wolfgang and Elisabeth Moravek, eds. *Oesterreicher und der Zweite Weltkrieg.* Vienna: Oesterreichischer Bundesverlag, 1989.

Novitch, Miriam. *Sobibor: Martyrdom and Revolt.* New York: Holocaust Library, 1980.

Nyiszli, Miklos. *Auschwitz: A Doctor's Eyewitness Account.* Translated from the Hungarian by Tibere Kremer and Richard Seaver. Greenwich, Connecticut: Fawcett Publications, 1960.

Pauley, Bruce F. *From Prejudice to Persecution: A History of Austrian Anti-Semitism.* North Carolina: University of North Carolina Press, 1992.

Pilch, Judah, ed. *The Jewish Catastrophe in Europe.* New York: American Association for Jewish Education, 1968.

Postal, Bernard and Samuel H. Abramson. *The Traveler's Guide to Jewish Landmarks of Europe.* New York: Fleet Press Corporation, 1979.

Press, Bernard. *Judenmord in Lettland 1941–1945.* Berlin: Technische Redaktion, 1988.

Przewodnik po Upamietnionych Miejscach walk i meczenstwa: Lata wojny 1939–1945. Warsaw: Drukarnia Narodowa, 1966.

Reder, Rudolf. *Belzec.* Krakow: Centralna Zydowska Komisja Historyczna przy C.K. Zydow Polskich, 1946.

Reitlinger, Gerald. *The Final Solution.* New York: Thomas Yoseloff, 1968.

Rosenberg, Heinz. *Jahre des Schreckens.* Goettingen: Steidl Verlag, 1985.

Rosenkranz, Herbert. *Verfolgung und Selbstbehauptung: Die Juden in Oesterreich 1938–1945.* Vienna, Munich: Herold, 1978.

Rozenblit, Marsha L. *The Jews of Vienna 1867–1914: Assimilation and Identity.* Albany: State University of New York Press, 1983.

Rudashevski, Yitskhok. *The Diary of the Vilna Ghetto.* Translated from the Yiddish by Percy Matenko. Israel: Hakibbutz Hameuchad Publishing House, 1973.

Rueckerl, Adalbert, ed. *NS-Prozesse.* Karlsruhe: Verlag C. F. Mueller, 1971.

Safrian, Hans. *Die Eichmann Maenner.* Vienna, Zurich: Europaverlag, 1993.

Safrian, Hans and Hans Witek. *Und Keiner War Dabei.* Vienna: Picus Verlag, 1988.

Schmidl, Edwin A. "Juden in der K. u. K. Armee 1788–1918." *Studia Judaica Austriaca* 11, Eisenstadt: Roetzer, 1991.

Schneider, Gertrude. *Journey Into Terror: Story of the Riga Ghetto*. New York: Ark House Ltd., 1979.

Schneider, Gertrude. *Muted Voices: Jewish Survivors of Latvia Remember*. New York: Philosophical Library, 1987.

Schneider, Gertrude. *The Unfinished Road: Jewish Survivors of Latvia Look Back*. New York: Praeger, 1991.

Schoenberner, Gerhard. *The Yellow Star: The Persecution of the Jews in Europe 1933–1945*. Translated from the German by Susan Sweet. New York: Bantam Books, 1969.

Schubert, Kurt. "Die Oesterreichischen Hofjuden und ihre Zeit." *Studia Judaica Austriaca* 12, Eisenstadt: Roetzer, 1991.

Schwarz-Bart, André. *The Last of the Just*. Translated from the French by Stephen Becker. New York: Atheneum House, Bantam Books, 1960.

Segev, Tom. *Soldiers of Evil*. Translated from the German by Haim Watzman. New York: McGraw Hill, 1987.

Sereny, Gitta. *Into That Darkness: From Mercy Killing to Mass Murder*. New York: McGraw Hill, 1974.

Snyder, Louis L. *Hitler and Nazism*. New York: Franklin Watts, Inc., 1961.

Stahlecker Bericht. Ordner A, Dokument 17, p. 30. Truppen der lettischen Hilfspolizei fuer "umfassende Beseitigung der Juden."

Starke, Kaethe. *Der Fuehrer Schenkt den Juden eine Stadt*. Berlin: Haude und Spenersche Verlagsbuchhandlung, 1975.

Sternfeld, Albert. *Betrifft: Oesterreich: Von Oesterreich Betroffen*. Vienna: Loecker Verlag, 1990.

Streim, Alfred. "Zum Beispiel: Die Verbrechen der Einsatzgruppen in der Sowjetunion." *NS-Prozesse*. Karlsruhe: C. F. Mueller Verlag, 1971.

Totenbuch Theresienstadt: Deportierte aus Oesterreich. Austria: Druck Brueder Rosenbaum, 1971.

Vereinigung Juedischer Hochschueler Oesterreichs and Juedischer Akademiker Oesterreichs, eds. *Das Juedische Echo* 34, no. 1. Vienna: Computer Publishing, 1990.

Vogl, Alfred. "600 Years of Medicine in Vienna: A History of the Vienna School of Medicine." *Bulletin of the N.Y. Academy of Medicine*, 2nd ser., 43, no. 4 (April 1967): 282–99.

Von Lang, Jochen and Claus Sibyll, eds. *Eichmann Interrogated: Transcripts from the Archives of the Israeli Police*. Translated from the Hebrew by Avner W. Less. New York: Farrar, Strauss & Giroux, 1983.

Vrba, Rudolf and Alan Bestic. *I Cannot Forgive*. New York: Grove Press, 1964.

Wasserstein, Bernard. *Britain and the Jews of Europe, 1939–1945*. Oxford: Clarendon Press, 1979.

Weinmann, Martin, ed. *Das Nationalsozialistische Lagersystem*. Frankfurt am Main: Zweitausendeins, 1990.

Weinzierl, Erika. *Zu Wenig Gerechte: Oesterreicher und die Judenverfolgung 1938–1945*. Graz, Vienna, Cologne: Verlag Styria, 1969.

Werth, Alexander. *Russia at War: 1941–1945*. New York: E. P. Dutton and Company, Inc., 1964.

Wiesel, Eli. *Night*. Translated from the French by Stella Roday. New York: Avon Books, 1960.

Wiesenthal, Simon. *The Murderers Among Us*. New York: McGraw Hill, 1967.

Willenberg, Samuel. "I Survived Treblinka." *The Death Camp Treblinka: A Documentary*. New York: Holocaust Library, 1979.

Zucotti, Susan. *The Holocaust, the French, and the Jews*. New York: Basic Books, 1992.

Zweig, Stephan. "Abschied von Wien." *Verbannung*. Hamburg: Christian Wegner Verlag, 1964.

The Merlin-LeWinter Family Tree

French Jew Jacques L'Hiver, came from Warsaw to Lemberg (Lvov), Germanized name to LeWinter

Bernhardt LeWinter = Shana Oppenheimer
(1801-1865)   (1801-1889)

Nachmann LeWinter = Chana Wertheim
(1822-1893)   (1825-1890)

Leon LeWinter = Bella Kaniuk
(1833-1890) (1835-1881)

Toya LeWinter = Jacob Merlin
(1845-1904) (1840-1903)

Yetty Dinah LeWinter = Bernhard Mandel = Irene Wertheim
(1858-1903)   (1838-1906)   (1845-1868)

① Nahum ② Paula ③ Bernhard ④ Abraham ⑤ Josephine ⑥ Ernestine ⑦ Leon

① Nahum Merlin-LeWinter = Chaja Wolfzahn*
(1863-1934)   (1864-1942)

Adolf   Augustine   Laura*   Jeanne   Jacob (Bubi)*
(1890-1968) (1847-1973) (1898-1942) (1900-) (1904-1945)

② Paula Merlin-LeWinter* = Hermann Rintel
(1865-1942)   (1860-1930)

Clara*
(1887-1942)

③ Bernhardt LeWinter = Charlotte Potocka
(1862-1946) (1871-1963)

Zygmund   George
(1845-1917) (1908-1991)

① Minna ② Jack ③ Hermann ④ Bertha ⑤ Joachim ⑥ Leon ⑦ Charlotte

Samuel Mandel = Clara Barbesch*
(1868-1941) (1878-1941)

Genia Mandel*
(1900-1941)

① Minna Mandel = Henry Whitman
(1876-1950) (1875-1924)

Henny   Betty   Murray
(1904-) (1915-) (1921-)

② Jack Mandel = Rebecca Finkelstein
(1878-1953) (1880-1968)

Diana   Millie
(1911-) (1917-)

③ Herman LeWinter = Fanny Grossmann
(1880-1938)   (1880-1947)

Diana	Margareth	Elizabeth	Alfred	Bruno
(1904-1918)	(1908-1990)	(1910-1977)	(1912-1952)	(1914-1952)

④ Bertha LeWinter = Abraham LeWinter-Merlin
(1882-1967)   (1870-1938)

Bernhard   Yvette
(1908-1967) (1910-

⑤ Joachim LeWinter* = Martha Koenigsberg*
(1884-1942)   (1889-1942)

Tusia*
(1911-1942)

⑥ Leon LeWinter = Regina Horowitz
(1894-1985)   (1896-1969)

Oswald
(1931-

⑦ Charlotte LeWinter = Pinkas Hirschhorn*
(1898-1982)   (1898-1945)

Gertrude   Rita
(1928-   (1930-

** The spelling of the names is often different from official records, but since the people used it in their correspondence and in prayer books, I have used their preferred version.

④ Abraham Merlin-LeWinter = Henny Rose Hirschhorn
(1870-1938)   (1876-1907)

Nachman*	Pinkas*	Jacques*	Antoinette*
(1896-1942)	(1898-1945)	(1904-1942)	(1905-1943)

= Bertha LeWinter
(1882-1967)

Bernhard   Yvette
(1908-1982) (1910-

⑤ Josephine Merlin-LeWinter = Roman Spielberg
(1872-1937)   (1870-1936)

Isadore
(1897-1951)

⑥ Ernestine Merlin-LeWinter* = Wolf Peczenik
(1874-1942)   (1870-1935)

Anna*
(1892-1942)

⑦ Leon Merlin-LeWinter = Lotte Wolfzahn
(1880-1914)   (1890-1975)

Albert Schmerer =
(1880-1925)

Siegmund   Martin   Max   Trudi
(1910-   (1912-   (1919-1994)   (1921-

* denotes DIED DURING HOLOCAUST

Index of Names

Index of Places

About the Author

GERTRUDE SCHNEIDER is Associate Placement Director and President of the Ph.D. Alumni Association at the City University of New York Graduate School. She has lectured and written extensively on the Holocaust and is the editor of the *Latvian Jewish Courier*. Among her earlier books is *The Unfinished Road: Jewish Survivors of Latvia Look Back* (Praeger, 1991), which is the last in a trilogy. The others are *Journey Into Terror: Story of the Riga Ghetto* and *Muted Voices: Jewish Survivors Remember*.